Best wishes
to Birdie Etchison
Marie Kramer
402-362-4357

Homestead Fever

by

Marie Kramer

© Copyright 1993

Published by

Tele: (402) 362-4357
Marie Kramer
York Mobile Plaza #20
York, NE 68467-9607

Printed by
Service Press
Henderson, NE 68371

Acknowledgments

Profound gratitude is due my Holt County, Nebraska, relatives, neighbors, and friends for sharing their stories and pictures with me and thus providing the material for this book. I regret that limited space denied me the opportunity of including more episodes from the file of stories that I have collected.

My deep appreciation also goes to those people who helped me find the ranch sites of the spreads where my father worked as a youth. I heartily thank the McGills, Roger Garrett, Sherrill and Eva Mae Emerson, and Shelly Joss Coffey in Wyoming; and Billy and Lucille Green as well as Dennis Mitchell in the Dakotas. As a child, I had often delighted in our father's tales about his experiences on the open range, and my excitement in finding the sites of those old ranches and the children and grandchildren of his former bosses could not have been greater had I been a Wizard of Oz enthusiast who had met the Tin Man walking on the Yellow Brick Road!

Sincere thanks are due the Monsons, the Moores, and the Teters for supplying stories of incidents about the families of my daughters-in-law and also for sending pictures. Each of them responded to my letters and calls with an interest and a swiftness which I found humbling.

The understanding and the support of my children and my grandchildren lightened my task considerably. My dream of providing this book for posterity was constantly nourished by their interest and also by their excited anticipation.

More people than I can list have answered my questions about dozens of details in the stories. I especially thank my Dobrovolny siblings and their spouses, my brother-in-law, Bill Krysl, and my cousins for their assistance. Also, I am compelled to mention my more recent sources located here in York: Dr. C.M. Wempe answered my questions about animals, their habits, and their diseases; and my present husband, Ray Kramer, and his friend, Bob Galaway, were always willing to turn aside from their work to explain a detail about an early-day machine or device. (My first husband, Don Krysl, died in 1983.)

I extend earnest gratitude to my daughter, Judy Krysl, to my brother John Dobrovolny and his wife Mary Ann, and to Amelia Peterson for their helpful suggestions in regard to the manuscript, and to Karla Noble and Sandi Staehr for coaching me in the wonderful processes of computer operation. Also, my daughter Judy's illustrations (pages 44, 116, 246, and 316) and those of my son, Vincent Krysl, (pages 39 and appendix 359) are greatly appreciated.

I ask all these people to stand with me in presenting this book.

Grateful acknowledgment is given to the University of Nebraska Press for allowing the inclusion of some of the legendary, open range, campfire tales which had already appeared in Ike Blasingame's book, *Dakota Cowboy*. These stories were a part of my father's account of his days in Dakota during the early 1900's, and I would have been sorry to have found it necessary to omit them.

Also, I thank Orlan Mills Studio for allowing me to reprint the pictures of the Fernando Leos family and the Bill Coventry family which appear in the photo album in the appendix.

MK

To my children

and their spouses

and to

my wonderful grandchildren

I lovingly dedicate

this book.

Above: The author showing her grandchildren, Vincent, Adrienne, and Renee Krysl, how the pioneers made hay twists to burn for fuel. Inset: Eve Willadsen. Lower: The author with her grandchildren, Stephanie and Robert Krysl, telling a story from the manuscript for this book. 1992 photos.

Foreword

In my minds eye, a young woman—my mother—sits on a short stool near the rocking chair of a crusty old cowboy, asking about the first penny he earned. When we arrived, he was a drawn, lonely, old man. Soon, his eyes shine with memory, and he is her affectionate uncle, teasing her.

My mind calls up a later picture of second graders engrossed in their teacher's energetic gestures and varying voice inflections. She becomes a living link between generations. The youngsters identify with children in a lake during a prairie fire. Will splashing water on their hair wet it enough so that it will not burst into flames?

Parents of the pupils told me, "Your mother should write a book."

I thought so, too.

When the time for reading came, I curled up with the manuscript, expecting to be wrapped in cozy, familiar tales. I suddenly recalled that I had never before heard the stories together, making a context for each other.

As the reading progressed, the familiar old-timers I'd known personally became symbols of all those who lived on Nebraska's barren plain at the turn of the century. The Sandhills become like a loom. Each story gave me characters who became colored fibers. They were parallel; they were opposed. They tangled; they merged. As they wove in and out of each others' lives, a cloth became recognizable. One cloth. A unique, strong, coarse, useful, unpretentious stretch of sky-scented fabric.

My life is also a thread in that hardy, textured material. My great-grandmother Antonija must be linked with other readers' grandmothers in common experiences. Therefore, all descendants of the pioneers must be cousins somehow. When I considered the words spoken by Chief Standing Bear, I knew his visual thoughts. He thought as I think before I paint—with a yearning to touch the deep, common places people share. Surely David Laravie, his great-great-grandson, and I are akin to each other even though I cannot boast a drop of Ponca blood in the veins under my pale skin.

People of every nationality had unalloyed visions larger than their own lives, but less complex than the potential of a maturing melting pot. Natives knew of a relationship with a Great Mysterious One, a Grandfather-God, and land no one could presume to "own". Immigrants, on the other hand, had believed promoters' promises of "free" land. Many longed desperately to be rid of oppression in Europe where, Antonija said, people spoke hopefully of a "Golden Amerika." How could such dissimilar philosophies interfuse into one, unified nation?

But in daily reality, frontier families struggled toward goals not because they believed in noble tenets, but because they wanted to survive. In spite of their opposing aspirations, they formulated a workable code. This happened not because they felt a part of an intellectually heroic experiment, but because they had to depend upon each other. Not only would these values help their offspring endure, they would be instrumental in producing greater spiritual and material riches than the wildest dreamer among them could imagine.

Those early settlers would be proud to see their descendants gathering to save the annual income of an ailing neighbor through the act of harvesting his hay. What a surprise to see their once desolate homesteads as productive meadows surrounded by numerous groves of trees. If they could sit with us in our churches and hear testimonies of God's work in our lives, surely they would be amazed at the miracles and the blessings of the past century. In a tangible sense, how would we explain—to those who lived in one dark room made of packed dirt clotted with grass roots—such wonders as refrigerators, bathrooms, televisions, computers, air-conditioned tractors, or recreational vehicles? What would the applier of a skunk grease poultice think of CAT scans and heart transplants?

This manuscript weighs little in my hand. But the accumulated impact of its stories convinces me that, for people who have worthwhile goals, there is a necessity to carry heavy, daily responsibilities.

Two of my desires build from our past. If you are reading this in 2093, I hope the many cultures in your neighborhood have unified into a textile artwork, with harmony, variety, and faithfulness to the materials. I also dream that you might have an exciting plan for passing that tapestry, that "Golden Amerika," to those who come after you. Therefore, in order that you would have those options, my generation has ponderous work to do.

As we grow through all our stages, parents educate us in so many ways that seem paradoxical. Somehow, my mother has a way of combining words to teach me more than mere words are expected to teach. I am grateful that she has done it again.

Judy Krysl
February, 1993

Contents

1. Early Days in America 1
2. Looking Back: The Old Country 53
3. The Great Blizzard and Indian Scares 71
4. Fire and Drought 101
5. Getting a Foothold 123
6. The Turn of the Century 143
7. Working on the Open Range 171
8. Back in Nebraska 227
9. Laughter and Tears 241
10. World War I and Beyond 279
11. The Great Depression 323

Appendix
    Photo Album 351
    Genealogical Diagrams 373

Ninety-two years after the building of Tom Dobrovolny's soddy, some of his great-grandchildren visited the site and in this photo are sitting on the mound which is the fallen soddy. From left: Mary Kay Dobrovolny, Judy Krysl, and Steve, Dick, and Joe Dobrovolny (grandchildren of the Joe Dobrovolny featured in this book).

Chapter 1

Early Days in America

Chilcoate's Land in Baltimore
about 1800
as told by Earl Moore

"One of our great-great-great-grandfathers was an Indian named Chilcoate who owned eighty acres of land in the heart of Baltimore. He leased it to that city for ninety-nine years and the contract expired about 1900.

"There were only two copies of the document: one of them was held by the city, and the other was held by a woman in Colorado who was a descendant of Chilcoate. She was a distant cousin of ours.

"When I was about seventeen (approximately 1925) there was a movement to locate all of the descendants of the old Indian and to make the city of Baltimore pay for the land. I signed an affidavit saying I was a descendant.

"An uncle in Indiana was actively involved in the movement.

"The people of Baltimore heard of this affair and sent a man to Colorado to bargain with the woman. He was able to buy the lease from her after which he destroyed it.

"Oh, boy! We lost it all! Some people were really upset, especially the uncle in Indiana.

"No one knows how much money the woman received, but we figure it was a considerable sum. Neither do we know

---

* Stephanie and Robert Krysl should preface the word *grandfather* with six *greats* instead of three.

how she spent it—or even what her name was."

Elja McCullough's Civil War Stories
1861-1865

Elja McCullough's* grandfather had fought in the Civil War on the side of the Union. One day Elja told her college class some Civil War stories, and said that when she retired from teaching she planned to write these stories for publication. Soon after her retirement, however, she suffered a stroke and died.
Here are two of the stories as remembered by a student.

William McCullough's** company of Union soldiers was ordered on a forced march through Confederate Territory. The soldiers were commanded to round up all the horses they could find on the surrounding farms, to mount them, and to ride south. It so happened that the horse which Will selected was not "broken to ride," and he soon was thrown off. His companions galloped on, leaving him lying in the dust. There he was, all alone in the middle of enemy territory. What should he do?

There was a small farm nearby, and Will walked over to it. It was occupied by a woman whose husband and son were both in the Confederate Army. However, she invited him in, made supper for him, and said he was welcome to stay overnight. She told him that morning would be soon enough for him to consider how he might rejoin his company.

Now it happened that her son's unit was also in the area, and he obtained an overnight pass to visit his mother. When he walked into the house, the two soldiers, one dressed in the blue of the North and the other in the gray of the South, stared at each other in surprise. Soon, however, they sat down and spent the evening in pleasant conversation.

There were two beds in the house, and the enemy soldiers slept together in one of them. In the morning they both departed, heading out to join their separate companies.

The Civil War was an extremely bloody war, probably

---

* Elja McCullough was the Holt County School Superintendent during the 1940's. Later she taught education classes at Dana College in Blair, Nebraska.
** The soldier's given name is unknown; the name William is used here for the sake of convenience.

because tactics had not caught up with the improvements in weaponry. So many men were killed in battle that it was difficult to keep a record of who was dead and who was alive. Thus, when Will heard that his younger brother had been killed in battle, he felt that it was possible for him to secretly slip away from his company, claim his brother's body, and take it home to his mother.

Through some cunning maneuvering, Will was able to secure passage on a train for himself and his brother's casket. After the funeral, he returned to the area where his comrades had been camped. There he discovered that, in a clash with Southern forces during his absence, his entire unit had been wiped out. It was supposed that he was a lone survivor of the battle, and he was assigned to another unit.

Eclipse of the Sun*
1869

While the Jan Ziska family lived near Diagonal, Iowa, they experienced an eclipse of the sun. It was a hot afternoon, and John and his older sons were working in the field near the buildings. They hadn't heard anything about an expected eclipse, and when the bright afternoon darkened, they were perplexed.

Frances, carrying her tiny baby Anna, hurried outside, followed by her eight-year-old daughter, Franny. The worried mother called to Anton, a toddler who was playing outside, and he ran to her.

Frantically she looked around for some explanation of the fact that the sun was "going out," for the sky was cloudless. The chickens, looking from right to left in confusion, walked to their coop and began flying up on the roost.

"Perhaps the world is coming to an end," thought Frances. Aloud, she breathed one word to her children: "Pray!" They all dropped to their knees.

By then, Jan and the older boys, John and Joe (ages nine and six), had walked the short distance to the house.

"I'm sure it must be an eclipse of the sun," he told his wife.

"But an eclipse isn't *this* dark!" said Frances.

"Sometimes—if it's total—it is," he assured her.

---

* Jan and Frances (Tasler) Ziska with children John, Frances, Frank, and Joe, came to America in 1866.

Albena Sobotka of Diagonal, Iowa. She is wearing a shawl and is posing by an immigrant chest, both being articles that were brought to America in 1866. She is a grand-niece of Frances Tasler Ziska. Background: Albena's daughter Dorothy. (1988)

When the sun began to reappear, the cows, who had come home to be milked, turned around and went back to grazing. They must have thought it was a short night.

Afterward, Frances said that it was a good thing that her baby had already been born; otherwise, as startled as she was, the baby surely would have been "marked."*

Albena Sobotka** said in 1988:

"The town of Diagonal did not come into existence until 1888, twelve years after the Ziska's arrived. Until that time they were forced to raise everything they needed—including enough food to supply them for the winter—or else do without. It was a two-day trip east by wagon to get their flour ground. Corn bread was their main food.

"They had no well nearby. Jan put a barrel at the corner of the house to catch rainwater. Frances' thirteen babies arrived

---

* It was believed at that time that a frightening occurrence which befell a mother could cause her unborn child to acquire a birthmark or some other defect.

** Second cousin to Ella Dobrovolny. The Sobotka's live in Diagonal, Iowa. Albena died in 1992.

in quick succession and she had all the laundry to do by hand while coping with a water shortage."

The Indians and the Twigs
probably in the 1860's or early 1870's

Burr and Annie Olson read the advertisements about the wonderful land in the Dakota Territory and moved in the fall of the year to a spot that is believed to be near the present town of Geddes, South Dakota. With them were their two little girls.

At that time there was only a sprinkling of settlers in the area. Most of Dakota belonged to Indian tribes, and over the winter the Olsons often saw their bronze neighbors passing by. At first the settlers were apprehensive, but after some months they began to feel at ease with the presence of the tribesmen.

Then one spring day several of the Indian men came to the Olson soddy and handed Annie some twigs that were about six inches long. Annie looked at them thoughtfully, rolling the sticks between her fingers as she pondered. Through sign language, she indicated that she didn't understand why they had brought them to her.

The Natives explained, using a series of gestures: "We claim this land. If you are still here when the grass is as tall as these sticks, we will kill you."

When the fright on Annie's face told them that she had understood the message, the Indians departed.

The Olsons hastily packed their belongings and headed east toward Iowa. The spring rains not only slowed the movement of the laboring team and the loaded wagon, but it also encouraged the growth of vegetation. The glory of the greening of spring was wasted on the Olson that year, for the lengthening of the grass brought only added terror.

How Annie hated the endless nights! The call of an owl or the howl of a coyote seemed to be the voice of a signaling Indian. Since she couldn't sleep anyway, she wished that they could travel on into the night; but the stop was essential, for if the plodding team were to get them to Iowa, the animals must have a chance to eat and rest.

Exposure to the chilly, damp weather could be expected

---

* The Norwegian grandparents of Luella "Ole" Olson Brady of Atkinson, Nebraska, whose husband was Frank Brady. She lives with her son, Elwood. Her nickname is pronounced Oh-lee.

to bring about sore throats and sniffles. However, as Annie thought back, she could not recall any indication that either of the children had a malady more serious than a common cold. Thus it was an unbelievable circumstance when the rising sun revealed that the four-year-old child had died during the night.

They were afraid to linger long enough to conduct what they felt would be a proper funeral, and the girl was hastily buried. (Later, Annie told her grandchildren that probably the grave was somewhere north of Yankton, South Dakota.)

The mother had no time to adjust to the shock of the child's death before she had to give her up, and she grieved for her for many years. Was the girl *really* dead? What if, in their haste and terror, they had been mistaken? How could she have died so suddenly when she hadn't seemed to have been ill? Had the parents been so preoccupied with their flight that they had failed to notice that she was sick? Annie tortured herself with endless questions.

The family traveled to Osage, Iowa, a Norwegian settlement, where they were satisfied to remain, having had enough experiences with frontier life.

The Ponca Trail of Tears
1877-78
as told by Ben Laravie, Standing Bear's grandson

The Ponca Indians lived on a triangular wedge of land on the Niobrara River in Boyd County, Nebraska. Their tribe, an off-shoot of the Omaha tribe, was made up of peace-loving people who calculated the greatness of an individual by the number of generous deeds he had performed. In addition to their farming activities, the Ponca also hunted buffalo.

The men were masters in oral expression, for they sang while they worked and each night gathered together to tell stories: legends and tales of historical occurrences, disasters, brave deeds, and of course, generous acts.*

After the U.S. Government allotted to the Ponca the sliver of land at the mouth of the Niobrara, the Indian Bureau seemed to have forgotten about the small, peaceful tribe; for when the government officials later made a treaty with the powerful Sioux, they made the mistake of including the Ponca lands along with the area granted to the Sioux. Always an

---
* See next page for footnote.

aggressive tribe the Sioux now felt they had every right to harass the Ponca and increased their attacks.

Eventually, the U.S. government decided they must renegotiate; but, in order to avoid dealing with the Sioux again, they asked the Ponca to accept new lands—in Oklahoma.

Since the Ponca objected, they were told that government officials would take a party of their chiefs to examine this wonderful, new land. While standing in Eastern Oklahoma and looking out across the humid marshlands, the chiefs (among them, Standing Bear) stated that the proposed lands were unacceptable. The angered white negotiators cracked their whips over the wagon teams and galloped away, abandoning the red leaders.

Because some of the chiefs were elderly, it took them many weeks to walk the seven hundred miles—facing the storms of winter—back to their homes on the Niobrara.

In spite of their objections, the following spring (1877) the Ponca were forced to begin the long trek south to Oklahoma. Unfortunately, the beginning of the journey was marked by a miserable, cold rain, and the travelers were poorly equipped to protect themselves from it. Falling ill with colds and flu was not a reason to interrupt the journey; after all, the soldiers in charge had their orders. The cold, drenched group trudged along, their tears of despair mingling with the rain.

The fact that two children** died during the first week gives one some idea of the difficulty of the journey. In the second week, several more died, one of which was Standing Bear's daughter, Prairie Flower. She was buried in a cemetery in southeastern Nebraska.

---

* Both times in 1990, when a guest visited the grandson of Chief Standing Bear, Ben Laravie of Verdel, Nebraska, she found him singing to himself as he went about his everyday tasks. During the course of their conversation, he said that he had given away his last book about Standing Bear to a "student from Lincoln." *"What was his name?"* asked his listener. "I don't know. He wanted the book for a class report, and I gave it to him. He said he'd send it back, but he didn't." There was no rancor in his voice. Obviously, he expected to be generous in such an instance.

** The first to die was White Buffalo Girl, daughter of Black Elk. She is buried in the Ridgeway Cemetery in Neligh, NE. Present-day Neligh citizens keep flowers on the little grave.

Left: Kim, Stacy, and Tracy Laravie, of O'Neill, Nebraska are the great-great-great grandchildren of Chief Standing Bear. The girls also have a brother, A.J.

Right: Ben Laravie of Verdel, Nebraska, grandson of Standing Bear. 1990 photos.

It continued to be a cold, wet spring, and by the time the tribe was in Kansas, adults were dying as well as children. However, the heat of summer was upon them when they, at last, came to the end of the journey in Oklahoma.

There they found no lodging and no protection from the blazing sun. Their food supply was depleted and it was too late to begin clearing ground for the planting of crops. Mosquitoes swarmed up out of the swamps, and malaria joined the other diseases that had been brought on by exposure and malnutrition. The Ponca continued to die. The government was deaf to their requests to be allowed to return to the Niobrara.

During the following winter, Standing Bear's eldest and last son fell ill. Before he died he asked his father to take him back to the land of their forefathers on the Niobrara for burial. Standing Bear promised.

It was January when Chief Standing Bear's clan—more than sixty people—departed from the reservation. They knew that many of them would die during the journey, but they were dying in Oklahoma anyway.

Their provisions were scanty, and they were not equipped for survival through the fierce Kansas and Nebraska blizzards. They trudged resolutely behind an old, broken-down team which pulled the cart that carried the body of the chief's son. The dead soon exceeded the space for transporting bodies, and a string of graves marked their desperate trail. About half of the little tribe, who tried to avoid white settlements so as not to be apprehended, perished.

The ragged, starving survivors were taken in by the Omaha Indians and nursed back to health. However, when the U.S. Government Agents found where they were, the Ponca were arrested, and General Crook was ordered to return them to Oklahoma.

The general, however, realized that these innocent people were being unjustly treated. A reporter from an Omaha newspaper publicized the plight of the Ponca and rallied public support. The question was: are Indians merely wards of the government—wards who have no rights—or are they "people" with the same guaranteed rights under the constitution as other people? To decide the issue, a trial was held.

The highlight of these proceedings was a moving speech made by Standing Bear. Possessing an eloquence developed by many years of story-telling, the Chief spoke in picturesque and poetic terms.

Standing Bear said that, in leading his people back to the Niobrara, it was as if he had been brought to a standstill on the bank of a deep, wide river with steep cliffs on either side. No man of his tribe had ever stood there before, which meant that there was no tradition to guide him.

Suddenly, he saw a path leading upward. There was a way! He would lead his people back to the quiet waters and the grassy lands of the Niobrara!

However, just as he was ready to guide his tribe up the rugged trail, a man appeared. It was a powerful man, backed by a multitude of soldiers.

"If he says I cannot pass," said the Chief, "I cannot."

Standing Bear pointed at the judge.

"You are that man!" he stated.

The judge ruled in favor of Standing Bear's little tribe who were then given land near the mouth of the Niobrara River.*

The following summer, Standing Bear's brother, an enormous man named Big Snake, organized a second group of Ponca to journey back to their old homeland. The government decided it must not let a trickle become a river and sent soldiers to arrest Big Snake. The Indian resisted and fought valiantly, but since the soldiers were both armed and numerous, he could not

---
* After Standing Bear's death, his daughters sold the land.

prevail. Finally he was shot and killed. Thus the Ponca tribe was split: Standing Bear's group remained on the Niobrara while the others, a larger group, were forced to stay in Oklahoma.

Accidental Shooting

The John Ziska family kept the awful secret from John's grandchildren for more than ninety years.

John's youngest sister, ninety-two-year-old Tillie Olson, was listing her brothers and sisters. She began with the oldest, John, and proceeded to herself, the thirteenth. However, when she came to the ninth, Vincent (Vaclav in Czech), a grand-niece interrupted her.

"Vincent? I don't remember hearing about a great-uncle named Vincent. What happened to him?"

"Your folks never told you? Well—he died when he was five. Two months before I was born. He's buried in Iowa."

"How did he die?"

The old lady looked down—paused—shook her head. Finally she spoke: "It was an accident. A terrible tragedy! Your grandfather John* was seventeen then. He was cleaning his gun when it accidentally discharged, hitting Vincent in the head."

For a moment, everyone in the room was stunned. Then the old lady muttered, "John had to live with that all his life."

Vincent (Vaclav) Ziska was buried in the old Bohemian cemetery near Diagonal Iowa. The message on his tombstone states that he was born on April 2, 1872, and died on August 9, 1877. Photo: 1988.

---

* John Ziska was six years old when he came to America with his parents, Jan and Frances Tasler Ziska, in 1866. They first settled on an acreage near the place where Diagonal, Iowa, was later established.

This disclosure answered several questions that some of John's grandchildren had wondered about for many years. Now they understood why, if there were ducks on the pond, it was John's wife, Mary, rather than John, who went with the gun to shoot a duck for supper. They knew why other young people went rabbit hunting and carried rifles on their trap lines, while John's children and grandchildren were not permitted to do so until they were older than their gun-shooting friends. Now, too, they realized why it was that their grandfather was always the one in family pictures who was easy to find because of his sad expression: undoubtedly, he was thinking that, except for him, one more brother would be there with the group.

Joe Ziska* was twelve years old at the time that his little brother Vincent was killed. Of course, everyone was stunned by the accident, but Joe was especially affected. For days, he seemed to have lost his power of speech. He walked about in shock, and repeated one phrase over and over:
"*Ahle thaukee,*" he muttered.
The phrase is a Bohemian expletive. A comparable English expression might be: "Oh, Golly!" or "Oh dear!"
It was several months before Joe began to use meaningful speech again, and when he did so, it was a few words at a time. He seemed to find it necessary to relearn how to talk. Even though he lived to an advanced age, he remained a quiet man, being more inclined to listen than to speak.

Courageous Ancestors of the Segers**
1880

John and Margaret Christ** (pronounced Krist to rhyme with list) and their little girl, Catherine, suffered shocking misfortune when they first came to the Atkinson community. They set out from Wisconsin in 1878 and settled for two years in Platte County, Nebraska. They then yielded to the intoxicating urge to press westward to the frontier where they could obtain free land. John was handy with tools and constructed a canvas cover for their ordinary wagon.

---

*Told by Joe Ziska's daughter, Mary Ziska Krysl.
** John and Margaret are the great-great grandparents of Leo Seger of Atkinson (1992). The little girl, Catherine Christ, married Paul P. Seger in 1897.

Margaret had baked bread before they began the trip, and whenever they stopped to eat, she made coffee. For a stove, she used a flat, square piece of sheet iron that was propped up on either side by a few shovelsful of sod. Under this iron they made a fire, using dried grass.

After two weeks of travel, they arrived at the place (about ten miles north of Atkinson) where they intended to homestead. At the time, it was assumed that Atkinson would spring up south of the river, but even though the town had been platted, there were no buildings on that location. However, on the north side of the river was Bitney's little frame cabin which was simultaneously a general store, a post office, and a drug store.

The Christs were disappointed in their new home site, for there was absolutely nothing to be seen except prairie and sky—a *limitless nothing* on every side.

It was nearing dark, and John was anxious to unhitch the horses and prepare for the night camp. As he was doing so, one of the horses—for some unexplainable reason—lurched and fell on him, pinning him to the ground. Probably the animal had either a heart attack or a stroke.

The terrified wife and daughter worked frantically to move the animal aside and managed to do so before John smothered.

Little Catherine was only nine, and it required several hours for her and her mother to get the broken man into the wagon and onto a make-shift bed spread on top of their boxes of belongings.

There was no doctor for many, many miles. The injured man lay all summer, unable to do anything toward making a home or planting crops.

Finally, with winter approaching, he dragged himself out of the wagon and began to consider how they might fashion some kind of shelter for Margaret and Catherine, for he must use the wagon to go to Neligh (seventy miles distant) for supplies.

First of all, they dug a hole about a foot deep and six feet square and placed sticks and poles—whatever they could find among their few provisions—in the corners. These sticks were leaned together at the top, teepee fashion, after which dried grass was collected and piled against them. They could gather only enough grass to enclose three sides, and thus the south side was left open. This little structure would be the canopied bed for Margaret and Catherine.

The shelter was so low that it was necessary for them to creep in on hands and knees. They spread their blankets inside, and at one edge, they piled their clothes. After John departed with the wagon, this covered bed was their only protection against foul weather.

One night a heavy blanket of snow fell. They could do nothing but huddle under their quilts, shivering, while the snow piled up more and more deeply as the hours passed. How difficult it was to creep out of their nest the next day when the storm ceased, and face the task of getting their clothes and bedding out from under the snow bank! However, once out, they found a shovel among the field supplies that were piled nearby.

As they removed the snow from the outside of their hut, they piled it on the south side, molding it to form the fourth wall of their tiny bedroom.

After about ten days, John returned with food and fuel.

Suffering from one snowstorm to the next, this courageous family did manage to survive the winter. In the spring, John, even though he was still crippled, managed to break some sod. He, with the help of his wife and child, built the walls for their soddy.

Next, he went thirty miles (probably to the Niobrara River area) to get trees and branches to form the roof. Last of all, the family removed the hay which covered their bed and placed it on top of the new dwelling.

When the spring rains began to fall, they discovered that their thatching ability was deficient, for the roof began to leak. That night at bedtime, Margaret opened an umbrella, and they huddled under it as best they could. By morning it was raining harder in the soddy than it was outside.

The leaky roof turned the earthen floor into a mudhole. Each morning Margaret removed the ashes from the stove and spread them underfoot. The mud eventually dried, and the ashes made a hard floor—until the next time it rained!

When John traveled to the Niobrara River area to gather wood, he had to be alert and careful. The Indians claimed the trees and did the best they could to frighten the settlers away from them. Once, they shot a gun, striking John's wagon wheels. The loud explosion (probably coupled with John's quick application of the whip) frightened the horses, and thereafter the team was skittish, jumping at every sudden noise.

During times when there were Indians camped nearby, the Christs kept their horses harnessed day and night in the event that they would need to make a fast get-away. However, their home was never attacked.

The Leopold Seger family also came in 1880 and settled south of the Elkhorn River five miles west of Atkinson. They had first lived in Chicago where they operated a brewery which burned in the Great Chicago Fire. Journeying to Omaha, they built another brewery. When this business also burned (they suspected a rival of arson) they decided to respond to the enchanting call of the frontier.

The family traveled by train to the end of the railroad at West Point and proceeded from there in wagons. After many days, they came to a lone store located near the Elkhorn River, and Leopold sent young Paul to ask the way to Atkinson.

"Sonny, you're here!" responded the storekeeper.

Since the family had lived in Chicago and Omaha, it had not occurred to them that a townsite at the far reaches of the frontier might consist of a single building.

Atkinson did not begin to develop until the railroad came through the following year—1881—after which it mushroomed.

Buffalo Bill's Ranch Hand
early 1880's
*to*ld by Earl Moore

John Frank Moore* (who usually was called by his initials, J.F., or else by his middle name, Frank) worked as a ranch hand for Buffalo Bill. The ranch was located at North Platte, but Buffalo Bill, himself, was usually absent. Most of the time he was on tour with his Wild West Show in various parts of the United States or Europe. (As a youth, Bill Cody was a Pony Express rider; later, he was hired to kill buffalo to supply railroad workers with meat—hence his nickname: Buffalo Bill.)

After Frank homesteaded ten miles southeast of Bartley, he spent the winter months on his land, for he had to occupy it for a specified amount of time in order to "prove up."** From

---

* John Frank Moore was the great grandfather of Shirley Teter Krysl. (See appendix for genealogy.)
** After five years of meeting specific requirements, a homesteader could receive a deed for the land on which he had homesteaded. To have "proved up" was a term used to state that one had met those requirements.

— 14 —

spring and into the fall, he continued to work for Buffalo Bill.

One summer when Frank was a member of a hay harvesting crew on Buffalo Bill's Ranch, a man whom we will call Jim arrived, riding a beautiful, spirited horse. The other hands took one look at the man's ragged clothes, untamed hair, and tangled beard and decided that he was a bum who had stolen someone's fine animal.

"Can you use another man?" he asked the foreman. "I need a job."

"What experience have you had mowing hay?"

"I grew up on a farm and have both raked and mowed, but usually I was the one who did the stacking."

"Then climb on the stack and go to it!" said the foreman.

Since Jim forked hay all day in the blistering sun, it would seem that he would be exhausted by evening, but after supper he mounted his horse and rode away.

The next morning when the ranch hands went to the barn to harness the teams, there stood Jim's horse, streaked with sweat. The bum obviously had only recently arrived back at the ranch from a long, hard ride. Jim stacked hay all day and seemed to ride all night *every night*. Since he was a punctual, untiring worker, no one said anything to him about his unusual habit. The other men were satisfied to leave him to himself, for they surmised that his tattered clothes and straggly hair were probably full of graybacks (body lice)!

After a couple of weeks, there came a morning when the bum was missing. About ten o'clock, a neat, clean-shaven, well-dressed man came riding in on Jim's horse. When he began to speak, the other men recognized him: it was Jim, himself! He led a second horse upon which a handcuffed man rode.

"I'm a U.S. Marshall," said Jim, "and I've been on the trail of this outlaw for some time. Now that I have him, I'll be riding on."

The ranch foreman took out his checkbook and began to figure Jim's work time.

"Oh, no," said Jim. "I won't accept any pay for the haying job. The government is paying me." He rode away.

Frank Moore was a descendant of the Indian chief, Chilcoate, who is thought to have been a member of the Cherokee Tribe. It is not known how much Indian blood flowed in Frank's veins nor when the Moore name entered the family. Since he died at a relatively young age, his children learned very little about him.

Frank's wife, Mary Etta, daughter of Gratius and Isabelle Miner, was a wonderfully kind and gentle person. She and Frank were married on September 26, 1888.

In spite of her difficult life (she lost her husband while many of her children were small), she remained cheerful. With the help of her family, she did all the tasks of the pioneer homemaker: baking, churning, washing clothes by hand, ironing, milking, gardening, sewing, soap-making, fuel collecting, and food preserving. Also, she and her ten-year-old son Lark were responsible for operating the farm.

She taught by example, and also had a great store of appropriate proverbs which she called upon to impart her wisdom. One of those wise sayings remembered by her granddaughter, Marva Moore Teter follows: "A man of words but not of deeds is like a garden full of weeds."

She sewed her own clothes as well as those needed by her children which made it necessary for her to dress plainly. Whenever she went outside she wore a sunbonnet.

One day Mary Etta was reaching to a high shelf to get some lye in preparation for making soap. Some of the caustic powder sifted down and fell on her lower eyelid. The scar from the resulting burn caused several of her eyelashes to grow inward, and periodically, someone had to tweeze them out.

Also, Marva remembered her grandmother's answer when someone asked her which grandchild was her favorite.

"The one I'm holding at the time," she said.

Green Valley
1882-83

After the shooting accident, John Ziska seemed to welcome working away from home. He was aware that his parents and siblings suffered twice: first, for the little boy that had died, and second, for him, the brother who was drenched in guilt for the child's untimely and gruesome death. He knew he would not outlive that aching guilt, and he felt undeserving of his family's sympathy.

Since the other children had reached an age when they could help with the work at home, John took a job with a neighbor where he earned enough money to buy a span of mules named Jenny and Gin. Whenever possible, he and the mules did field work for pay.

In 1882, he learned from a newspaper article that men and teams were needed to break sod* near Wayne, Nebraska, a distance of roughly two hundred miles from his Iowa home. He set out for Wayne, riding in a wagon pulled by Jenny and Gin. Just why the plowing was being done is not clear, but it seems that the crew worked into the late fall.

While there, John heard stories of the frontier which, by then, was in Holt County. The exciting words—the entrancing words—were: "Free land!" When John finished the job in Wayne, he left the worked-down mules in the pasture of an acquaintance while he traveled west to Holt County to see that exciting Promised Land! Stepping off the train in Atkinson which then consisted of several scattered buildings, he saw a couple of men unloading lumber from a flat car and heard the staccato blows of several hammers.

The town had originally been laid out (by General John O' Neill in 1876)** south of the Elkhorn River. However, the railroad came through in 1881, passing on the north side of the river. Frank Bitney's store and post office had preceded the platting of the town, and was already located on the north side. General O'Neill's colony knew it would be to their advantage to be near the railroad and decided to move to the north side of the river. The town was replatted in the same area as the Bitney store.

When John Ziska arrived, the *second* Atkinson was only about a year old. The few dwellings there were either make-shift or else under construction. He found the building activity and the aroma of new lumber exhilarating.

John entered the Bitney store which also served as the post office. Frank Bitney told him that the land in the vicinity around town had already been homesteaded, but that there was a lush grassland to the southwest that ran all the way to the rolling

---

* The term "break sod" means to plow virgin prairie.
** John's granddaughter has the original ink-drawn plat of the town of Atkinson situated on the N 1/2 of Sec.6. (First location of Atkinson.) This plat shows that Gen. O'Neill was expecting a quick growth of the town, for it consisted of 72 blocks, each of which was divided into lots. All of the names of the streets were different from those of present-day Atkinson. One block in the center of town was designated as a park, and the business district was planned to surround the park in such a way that the store fronts would all face it.

sandhills visible in the distance.

Bitney pointed to a shed, the walls of which were constructed of double "fences" of woven wire between which hay had been stuffed. Such a building was called a "hay shed."

"That is the blacksmith shop," he said. "The smithy might have a horse he'd rent you."

After securing a horse, John rode southwest, and a few hours later he came upon a broad, unsettled portion of the prairie where the dry, winter grass slapped his legs as he rode through it.

The only people who lived in that part of the valley were the Whipples* and the Slaymakers. After spending the night in the Whipple soddy, John and Sanford Whipple rode through the expansive grassland which was already called Green Valley. John knew that this was where he would live. In Iowa, the land had been homesteaded prior to their arrival in 1866, and his father, Jan, had bought the family's farm which consisted of perhaps fifteen or twenty acres. But here on the frontier, a person could receive 160 acres of *free* land! There was a name for the excitement that burned on John's brow and set his blood racing. That name was *homestead fever*.

"I'll be back!" he promised Sanford the next day when he mounted the horse to return to Atkinson.

John drove his mules from Wayne back to Iowa. His family helped him gather needed equipment and provisions, including seed for planting his first crops. In January, 1883, just before his twenty-third birthday, he and his hardy mules again headed west. It was John's intention to complete the paperwork for filing on his land and to construct a dwelling before planting time arrived.

Most of the early settlers in Holt County built sod houses, but John had lived in a log home in Iowa. Also, he had not forgotten the bright, clean look of the new lumber nor the intoxicating odor of the sawdust from the frame building going up in Atkinson. He had saved his money carefully so that his home, too, would be made of wood and nails and shingles. It wouldn't be necessary to de-sod any of his precious land to build a house.

----
* Whipples moved to the land near Whipple Lake (also called Slaymaker's Lake) during the 1890's. Because the Midwest was baked from a drought, they were compelled to wander afar in search of game. They came upon a large slough which was green in spite of the lack of rainfall and resettled there.

Ziska Wagon train
1884

John's letters from Holt County portrayed an enticing picture of the land available for homesteading in Green Valley, and a number of families* in Ringgold County, Iowa, decided to travel west. Among them were John's parents, Jan and Frances Ziska, along with their other children.

Early in 1884, John's brother Joe came to care for the

Above: Jan and Frances Tasler Ziska. Left: Jan Ziska's home built in 1884. This tiny abode housed eleven people. The trees indicate that the photo was taken years later.

---

* Some families, in addition to Jan's family, known to be in the Ziska Wagon train were the Pachas, Taslers, Mlinars, & Freoufs. (Joe Freouf had married Jan Ziska's daughter Frances in 1880.)

Green Valley farm while John and his mules returned to Iowa to guide the group to Holt County. Late that winter, the Ziska Wagon train, consisting of twenty-two vehicles, embarked from Diagonal.

Since these families had been in America for some years, they were able to afford the expense of stopping at hotels on cold nights rather than being forced to camp on the trail. One morning Frank and Josephine Pacha carried their luggage to the wagon, and each thought that the other had loaded the basket which contained their baby, Effie. The wagon train was miles down the trail before they noticed the absence of the infant.

The worried parents returned to the hotel and found the wife of the innkeeper caring for the baby. She feared that they had intended to abandon the child, and she was considering what to do with it.

The Jan Ziska family homesteaded in the broad valley near the Pachas on the Correction Line. They built a small frame house with two rooms downstairs and a bedroom upstairs. One wonders how a family of eleven* could possibly fit into it, but in those days, people expected to be crowded.

Ella Ziska Dobrovolny remembered that when she was a tot, she stayed with her grandparents (Jan Ziskas) while her parents went to the Anna Kozisek and John Skrdla wedding. Grandma Ziska gave her a box of spools and she played with them beside a bed that was wedged into a corner of the kitchen.

In winter, most likely, Jan and Frances slept in the kitchen; the girls slept in the dining room, probably on feather quilts or husk mattresses that were spread at night and picked up in the morning; and the boys slept upstairs on husk mattresses.

In the summer, as was common in homestead days, the boys slept in the barn or corncrib.

An Anonymous Samaritan
late 1870's

The foreign-born settlers were nearly all poor. Some of them had spent all of their savings to get to America; others had money when they arrived, but because of the language barrier and because of the strangeness of the laws in their new country, they were easy prey for the unscrupulous and soon lost it.

---

*Actually, there had been thirteen children in the family, but two had died young, and two (John and Frances) had left home.

The Regal family was among those who had arrived with an adequate amount of money—enough to set them up comfortably in the New World. They came first to Howard County and later to Schuyler. At Schuyler they bought land and proceeded to build on it. After they had all their money invested in it, they found that the title of the land was not clear, and they had to relinquish it. The man who had taken their money had absconded with it, leaving them virtually penniless. They even had to sell their three cows to pay for legal fees.

At that time, Holt County was on the frontier, and Martin set off afoot to see if he could locate a homestead there. On the way he was picked up by two men, one of whom was named Hanley. Since Hanley didn't speak Czech, they couldn't converse; however, the second man could figure out much of what Martin was saying.

Hanley helped him file for his land which was located about eight miles west of Atkinson and loaned him mules as well as seed with which Martin planted his grain fields and garden.

The family had stayed in Schuyler, the house nearly barren of food as well as of money. Victoria had a few pounds of ground corn, and several times a day she made a thin mush to feed the children, now numbering five, for Baby Grace had joined the family. Victoria worried about what she would do when the corn meal was gone.

The children grew tired of corn meal mush as a steady diet. Mary, who by then was about ten or eleven, asked her mother if she could make cornbread for supper, but her mother said that it would use up too much of their only food staple.

One night there was a knock on the door, and when Victoria opened it, she found a box of food—flour, corn meal, beans, sugar, and coffee. A man was retreating in the darkness.

"Who is there? Who brought this food?" Victoria called in Czech.

"My employer sent me," the disappearing man called back. The Regals never learned the identity of their benefactor.

After Martin had the crops planted, he returned to Schuyler for his family.

In the fall of 1884, when Tom Dobrovolny traveled to Holt County to look for land on which to homestead, he stayed overnight with Regals. Martin pointed to a loaf on the table.

"That bread," he said, "is made from wheat that we raised right here on our own farm."

The Dobrovolnys in the New World
1870's

When John Dobrovolny came to America in the early 1870's, he obtained a job at the Fleischman Yeast Company in Chicago. After the company had begun to prosper, Mr. Fleischman, as John reported, invested money in some stocks which he later lost. He then was forced to lay off all the other employees in the factory, saying: "Well, John, we're back to just you and me again. We'll have to start over."

John saved his money and after a few years, bought eighty acres of land north of Fremont, Nebraska. Since he didn't have the full purchase price, he returned to his job in Chicago.

In 1878, John's brother Thomas, with his wife Antonija and their tiny infant, Frank, came to America. Antonija reported that at the harbor many of the people who were leaving their European homelands wept, but that she did not.

"Why do they cry?" she wondered. "We are going to a place where there is free land, which means we will be able to come back to visit any time we choose." [In Europe, landowners were wealthy, and Czech people referred to the New World as *Zlaty Amerika!*—"Golden America!"—because it offered free land!]

However, Antonija soon discovered, along with the other settlers, that the ownership of a piece of raw prairie did not mean riches. She reported that pioneer women watered the lonely, Nebraska plains with many a tear during the years to come as they faced the task of grubbing food for growing families from soil that was often dry and unwilling,

The Dobrovolny baby became ill on the trip across the ocean. He was covered with a rash which, Antonija thought, was brought on by bathing him in the ship's water. He cried incessantly and would not nurse.

When the little family reached a hotel room in New York City, Antonija bathed Little Frank in fresh water. He went to sleep and slept most of the time on the train trip to Chicago.

There was a considerable amount of rubble in the area of the Great Chicago Fire, and at first, Tom planned to get a job with the clean-up crew. However, John told him that, if he chose, he could live on his place north of Fremont up until the time when John, himself, was ready to move there. For rent, a portion of the crops Tom raised would go to John.

Ninety years later Frank Dobrovolny holds the tiny cap he wore when he crossed the ocean.

It didn't take Tom and Antonija long to decide in favor of the farm, and since it was already summer and late for planting, they quickly set out by train for Omaha. During the time that Tom's family lived on John's place, John walked from Chicago to Fremont each fall to settle the rent.

Grasshoppers
1878 or 79

While Tom's family lived on the farm north of Fremont, there was a grasshopper plague. Frank was a baby and didn't remember, but his mother told him that the hoppers arrived in a thick, black cloud that completely blotted out the sun.

Tom and Antonija went into the field, and using scythes, attempted to cut some of the grain in order to save it from the hungry horde. They left their tools in the field while they took a load of grain home. After quickly eating some lunch, they returned to the field.

The hoppers were everywhere. They flew up in a pattern in front of the harvesters, looking like grain coming out of a spout, and circled to light behind them. When Tom located their tools, they found that the scythes wouldn't cut. The insects had nibbled on the sharp edges of the blades and had covered them with their brown spit which hardened, dulling them. Also, the hoppers had chewed on the portions of the handles that were ordinarily grasped by a worker's hands. Tom and Antonija supposed that the sweat from their palms attracted the hoppers to that portion of the implement. The handles were rough after that.

Indian Trails near Fremont
1878

In the Early Days, the lowlands north of Fremont were marsh lands.* The Tom Dobrovolny family lived six miles from Fremont on the north edge of this marsh. When the Indians traveled from east to west and back, it was necessary for them to detour around the swampy ground, a route which invariably brought them past the Dobrovolny house.

Since the buffalo on the prairie had recently been slaughtered, the Indians had lost their main source of food. They often stopped at the Dobrovolnys and made eating motions to signify that they were hungry. When Tom was home, he gave them bread; but if Tom were in the field, Antonija kept a watchful eye, and if tribesmen approached, she was terrified. She locked the door, picked up her baby, and hid behind an immigrant chest (that she now used for a cupboard) until they departed.

The Baby with Copper-Colored Hair

At that time, a doctor named Joshua Shippley Devries** lived in Fremont. He and his wife Miriam had six children, one of whom was named Herbert. Herbert had a peaches-and-cream complexion, sky blue eyes, and bright red hair.

Indians often passed through Fremont, sometimes on foot and sometimes on horseback. One of their main trails wound across the edge of the Devries backyard on the west side of the house. Often, Miriam parked baby Herbert in his buggy while she worked outside. Houses were small in those days, and in addition to such outside tasks as gardening, bringing in water and fuel, and tending the chickens and the milk cow, many other chores were done outside if weather permitted: laundry, churning, and preparing vegetables to name a few.

One day passing Indians saw Baby Herbert and were fascinated by his fair skin and his brilliant hair. When Miriam saw them viewing him with excitement and wonder, she grabbed

---

* Later the marsh was drained, and it became some of the most productive farmland in the area.
** The granddaughter of Dr. Joshua Devries, Jane Byorth, married John Soukup, grandson of John and Barbara Dobrovolny.

the baby and clutched him in terror. The Indians conferred among themselves; then they collected objects from their packs. They displayed blankets, beads, and tools—and, through sign language, offered them to Miriam in exchange for the baby. The frightened mother kept shaking her head frantically, and finally the Indians departed. After that, Miriam kept the baby inside as much as possible.

Usually, Indians didn't knock on doors; they simply appeared. A knock meant that a fellow settler was at your door—or so Miriam thought. One day someone knocked and Miriam, who happened to be holding the copper-headed Herbert, opened the door. There stood five husky braves one of whom moved forward enough so that she could not close the door. Numb with fright, she stood firmly in place, fearing that if she retreated, her visitors would follow her into the room.

The Indians held up their offerings: blankets, beads, robes, tools, trinkets of all kinds; and they indicated that they would trade them for the baby. At first she was too terrified to respond, but finally she collected her wits and showed them by sign that the baby was hers and that she would not trade it. Finally, one by one, the Indians gave up, returned to the trail, and went north.

When only two remained, one of the braves pulled back the several blankets that were fastened around his neck (all having been brought as items for trading) and produced a pair of tiny, white deerskin moccasins that were decorated with blue beads. He presented them to Miriam.

Thinking they were one more item being offered in trade, she kept pushing them away and saying: "No! No!"

Finally, the Indian laid them down, signing that they were for the baby, and he backed away. Apparently, since he could not have the infant with the brilliant halo, he wished to make a gift to him. Later, the same Indian brought his wife to see Herbert, and, once acquainted, the woman returned several times more to visit the apprehensive Miriam and her baby. The mother felt the need to guard the boy during his entire childhood, being especially worried after he entered school.

When Herbert was a teenager, bands of gypsies were common, and Miriam continued to be concerned for his safety.

No one knows what became of the little moccasins. Probably Miriam, wanting to avoid being reminded of the anxiety she experienced while Herbert was growing up, did not save them.

Quick Trip for Help
1879

Antonija was alone on the chilly November day on which her second child, Thomas Jr., was born. When it was obvious to her that she would give birth, she put a bucket of water on the back of the stove to warm, spread some newspapers and blankets on the bed—and prayed. She knew almost nothing about delivering a baby. When her first baby was born, she had been in Czechoslovakia and was surrounded by her mother and her aunts. They had taken all the responsibility of seeing that everything had gone right and had provided experienced and loving care for both mother and babe. Had they not been available, there would have been a dozen near neighbors to help her. But here on the barren Nebraska prairie Antonija's only companions were fear and loneliness—and her eighteen-month-old son, Frank.

The new baby was unconcerned about the fact that there was no one to attend his birth. He arrived anyway. Once he had put in his appearance, Antonija picked him up.

It was obvious that what this small, noisy character needed was a bath. Antonija tested the temperature of the water in the bucket. It was not as warm as she would have chosen, but it would have to do. She dipped the baby into the bucket, and attempted to rinse him off. She was alarmed when he screamed lustily. She didn't know how or where to tie the umbilical cord and, feeling there surely was a right and a wrong way, was afraid to guess.

Finally, the anxious mother decided that she must walk to the Hespens, who lived a little more than a half mile away, for help. But what should she do with her older child, Frank? She couldn't possibly carry him along with the new baby. Deciding quickly, she seated him on the floor and gave him a tin cup with a little sugar in it, and also a box of teaspoons. She hoped he would entertain himself with these items until she was back home.

Antonija put on a heavy coat, rolled the infant in a blanket, and walked to the Harms Hespen place. Since the Hespens were Germans, the two women could not communicate through speaking, but when Antonija unwrapped the newborn baby, it didn't take much in the way of sign language to indicate that she needed help. Impossible as the idea seems, it is the opinion of descendants that Antonija had come all that way with the umbilical cord intact.

The Hespens were aware that the Dobrovolnys had a toddler, and Antonija was able to make them understand that he was home alone. Someone was sent to care for him. Later, Antonija and the new baby, named Thomas, were returned home in a wagon.

Red Underwear
about 1882

As a boy, Joe Dobrovolny wondered, when he saw his father's long, winter underwear hanging on the clothesline, why the legs and the front were reddish-brown. One day he commented about it to his brother Fred, and their mother, overhearing their discussion, explained.

When they lived in Schuyler (early 1880's)* there was, in addition to the sod house they occupied, an older dug-out in which a sow and her young pigs were housed. Since the dug-out was in the side of a hill, the door was on low ground. Tom had ridged up dirt around the door to keep water from running in when it rained. However, one spring they got a cold, three-day rain, and so much water collected in the valley near the door that it was beginning to turn the low, red-clay floor of the dug-out into mud.

Tom brought some tree branches from the creek and fashioned a crude pen on high ground, but since this new enclosure provided no shelter, he chose not to move the pigs unless it became absolutely necessary. He watched closely the next day and was relieved when, late in the afternoon, the rain stopped, and the sun came out. The weather seemed to be settled.

Then, in the middle of the night, the rain began to pour down again, and Tom knew the pigs would drown before morning unless he moved them. He and his wife Antonija went to the dug-out where they found, with the aid of dim lantern light, that water was rolling in. The earthen floor was a quagmire and was getting worse by the minute.

While Antonija carried the lantern, Tom wrestled the slippery, clay-covered pigs up and out of the dug-out and into the

---

* When John moved from Chicago to his land near Fremont, Tom moved his family to a farm located on school land, north of Schulyer, Nebraska. (about 1880-85)

pen. By the time they were finished, Tom's clothes sagged with the weight of the thick, red mud that clung to them. Standing outside in the rain, he undressed, laid his garments on top of the low soddy, and washed himself in the rain water that had collected in the little valley. It was a cold bath, but was bearable when one considered the alternative: the trouble of carrying in the laundry tub (which doubled as a bathtub), bringing water from the creek, and starting a fire to heat it.

The next day, Antonija scrubbed the muddy clothes. However, even with generous applications of her home-made lye soap and vigorous rubbing on the wash board, the red clay remained colorfast for the entire life of the garment.

Tragedy at Malloy's Peak
1882-1884

The tall, cone-shaped hill in west central Holt County was unnamed when Dick Malloy agreed to teach in the sod schoolhouse on the edge of the frontier which was then roughly five miles south of the budding town of Stuart. Dick approached Jeremiah Murphy who lived about a quarter of a mile north of the school, and asked if he might secure room and board from them. Since the Murphy soddy was the one nearest the school, Jeremiah would have liked to have accommodated the young man, but Bridget was expecting a child.* This child would be born in their one-room home which allowed scant privacy for any of its occupants. Therefore Jeremiah asked Dick to seek board elsewhere, and the young man then found lodging at the Mathias place which was about a mile northwest of the school.

The Regal family, who had four children** old enough

---

* The baby born to Jeremiah and Bridget, Jan. 28, 1883, was J.P. Murphy, father to a large family, including Frank, who now (in 1992) lives on Jeremiah's old homestead. Frank's son, Dan, lives on the old school site. In addition to Frank, J.P.'s other children are Mary, Catherine, Cornelius (Connie), Henry, Sophie, Jane, Eileen, James, Elizabeth, Rita, and John.

** The eldest Regal child, Mary, married John Ziska and they became the parents of Freddie, Annie, Ella, and Jim; Antonia married Joe Ziska and they became the parents of a large family; Jim Regal married Emma Dibble who was a tot at the time of this story; and Josephine Regal married Stanley Johnson, and was the grandmother to Dorothy (Runte) Straka.

to attend classes, lived about a mile east of the school. The Dibble family, who had several daughters, lived near the Regals.

One winter day, Mr. and Mrs. Dibble went to Atkinson for supplies and before they left, cautioned the girls not to admit any outsiders during their absence. They must especially be on guard should any young fellows happen along, for proper young ladies must not entertain a male acquaintance unless they were chaperoned.

During the late afternoon a blizzard moved in, preventing the senior Dibbles from returning. The girls, thinking their parents might be out in the storm, put a lamp in the window to guide them homeward.

In the schoolhouse, Dick hastily put his after-school work aside and set out for his boarding house. The blowing snow was blinding, and since there were no trails nor fences to follow, he was soon lost. Night descended bringing total darkness and scant hope of finding shelter. We can only imagine the young man's sense of relief when he caught sight of a faint glimmer of light. The feeble rays, seen between gusts of the storm, guided him to the Dibble soddy. The girls, some of them his students, answered his knock, but they had been well-instructed.

They explained that they were forbidden to allow outsiders in the house during their parent's absence. The man replied that he was already very cold, and that he felt he couldn't possibly find other shelter in the darkness of the raging storm.

"If you will only let me in, I will do anything you say. I'll sit in a chair by the stove all night or curl up in a corner and not move out of it."

The girls went to the opposite side of the room to confer. When they came back, they told him they were sorry, but that they must not disobey their parents.

They were the last people to see Dick Malloy alive. We do not know how long he staggered about in the storm before he gave up, turned his back to the wind, and let it push him into unsettled country. He was about twelve miles south of the school when he perished.

A year and a half later, in July of 1884, his body was found about 300 yards southwest of the large sandhill that has, ever since, born his name: Malloy's Peak.

During the dry thirties a blowout began eating its way into the top of the giant cone, but until the 1950's this hill could

Malloy's Peak in 1980. The dotted line shows an approximate assessment of how the big hill looked from 1880 until about 1950.

be seen from a distance of thirty miles. However, by now (1992) the entire top has blown off, robbing it not only of some of its height, but also of its distinguishing shape.

Roughly a century after Dick Malloy's death, a curious citizen decided to visit the famous hill, and knowing that it is located on Jones land, she first contacted Keith and Amy Jones.

"It is in the second range of hills from here," said Keith. Once you get over these closer hills, you will see it."

"Since it is in a range of hills and since its shape has been altered by the winds, how will I know which one it is?"

"You won't have any trouble," he answered. "It is still the biggest thing out there."

He was right. It is.

More Blizzard Stories
1870's and 1880's

Looking from the viewpoint of the present time, it is difficult to understand why the girls refused shelter to Dick Malloy, particularly since the settlers *expected* to feed anyone who happened along and *expected* to offer night lodging to anyone who came late in the day.* Such actions were considered common courtesy.

----

* How did one manage overnight guests in a crowded one-room soddy? "No problem," reported Fred Dobrovolny. "Dad carried in a few armloads of hay, and put them on the floor. Mother got out whatever blankets she had. Someone might sleep under the table and someone else in front of the washstand. It wasn't like now, when people think they have to have guest rooms."

However, these rules did not apply to single women. The reputation of such a person who kept a male guest overnight was, if the people in the community were aware of the act, soiled—sullied—besmirched—not momentarily, but for life. An extremely difficult situation arose whenever it was necessary for a man to seek refuge in the home of an unmarried woman.

Consider this incident:

Tillie Olson, aged 91, was asked by a grandniece if she knew what her brother, John Ziska, was doing on the day of the Blizzard of 1888.

"He was at his home," said Tillie. "He took care of the stock the best he could, and waited it out. But when John was in his teens—it was shortly before I was born—he got caught in a blizzard and had to spend the night away from home. We were in Iowa, then."

Tillie's guest, sensing a story, asked for details, but the old lady was reluctant to answer. She looked down, obviously embarrassed, and nervously smoothed the wrinkles in her apron. Finally, she looked up.

"Well, I guess it is all right to tell now. Everyone involved has been dead for many a year.

"It was a nice winter day to begin with, and in the afternoon the boys turned the animals out of the stable so they could clean it. The horses were out in the field, pawing around in the snow trying to find something different to eat. John noticed they were wandering quite far and figured he'd have to be going after them soon.

"Then suddenly a blizzard swept in from the northwest. John immediately hurried after the horses, but they were traveling with the storm and were going farther and farther away from home. When John finally caught up with them, they were on the sheltered side of a couple of cabins, and dusk had fallen. One cabin was vacant, but the other was occupied by a widow.

"John knew it would be foolhardy to try to find his way back in the dark. In those days, there weren't any fences or roads to guide a person across the prairie. So John put the horses in the vacant building and went over to the widow's house.

"The widow agreed that John should not try to get home until the storm blew over. She said he could stay the night if he would promise not to tell anyone except his family.

"The folks were scared when John didn't return. Mother cried and prayed all night. They were really grateful to the woman for keeping John there. In appreciation, the next spring our father plowed some ground for her and broke one of her young horses to the buggy."

"If you weren't born then yet, how did you find out about it?" asked Tillie's visitor.

"Years later, my older sisters told me; but no one ever mentioned it outside the family. If people found out, it would have ruined the widow's reputation. I guess it's all right to tell now, though. She's been dead about fifty years."

A second incident follows:

An old man had finished telling a visitor about various blizzards. Thinking the conversation was over, she closed her notebook and prepared to leave.

Suddenly, he grinned at her and said, "I'll tell you a really good one if you promise not to say where you got the story. Everyone involved is dead, but I still don't want people to know that I was the one who told."

Then he related this amusing tale.

On Saturday nights, several settlers were in the habit of getting together to play cards at the home of a bachelor friend. Two of the players met earlier in the day one Saturday, and both stated that they planned to attend the usual gathering. We shall call them Ed and Henry.

That evening, however, it began to blizzard. When Henry did not arrive as expected, the others were concerned. To venture out in search of him on the stormy night was too dangerous to be an option. However, the morning dawned clear but cold, and the group set forth.

Actually, what had happened the night before was that Henry had left home a little later than usual, and the storm closed in while he was en route. He took refuge in the only soddy in the area, a one-room home occupied by a widow whom we shall call Emma. She admitted the snow-clad figure, and when the blizzard continued to howl, they both realized that the only safe solution was for Henry to remain for the duration of the storm.

But what about Emma's reputation?

Henry assured her that no one would know that he had stayed with her. He would tell his friends that he had burrowed into a hay pile to wait out the storm. Never, *never* would he breathe a word about this night in her home! Emma put a quilt on the floor and he rolled up in it. She sat in a chair and laid her head on the table. Neither of them even glanced at the bed.

The next morning as Henry prepared to leave, he saw his friends approaching. Since the frantic Emma insisted that he hide, he quickly slithered under the bed.

The men arrived. Had she seen anything of Henry? No? Well, could they come in and warm up? It was mighty cold out. Below zero.

Reluctantly, Emma stepped aside and they crowded into the tiny space that was available. Suddenly, there was a commotion under the bed, and Henry came scrambling out.

"I don't care who knows I'm here," he shouted. "I've been snakebit, and I need a doctor!" He pulled up his pant leg and there on his ankle were two red marks. "Its a rattlesnake," Henry groaned. "I heard him rattle just before he struck."

Emma looked more closely. "That's not a snakebite," she said. "It's a henpeck!"

Wanting some early chicks, Emma had set two hens in boxes under the bed. One of them was a feisty creature who tolerated no disturbance. Henry had gotten too close to her nest, and she had made the deep-throated, rattling sound common to setting hens and had pecked him sharply on the ankle.

When the excitement abated, the group considered the widows predicament. Could every man present be trusted to keep the secret that, should it become known, would be Emma's social downfall? They swore that they would! And for as long as it mattered, they did.

Thus you can see that the decision which the Dibble girls faced was not an easy one. Also, it was a time when obedience to parents was the norm. There were no saucy radio and television characters which provided patterns for disobedience. Thus the Dibble children felt compelled to follow their parents' command: "Don't let any outsiders in while we are gone."

Curly's Sad Fate
1884

Tom Dobrovolny and his six-year-old son Frank had gone to the creek about a half mile from their place to get water as they had no well on their farm near Schuyler. A neighbor was at the creek, drowning a litter of unwanted pups. As the animals tumbled about in the swift current, little Frank watched in horror—silent horror, of course, for a child was not allowed to question the actions of an adult.

Finally the struggles of one of the puppies brought it near to the bank of the creek, and Frank was able to rescue it. He snatched it and ran toward home, expecting any minute that the adults would call him back and toss the puppy back into the water.

Frank was both out of breath and vastly relieved when he reached home with his new pet. Even though it was half drowned and was quite young to be taken from its mother, it lived. It was a black dog with a wide, white ring around its neck. Frank gave him an English name—Curly.

Antonija didn't like the dog's name because she couldn't learn to pronounce the English "r" sound.

"Heh, Cu-uh-ly! Heh, Cu-uh-ly!" she would call to him.

["I can hear her yet," mused her son Fred about eighty-five years later. "She always tried hard but never could say it right. Curly understood, though. He came. Good old Curly!"]

In a world where the major concern was that of providing food for a growing family (by now there were five little boys), the children must invent their own toys and games. Curly immediately became the source of their entertainment—a committed friend, a ready companion. While facing the deprivations of the raw prairie, how wonderful it was to pat the silky back and be rewarded with a canine grin and the soft-eyed gaze of complete devotion!

The next year when the family moved to Holt County, Curly went along.

Frank Dobrovolny, John Boettcher, and Joe Balloon were herding cattle on the Jules Balloon quarter.* When Whittler's dog, Fido, heard their voices, he trotted over to play with them. Being a boy who loved dogs, Frank befriended Fido who followed him about. Several times Whittlers got the dog and took him back home, but Fido would soon leave and return to the Dobrovolny farm. Whittler finally told Frank he could keep the dog, and the Dobrovolnys then had two dogs.

A Polish man who lived in the neighborhood repeatedly asked Tom (Frank's father) if he could buy Curly. Since the dog

---

* That quarter later became the NE pasture of the Wright land and was owned by Joe Dobrovolny. Now in 1992 it is the property of Joe's son, Fred.

belonged to Frank, Tom refused to sell him. Finally, when the Polish family was moving away to the Burwell area, he decided to let the dog go. He reasoned that Frank was now working away from home (herding cattle for a neighbor) and that they didn't need two dogs.

The Polish man tied the dog in his wagon and departed.

A year or two later, this same fellow returned to visit his old friends. He wore a beautiful jacket, the back and front of which were made of black and white fur. Fred and Joe, Frank's younger brothers, were horrified when they saw the garment, for they recognized the markings on the back of the jacket as those of their old pet, Curly!

It seems that the Polish man had a black and white dog of his own, but the hide of one dog was not adequate for a garment. Thus he kept bargaining for the Dobrovolny dog because the fur of the two dogs was well matched and was enough to make him a fine jacket.

When the man saw the boys' stricken gazes, he realized that they recognized their pet's fur. He removed the jacket and laid it in his wagon; then he reached into his pocket and pulled out a nickel which he handed to Fred.

With lowered heads, the boys walked to the back side of the soddy and sat down. Tears rolled down their faces.

["Oh," remembered Fred, "it was a hard life! A hard life! Curly had been like a member of the family."]

After some time, Fred opened his hand and revealed the nickel. The boys examined it. They had never seen one closely. They turned it over, polished it, passed it back and forth, let the sun play on it. For a few moments they were engrossed—but then they thought of Curly.

"If the nickel were mine," said Joe, "I'd bury it."

Fred considered thoughtfully for a moment. Neither he nor Joe knew anything about "memorials" or "paying tribute to a memory," but in his heart, the suggestion seemed right.

"You dig a hole," said Fred, "and I'll find something to wrap it in."

They buried the nickel.

(A few days later Fred reclaimed the coin. It was too great of a treasure to give up permanently.)

Sophia Kaup and the Indians
late 1800's

Herman and Sophia Kaup* raised their family in rural Cuming County. On occasions, Herman went on week-long trips to the Elkhorn River to cut logs.

One day while her husband was gone on such a trip, Sophia was working in the garden when she heard a noise, a quiet "Whuff! Whuff!" Startled, she looked up and saw Indians on horses standing in the tall prairie grass.

The visitors dismounted and approached. They made signs indicating that they wished to have the family dog.

It was the children's pet, and very nearly the only thing they had to play with. Sophia didn't want to give up the animal.

She turned her head toward the barn, cupped her hands around her mouth, and shouted: "Herman! Herman!"

The Indians mounted their horses and galloped away.

Obstinate Cows
1885

Antonija had driven the two cows a distance of about sixty miles before she gave up. However, during that time, she probably walked four or five times that far, for the sixty miles is figured "as the crow flies" and those unruly cows darted about, completely oblivious to the trail or to the flight of the crow. The early growth of green grass that peeked out in the low spots and around the scattered buffalo bones was the attraction, and the headstrong animals each insisted on going a different direction in search of the tender blades. Antonija was exhausted from trying to keep them headed in a northwesterly direction.

It was early spring, and the Dobrovolnys were en route from Schuyler to Holt County where, the fall before, Tom had chosen land on which to homestead. Tom drove the team and wagon** loaded with their few possessions and their five little boys: Frank, nearly seven years old; Thomas, five; Anton, nearly four; Joe, two; and Fred, one. Frank, small as he was, did

---
* Grandparents to Grace Weichman and to Paul and Bernard Kaup—as well as a great number of other Kaups living in the Stuart area. Grace told this story.
** One precious object on the wagon was a White sewing machine. It is now owned by a great-grandson, Don Krysl.

the best he could to care for the younger boys while Antonija chased after those cows. She and Tom could not exchange jobs: Tom's experienced hand was needed in driving because one of the horses was blind in one eye, causing him to spook easily.

A second wagon, pulled by a yoke of oxen driven by Tom's youngest brother, Fred, accompanied them. Fred had more recently immigrated from Czechoslovakia to America.

When the wagons camped near Norfolk, a local citizen noticed how footsore and exhausted Antonija was.

"How about selling me those cows?" he asked Tom, speaking in German.

Fred who could speak several languages translated the request into Czech and Antonija overheard.

"We need the milk," she insisted. "Little Fred is yet a baby, and the other boys are small. They need milk to go with their bread."

"Explain to him," Tom told Fred, "that we need the milk."

The man knew they spoke the truth—they did need the milk. However, he also surmised that Antonija was the one who would be responsible for driving the cows, and he was sure she could not chase them much farther. The next day he rode down the trail to see how she was managing.

He found her sitting by the wayside, holding an ill-fitting shoe in her hand and considering what to do about her bleeding heel. She had no proper bandage, and the make-shift one she had applied in the morning had already been rubbed aside by her shoe.

The man could not understand her words, but had no difficulty interpreting the motions she made with her hands.

"You can have them! I give up!"

He rode ahead to the wagon and bought the cows from Tom. Antonija had a hard time hiding her tears as he, being horseback, quite easily drove them back along the trail.

For the remaining hundred miles of the trip, which at oxen pace was more than a week's journey, the family ate bread without milk.

After Antonija was free from herding the cows, she rode in the wagon to give her blistered feet a chance to heal. Since she was now able to keep watch over her smaller boys, she allowed the older ones to get out and walk. It is said that Frank and young Thomas enjoyed hiking along with the dog Curly and that three-year-old Anton happily wore himself out trying to stay ahead of the wagons. He was fascinated by the birds, and wanted to be the first one over the trail in order to flush out any feathered creatures hiding in the prairie grass. His parents were not surprised, later, when he became the wildlife enthusiast in the family.

When they reached Holt County, Antonija and the boys stayed a few miles southwest of Atkinson in an extra soddy located on the Zahradnicek place. It seems it was originally built by the Coufals who later moved to another place. Both Coufals and Zahradniceks had lived near Schuyler before coming to the frontier.

Tom and Fred began building Tom's soddy on his homestead quarter which was about fifteen miles southwest of Atkinson. Haste was necessary because already it was late for plowing and planting the fields.

Constructing a Soddy
1885

Tom's soddy was a one-room dwelling with the door facing the east. Years later, using a box of dominoes, Tom's son Joe demonstrated how sod was placed to construct a building. The walls were surprisingly thick—from two and one half to three feet thick—and were made of a double wall of sod.

First of all, the site for the building was carefully leveled and the grass was cut from the turf to be used. Slashes which formed the ends of the blocks were cut into the earth with a sod cutter after which the sod was plowed with a "grasshopper plow" in furrows that were perpendicular to the slashes. The blocks of sod were 15" by 30" for a wall that was two and one half feet thick; they were 18" by 36" for a wall that was three feet thick.

The diagrams show how the first three layers of sod were positioned. These three layers were repeated until the walls were as high as needed.

The door frame (as deep as the thickness of the walls) was set into place on top of the second or third layer of sod. Window frames were added when the walls reached a height of a foot or two. The sod then was built up around them. When the walls reached a height that was perhaps six inches above the door and window frames, strong beams were laid across these frames, and the building proceeded. The few inches of vacant space above the door and the window openings were necessary

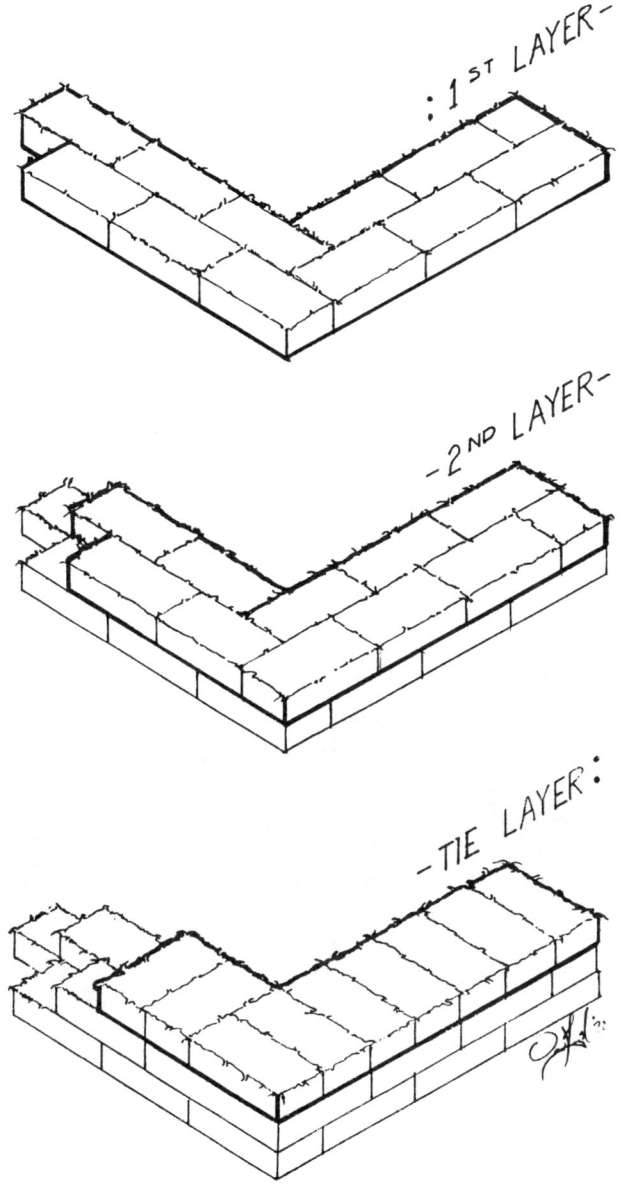

Building a Soddy   by Vince Krysl

because they allowed the walls to settle without damaging the frames. These vacant spaces were stuffed with paper or rags or hay. Tom packed gunny sack material in those openings in his house.

It was imperative to make the inside walls vertical, for a leaning wall would soon collapse. People used levels and plum lines to keep the walls straight.

The two end walls were built to a peak that formed the gable, and a sturdy ridge pole was laid across to form the spine of the roof. It might be a strong, straight tree or it might be a heavy, sawed beam. Shorter timbers slanted down from the ridge pole to the top of the wall, forming the "rafters." Tom's soddy had a board roof over the timbers with sod placed on top of the boards.

Some people went to the Long Pine area and cut the ridge pole and the "rafters" from the tall pines which grew there, but such construction produced rougher, less-durable shelters which were more inclined to leak.

Because a sod-covered roof was extremely heavy, the

Tom's one-room soddy (sketched by Joe's daughter according to directions that he gave) looks small to house seven people, but consider that it was even smaller inside than it appears, for the walls were two and a half feet thick. Joe lived in this soddy until he was eleven.

In winter, the five boys slept on a husk mattress which was spread on the floor at night and was stored on top of their parent's bed during the day. In the summer, the boys, as was a common practice then, slept in the granary.

ridge pole needed strong supports both at the ends and the middle. Tom's dwelling thus had a couple of pillars in the middle of the house. Nails driven halfway into them provided hanging space for a number of articles: one was called upon to display pots and pans while the other was adorned with clothing. The door was set to be flush with the inside wall and opened to the interior, while the two windows were flush with the outside wall, an arrangement which left a deep, window seat at each one.

To finish the interior, Tom examined his land and chose a spot of fine alkali soil. He collected some of it and mixed it with water to make mud. This mixture he used to plaster the walls. The next fall he purchased a dime's worth of lime which he combined with water to make whitewash.

"I remember when Dad slacked it—that is, mixed the lime with water," said Joe later. "He sent us kids into the house, but Anton and I watched from the window.

"When you first add lime to water, it bubbles and boils and gives off strong fumes. But once it is mixed together and cooled, it loses its power to burn.

"Mother painted the inside walls with the whitewash. It was quite a surprise to us boys because those dirt walls became as white as chalk."

While building the soddy, Tom and Fred went on weekends to visit Antonija and the boys. This arrangement allowed them to change clothes and to get a new supply of bread. One Monday morning when they returned to the work site, they discovered that the pile of lumber (that Tom had purchased for the roof of the soddy) and also his plow had been stolen. They followed the tracks and found these items at the home of a settler named Ben.

Tom could identify the plow because of a bolt he had replaced and because of the way the plow share was worn.

"You have my plow and roof lumber!" exclaimed Tom.

"That plow is mine," said Ben. "And those boards, too. You can't come onto my place, lay claim to my property, and simply walk off with it."

Tom went to court. Since the Dobrovolnys knew very little English, they were forced to rely on an interpreter, making the proceedings clumsy and difficult. Tom used all the money he had on legal fees.

Because of insufficient evidence, he lost the case. He had to borrow money to pay the court costs as well as to replace the lumber and the plow. Discouraged, he considered going back to Schuyler, but the return journey would make him too late for planting.

As soon as the soddy was completed, Tom began breaking sod while Antonija followed and planted corn with a hoe. Because of the lateness of the season, they weren't able to get as much planted as they would have liked, though they did raise some corn.

The potatoes were planted too late and didn't grow well because the heat of summer stunted the young plants. That first winter the family's diet was heavy with squash, pumpkins, turnips, and corn bread. Tom bought a cow which provided milk, cottage cheese, and butter for a part of the winter—until she went dry.

Kodyteks came to America several years later than most of the Green Valley settlers. Mlinars helped them build their soddy, and by then had designed some improvements. On a regular soddy, it took a considerable amount of lumber to make the roof because it must extend to the outside of the thick sod walls. On Kodytek's soddy, Mlinars first made a wooden wall and next piled sod on the outside for insulation. The roof then need not extend over the sod walls. The lumber saved in the roof construction was about half of what was required for the wall.

Marijuana
late 1800's

Was there marijuana in Nebraska when the settlers came? Probably not, for initially the prairie was covered with deeply rooted grasses. Many of the weed seeds were introduced along with the grain seeds brought by the settlers, and others followed newly constructed railroad beds.

It has been said that during World War I, marijuana was introduced in the midwest as a crop because its tough, fibrous stem-covering could be used for making rope. However, Louis Zahradnicek says that marijuana—known then as "stink weed"—was here before then.

One of the early settlers who rented the Zahradnicek's extra soddy raised canaries. Since songbirds were then the fashionable pet, it was easy to sell them in the nearby towns.

These enterprising bird-growers used commercial canary

food which included varieties of weed seeds. When they emptied the litter from the cages, numerous seeds were discarded, also. After the family moved away, the yards around the soddy grew up into seed-producing weeds. One of the most tenacious of these new plants was stink weed (marijuana). After the Zahradnicek soddy was vacated, it fell down and the marijuana took root on the mound that remained. People often came to pick the seeds to use as feed for their canaries.

One can easily imagine how the seed would spread. It was emptied out of bird cages in other yards, was transported to new places in pant leg cuffs or in the woolly fibers of socks or sweaters, was carried in the fur or feathers of animals, and was blown about by high winds.

Ordinarily, stink weed did not take root in pastures or meadows where the earth was sodded. However, it was often found around farmsteads, near the edges of fields, or in groves. Once established, it was difficult to eradicate because of the multitudinous number of seeds that it produced.

Baby in the Well

Tom Dobrovolny's brother Fred helped him make the well that was located east of their new soddy in Holt County. While they dug, Antonija was busy planting some garden in a plot she had spaded the night before. Now that they were going to have a well, she could carry water to her plants, hurrying their growth. She desperately needed something more to nourish her five little boys who were subsisting, as were she and Tom, on bread, dumplings, lard, an occasional rabbit, and milk.

After finishing the pit, the men put the ladder beside the soddy, and walked south toward their brother John's place.

Presently Antonija looked up and asked, "Where's Little Fred?"

"Well, say," said young Thomas, "come to think of it, I did hear a splunk at the well."

Antonija ran to the pit which as yet had no cover, and saw year-old Fred lying in the water below.

She screamed to the men who by then were about a quarter of a mile away.

"Help! Help! The baby is in the well!"

She dragged the ladder to the excavation and quickly lowered it into the deep hole, fearing the whole time that she might be setting it on the child.

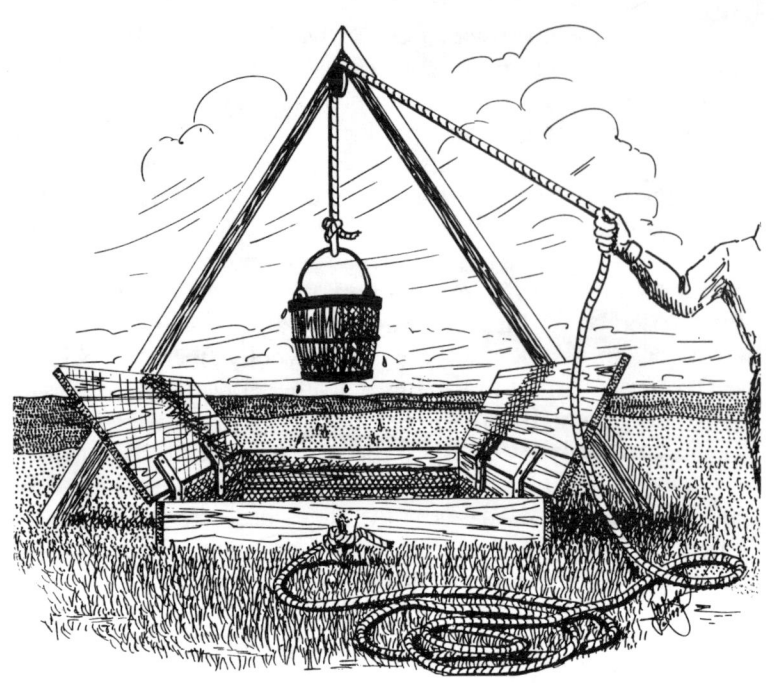

Top: Pioneer well as described by Henry Dickau. There was no crank to lift the bucket; rather, it was pulled up by hand. Drawing by Judy Krysl.

Bottom: About 50 years later, the Dobrovolny brothers: John who was visiting from Fremont; and Tom and the elder Fred from Holt County.

When she had scrambled to the bottom and had snatched up the infant, she was further terrified to discover he was not breathing. She hurried up the ladder, and since it was too short to reach the ground above, she couldn't get out of the well while holding the baby in her arms. She tossed him up on the pile of sand just as the men arrived, Fred in the lead.

They held the baby up by the feet, and water poured out, but still he was not breathing. Running into the soddy, Tom got a bottle of camphor from the shelf inside the big clock and put some of the pungent medication on the infant's nose. Little Fred gasped, coughed, and began to cry.

Later, in telling about their wild dash home, Tom always said, "Brother Fred outran me!"

John and Barbara Dobrovolny had moved from Fremont to Holt County that same spring. They went to the land office substation in O'Neill and "took out papers" on a quarter of land northwest of Tom's place. However, Joe Freouf had chosen the same land, and had filed his homestead papers in the main office in Niobrara, thus negating John's application.

Since it was already time for planting, John did not want to risk making a second such mistake, and he rented a horse in O'Neill and rode to Niobrara. He discovered that the quarter east of Rosenberry (Wright's) Lake had not yet been taken, and he filed homestead papers on it.

The Balloons who lived nearby were disappointed with their new neighbors because they had hoped to have their eldest son file on that particular quarter.

New Coffin
about 1887

The only corpse which Fred and Joe saw before their brother Thomas died was that of Henry Schwering who had died of consumption. The little boys, tots probably three and four years old, walked with their mother to the Schwering place,* a distance of about three miles. Mr. Schwering had been laid out in a freshly-painted, brown coffin.

Al Schwering, afraid that the little boys would touch the wet paint, repeatedly cautioned them: "Get back! Get back!"

Coffins were made-to-order, in those days, after a

---

* Where Keith and Amy Jones now live.

person died. Kubarts and Wonderchecks both made coffins when the need arose.

Seasick Mother
1886

Gregor and Johanna Hytrek had three children when they sailed across the Atlantic to America: Roman, seven years old, Paul, two, and Stella, a nursing baby. Their friends, Joseph and Mary Dlugosh, were traveling with them. Because Mary had a severe bout of seasickness, she wasn't able to eat and thus didn't produce enough milk to feed her baby, Little Joe.

Luckily, Johanna Hytrek had an abundance of milk, and she nursed Joe along with her own baby, Stella.

Both the Hytreks and the Dlugoshes went immediately to Holt County, because Gregor's brothers, Fred and Stanislaus (Gregor's twin), were already on homesteads there.

The Dlugoshes settled a few miles northeast of the Hytreks.

When the children were grown, Stella Hytrek married Little Joe's brother, Frank Dlugosh.

The Krysls Arrive
1891

Vaclav and Mary (Motis) Krysl married in 1880 and lived in Pilsen, Czechoslovakia until their emigration to America in 1891. At that time they had three children: Christina, 4; Vencil, 2; and Annie, a tiny baby.*

Vaclav's parents, Albert and Anna Slamova Krysl, accompanied them. After disembarking at New York City, they walked across a huge railroad yard. Mary was carrying her tiny baby and her mother-in-law Anna was carrying Vencil. Anna stumbled on one of the railroad tracks and fell. Little Vencil got a bruise on his head, but was not seriously injured.

Most of the land in Holt County had been settled by the time the Krysls arrived, but they were able to secure homesteads at the edge of the Sandhills in the western part of Green Valley.

---

* Years later, Christina married John Krobot, and Vencil (V.J.) married Anna Hytrek. They lived out their lives south of Stuart. Vaclav and Mary's baby Annie later married Bill Hytrek, cousin to Anna Hytrek Krysl, and they moved to Glendo, Wyoming.

Vaclav at the Gravel Pit
1891

It was Vaclav's wife Mary and his father Albert who broke the sod and planted the crops when the family first came to America. Mary led the oxen and Albert, a huge but aging man, guided the plow.

In order to earn some hard-to-get cash for the family, Vaclav worked at the gravel pit located halfway between Stuart and Atkinson. Since the distance was too great for walking home each night (about eighteen miles) he slept near the job site—mostly under the stars—and went home on weekends. If the family needed flour, he walked first to Atkinson where there was a grinding mill after which he carried a fifty-pound sack of flour on his back for the twenty-two miles home.

One miserably cold, rainy day, the gravel pit crew got soaking wet and chilled to the core. In the evening, Vaclav and two other workers flipped over a wagon box and crawled under it for protection. Since it was impossible to have a campfire, they had no way to make biscuits nor to dry their clothes. They thought their condition would be improved if they had a bottle of "spirits" to numb their senses.

Any of them would have been willing to walk the five miles to Atkinson to get a bottle, but all of them were recent arrivals in America, and they did not know the English word for the product they desired.

Finally, one member of the party recalled a word which sounded right to them all. They pooled their coins, and sent him out into the stormy night.

"Now don't drink it all on the way back," said one of the men.

"I'll not even unwrap it," he promised.

Hours later he returned, and true to his promise, the bottle was still neatly wrapped. With a whoop, one cold, thirsty fellow grabbed it and tore the paper off. Imagine their dismay when they found that the package contained a bottle of horse liniment.

(On the next pages are pictures of the generations of Krysls from pioneer Vaclav down to Stephanie, Robb, Vince II, Adrienne, and Renee.)

Vaclav Krysl Family-1901 Back: Christina, Annie, Vencil.* Seated: Vaclav* & Edward, Frank, Joe (front), and Mary* with Albert. Later, three more children were born: Mary, John, and Agnes.

V.J. and Anna Krysl Family. Back: Christine, Leo, Donald*, Bill; front: Josephine, V.J.*, Anna*, & Amelia.

*Direct ancestors of Judy, Vincent, and Donald II. 1941.

Top: Donald and Marie Dobrovolny Krysl Family. Judy, Don Jr., Don Sr., Marie, and Vince. 1966. Lower: Judy, with nephew Vince Jr. and nieces Renee & Adrienne. 1991. (After Don's death, Marie remarried—thus the name Kramer.)

Top: Vincent and Patti Monson Krysl Family, 1990. Back: Vince Sr., Patti, Eve Willadsen; front: Vincent Jr., Adrienne, and Renee. Bottom: Donald Jr. and Shirley Teter Krysl Family, 1988. Don, Stephanie, Shirley, and (front) Robert.

V.J. Krysl and His Dog

**The Krysls all have special
relationships with their dogs!
This picture was taken in 1951 when
V.J. was ill. He died
a couple months later.
V.J. is the eldest son of Vaclav.**

Vaclav Krysl in his German
army uniform, about 1879. A dozen
years later, he and his wife Mary
and babies Vencil and Anna
came to America.

Chapter 2

Looking Back: The Old Country

Old Country Army Stories
1860's and 1870's

Since Germany had conquered the Polish and Czech lands, the young men of these two oppressed countries were required to serve in the army of their old enemies. Such was the case of the Czech Krysl, Dobrovolny, Ziska, and Regal men and also of the Polish Hytrek men.

Fred Dobrovolny, the youngest brother of Thomas, had been in battle someplace in Europe. When his nieces and nephews asked him about it, he responded with a loud mixture of Bohemian, German, and English phrases accompanied by wild gestures. Sometimes he jumped to his feet to demonstrate how they loaded and shot the cannons, and he would jerk back to show the recoil of the big guns. Unfortunately the children could not understand the tumble of foreign words that described his actions.

After Fred had completed his required term of duty in the army, he was required (as were all other servicemen) to remain in the reserves for some years. During that time, it was impossible for him to obtain permission to leave the country. However, Fred's brother John had been in the New World for several years, and more recently his brother Thomas had gone to America—the land where people enjoyed an independence unimagined in the Old World and where land, itself, was free!

Wanting to immigrate without further delay, Fred put on several layers of clothes (in order to have some extra clothing without taking luggage) and walked out of Czechoslovakia into Austria. From there he obtained a passport to London and later to America. Fred's naturalization papers incorrectly give Austria as his homeland.

Thomas Dobrovolny, being older, had served his active duty and his reserve time before he embarked for America.

Grenadier Johann (Jan) Ziska was discharged from the

Top: The fragile paper inside Vaclav Krysl's metal dog tag. Bob Ziska, Vaclav's grandson, has the original.

Left: This photo was found among the keepsakes of Ziska relatives in Iowa. It is believed to be Jan Ziska, as he was a grenadier (palace guard) at one time. Courtesy Artha Frickel.
Right: A photo of Tom Dobrovolny. It was found among the mementos of Tom's son, Fred.

Genealogical diagrams can be found in the appendix.

Austrian Army on December 31, 1857. He was 31 years old and had served for more than nine years. He fought in Italy during the year of 1849.

Later, while serving his time in the army reserves, Jan worked as a shoemaker.(Jan is the Czech spelling for John.)

Gregor Hytrek had served his active duty and his reserve time before embarking for the New World. However, his brother Frederick, the first of the Hytreks to come to America, didn't care to wait that long. While home on leave from the army one day, he took off his uniform, threw it into a corner, and exclaimed: "Well, that's enough of that! I'm going to America!"

Taking no luggage at all, he sneaked out of the country and headed for the new land that was supposed, since it had oceans on both sides, to be free from war.

One story of Frederick Hytrek's army days has been handed down through the generations. He was stationed in France, and he and several other soldiers were walking down a road when they came to a field where several French girls were digging potatoes. The young men picked up some potatoes and playfully threw them at the girls. The girls quickly fired back. For a few minutes there was an exchange of laughter, French and Polish exclamations—and flying potatoes.

Gregor Hytrek played an accordion, and he often mentioned times when he entertained the troops with his music.

Vaclav Krysl was once stationed in (or near) Turkey. One Turk had about a dozen wives. Vaclav said that on some nights the Turk would carry a blanket to the middle of the yard and would sleep on the ground by himself.

Bunny Stew
1877

In Czechoslovakia everyone lived in cities, towns, or villages. The plots of farm land were small and scattered, having been divided by heirs as the centuries rolled by. Thus each landed family possibly owned a number of scattered plots. In the morning members of a village household might leave the cluster of cottages and walk to one of the plots of land they owned. After completing the days work, they returned to the village. No one lived on a farm in the country as people in America do.

Each family, whether or not it was among the prestigious landowners, kept a milk cow. Near the villages were wooded areas which belonged to all, and people could go to these groves to gather grass for their cows or to collect firewood.

Just as did other women of their country, Anotonija Dobrovolny went to the woods near their village of Radkovice to cut grass each day. She carried a large shawl, perhaps six foot square, on which she piled the grass, after which she tied the corners in a certain way, slipped her arms through the top of the bag, and carried it home. When she noticed that a rabbit was in the habit of frequenting the part of the woods where she worked, she told her husband Tom about it.

Tom thought a pot of bunny stew would be quite delightful, but all hunting of animals in the woods was forbidden to the common citizens. Any of them caught poaching would be fined and would lose their rights to collect grass and firewood there. Tom decided that if he were going to bag a rabbit, he had best lay plans carefully.

For a few days Tom observed the habits of the rabbit. Then one evening he took his gun, an illegal possession, out of its hiding place, went to the woods, and shot the animal.

Ka-boom!

The explosion split the night air, shocking Tom by its mighty blast and making the hair stand out on the back of his neck. He knew that everyone in the village had heard the thunderous noise, and that his neighbors would be coming to investigate. Quickly he hid the rabbit and his gun and circled away from them. As inquisitive people began to arrive, he joined them, pretending to be as curious as they were.

The next morning Tom instructed Antonija regarding the location of the gun and the rabbit. She concealed them in her bag of grass and, in that way, took them home.

The Discarded Coffin
probably 1860's

After more than 125 years, there is no way of finding out what it was—illness or accident—that put Martin Regal (older spelling: Rigl) in the coffin. But there he lay, cold, stiff, and ready for burial. Although his appearance gave every indication that he was dead, actually, he was not. He heard the men who had kept the nighttime vigil as they put away their playing cards and refilled their coffee cups from the big pot on the stove. He assumed that dawn was breaking, but he could not know this for certain, for his eyes were closed so tightly that, no matter how desperately he willed them to open, they remained still.

What an incredible nightmare!

The only one of his senses that remained intact was his hearing, and that particular sense did nothing to help him signal to his grieving relatives, saddened neighbors, and sobbing wife, Victoria, that he was not dead. Would he actually be buried alive? The hideous thought was enough to make a person stiff with terror.

Victoria's sister-in-law arrived and began making breakfast for the men who had kept the all-night wake. Her own husband, Joseph Kopecek, and his brother John (both of whom were brothers of Victoria) were among the group.

Martin knew that as soon as breakfast was over the men would approach the coffin in a customary salute that was at once a prayer, a morning greeting, and a part of their final good-bye. Afterward they would go home to dress for the funeral. Martin prayed desperately. He shoved the terror brought on by his predicament to the far corners of his mind and mentally begged God for a way to signal his friends.

Just as Martin had supposed, once breakfast was over, conversation stopped, and the men, one by one, shuffled over to the coffin. He heard their footsteps, heard the rustle of their clothing, even heard their breathing. He tried to move his hand, but it was too stiff, too heavy, too disconnected from his mental commands. He strained to open his eyes, to move his mouth, to draw a breath—anything to show them that he was alive—but his efforts were useless. His eyelids seemed to be pasted shut, and his ribs would not expand to draw in air.

Then suddenly one of the neighbors cried out, "In the name of heaven, get a doctor! Martin is not dead!"

Everyone turned toward the speaker. What had come over him? Had he lost his senses? Of course Martin was dead! They all knew it.

"I saw his eye move underneath his eyelid," insisted the man. "He's alive! I know he is! Call a doctor!"

He was so determined that there was nothing to do but call a doctor, though everyone else was certain that it would be wasted effort and wasted money. The man had probably seen a shadow brought on by the flickering candle that stood by the coffin, or else his own tired eyes had played a trick on him.

The doctor arrived and was able to ascertain that Martin, indeed, was alive. How long he remained in this catatonic state is not known, but he did recover. He fathered ten children, moved to America, and lived to be 84 years old. His body is

Left: The parents of Victoria (Kopecek) Regal. **Right:** The European Kopecek home. Victoria was born in this house, and now (1992) it is the home of Victoria's grandniece, Marie Chvatalova. In the 1800's, the right side of the building was the residence and the left side was the barn. The middle portion was used to store a wagon or carriage.

buried in the St. Joseph's Cemetery in Atkinson, Nebraska.*

The near-death experience changed Martin's life, making him a more God-centered and forgiving person. Joe Dobrovolny, the husband of one of Martin's granddaughters, said, "Martin Regal was the kind of man, who, if you were to throw a rock and hit him, would probably turn around and offer you bread."**

The Second Mary

The Regals had four children when they came to America: Mary, eight; Antonia, six; Jim, two; and Josephine, six weeks. Although Mary was the eldest child, she was the fourth-born and also was the second Mary. Three older children, thought to have been named Frances, Anna, and Mary, had died. Mary was the first to die, but when a new baby was born into the family and they were discussing what to name it, Frances said:
"I don't care what you name her, but I am going to call

---

* All his life, Martin Regal was more inclined than most people to attend funerals. If no minister were present, Martin conducted the service and offered earnest prayers for the soul of the deceased. If a priest or minister were present, Martin waited until the regular service was completed and then arose and came forward to offer more prayers. Some of Martin's kinfolk thought that perhaps his near-death experience was responsible for this unusual interest in funerals and in praying for the dead.
** This forgiving quality was not, it seems, an outstanding quality of his wife.

her Mary." Thus it was that they named the new baby Mary after her dead sister Mary.

One day when Frances was talking about getting a new dress, her sister Anna said, "Why do you want a new dress? You won't need it."

Later the family recalled these words and considered them to be prophetic, for both Frances and Anna died.

Ella Ziska Dobrovolny thought the children probably died of "summer complaint," which was actually food poisoning. No refrigeration and no running water in the homes made the disease common, both in Europe and in early American days.

Childhood Days in Europe

In her old age, Antonia Regal Ziska (usually called Toni) gave this account of their life in Czechoslovakia. Since she was a devout person, she often mentioned the Supernatural in her stories as well as in ordinary conversation.

I was born in Caslavice, Moravia in Czechoslovakia on May 10, 1871. Although we lived in the country, the houses were close together just as in a town. Someone in the neighborhood had a store because in those days, people traveled on foot, and the town was quite a distance away.

Each farm family had a small patch of land on which they might have a little flax and maybe some red clover. No one raised corn, but a few people planted wheat or oats. As was usual in that area, we had a couple of cows and a team of oxen.

People farmed by hand and used a flail for threshing. The flail was made with a long, wooden handle that had a shorter stick fastened on one end with a leather hinge. This stick would flop back and forth when it was swung at the bundles of grain. The straw from the grain was cut up and fed to the animals.

I remember when I went with my mother to get grass for the cows. She carried a large cloth—maybe six foot square—and went into the orchard. She cut the grass with a scythe, tied it in the cloth, and carried it to the cows. The red clover was cut the same way, but I think it may have been dried in the sun and piled to use in the winter for hay.

Even though we didn't have much land, we had a nice orchard with apples, prunes, pears, and cherries. Some of the fruit we dried, and it was used to make kolace for special occasions. *[Kolace* is the plural of *kolac;* however, many American people use the English method of forming the plural and say *kolaches.]* In the fall we also put apples in piles and covered them with oats or bran to keep them from freezing.

When we had evening guests, we served apples. I was really shy, but sometimes I passed the apples to the company anyway. Then our mother would cut some apples in two and give each of us children a half apple. Oh-h-h! They smelled so good—and tasted good, too. I ate mine with tiny nibbles to make it last as long as I could. We ordinarily ate a lot of potato soup and bread, and any kind of fruit was a great treat to us.

Our neighbors had currants in their garden. I used to walk around them and look, but I didn't pick any. Our parents had forbidden us to pick fruit or vegetables in the gardens, but some of the other children were really bold. Once they decided to go into a pea patch. I went with them part way, but then told them that I couldn't go into the patch and pick peas because it would be stealing. I also told them that while they were in the patch, to get some peas for me. Isn't that something! I wouldn't steal, yet I would eat the stolen peas. Of course, I was small and didn't understand such things very well.

Another time I was with some kids who decided to pick some poppies in the neighbor's poppy patch. I knew we shouldn't pick the poppies, and so I sat down at the edge of the patch and was collecting the fallen petals and was stringing them on a stick. A man came out when he saw the kids in the patch and shook his fist at them. They came running past me and scurried away, but I just sat where I was. When the man came and looked down at me, I stood up and showed him the stick with petals on it. He smiled, but I was shy and a little frightened which made me take a few steps backward. I stumbled on a clod and fell down. As soon as I could get onto my feet, I ran away. He stood there chuckling.

Once when I was about three years old, one of my cousins was carrying me on her back toward their place. As luck would have it, we happened to meet Santa Claus. Being afraid, I begged my cousin to put me down so that I could run home.

"Don't be afraid," she kept telling me, but I was scrambling around on her back, trying to get down. She took me home, after which Santa Claus came to our house. I'm sure that a group of neighborhood men had gotten together and had dressed someone up to go around to the various houses to startle the kids. It wasn't planned ahead with the parents. Anyway, the

Santa had switches, and he said we should pray. My sister Mary ran and hid, but I didn't think of that. I knelt down beside the trunk and began to pray. I kept praying even after my parents called that it was enough. Then the Santa passed us some candy and nuts.

Some days later, the three kings came. We again were scared, and we called to our mother who was outside. As soon as she got to us, she told the men to go away, and not to come anymore because we were small and easily frightened.

Another time, a man came to our house, carrying a stick with a bundle tied on the end. When he shook the bundle, it rattled. He said he could do plastering and other kinds of masonry and asked if he could stay overnight. My mother said that there were other people in the neighborhood who had more space in their houses, and he went to my father's brother's house. In the middle of the night, my uncle tapped on our window.

"We have been robbed," he said. "The man we took in for the night stole all the clothes from our trunks and also our money. Everything is gone!"

I recall a time when my parents went to a wedding, leaving us children home with an old lady whom we called Petsy. Well, we all, Petsy included, kept thinking about those good *kolace* (Czech fruit rolls) that would be served at the wedding, and Petsy finally concocted a plan to get us some. She dressed us girls in our best dresses, tied on our red aprons, and sent us to the wedding reception which was being held in a home in the neighborhood. There was a large crowd there, both in the house and in the yard. We went into the house and crawled under a bench so that our parents wouldn't see us. After some time, a man discovered us there.

"Why, here are two little girls!" he exclaimed, drawing us out from under the bench. "Someone bring them some *kolace!*"

The ladies who served us encouraged each of us to take both an apple and a prune *kolac*. As soon as it was possible, we sneaked out and ran home as fast as we could go. Petsy had come a little way down the road to meet us. She divided the four *kolace* into parts, and we three had a most pleasant tea party. You may be sure that our parents did not hear about this incident until we were grown. (See appendix for the *kolac* recipe.)

Mary was old enough to go to school in Czechoslovakia, but I wasn't. However, I sometimes walked to school with her, and after she disappeared inside the school, I went back toward home and stopped at my grandmother's house. Since they milked a couple cows, she churned butter which she sold at the little grocery. Most of the rural people in that area sold or traded their extra butter and eggs to the store. I think the storekeeper probably took these items to the town nearby a couple times a week. My grandmother usually churned in the cool of the morning because cream churned better if it wasn't too warm.* I would wait until she finished, and she would give me a piece of bread with fresh butter on it.

Even though I didn't get to go to Bohemian School, some years later I did learn to read and write the Czech language.

In those days, my folks had quite a lot of money, some of which had been found. Before my mother was married, her family found some treasure on a place that they were renting out, as they had two different places. Once one of her brothers claimed that he dreamed that there was money buried under a big rock that was in the yard of their rented place.

"Of what good is a dream?" said his father, shrugging.

But my uncle insisted that it was an answer to prayer and persuaded his father to go with him to investigate. Just exactly how my uncle got the information, we will never know.

After rolling aside the rock and digging energetically for some time, they came to a large, rotted, leather bag. Since the bag fell apart, they were scooping out its contents—hundreds of old coins—along with the dirt around them. The lady who was renting the house came out and began raking the money into her apron. She ran inside, emptied her apron, and returned to gather more of the coins. Finally, my grandpa said to her:

"Wait, lady! We found this money and it is on our land. We are willing to give you a share, but you can't take it all."

Thus it was that my mother had quite a large sum of money. My parents decided to use some of it to build a larger house, and they had the plans drawn and the foundation laid out. Then, because there was talk of more war, they decided we should come to America instead. We set sail on May 1, 1877.

I enjoyed every bit of the three or four weeks that it took for us to get across the ocean. I could hardly take time to eat my meals because I was so interested in watching the big waves and in looking for huge fish.

One night there was a storm which rocked the ship back

---

*Cream that is too cold doesn't churn well either. It is inclined to whip, after which churning is much more difficult.

and forth in a frightening way. The captain called everyone together and asked us to pray. As we were doing so, one woman jumped up, began waving her arms, and screaming curses. The captain had her taken out of the room so as not to disturb the rest of us. After some time the storm ceased.

Saying Farewell to Europe
1877

Mary Regal, who was eight years old at the time they left Europe, later told her daughter Ella* about their departure.

After we had everything packed for the journey, the family visited the cemetery. Toni and I placed poppies on each of the graves of our three sisters, and our mother had flowers for the graves of other relatives.

At the time that the family was getting ready to board the ship, we were standing in a crowd of people, some who were soon to leave Europe and others who were there to see relatives and friends off. A young man named Clint was among those who were embarking for the New World. His father, stricken by the fact that his son was leaving, wept and told him always to be faithful to God. Wanting to emphasize this request, the old man finally fell to his knees and implored his son:

"Remember every day of your life to stay near the Lord. Promise me! Be faithful to the commandments." The son promised.

We children thought that the ocean voyage was a great adventure. The fact that the adult travelers were free from their usual occupations gave them more time to talk to us. They gave us treats, told stories, and fashioned surprises for us. Toni celebrated her sixth birthday on the ship, and on that day she and I were both showered with attention.

We all enjoyed watching the enormous, rolling waves and the occasional appearances of the huge fish. However, my pleasure was somewhat dampened by the fact that one of the women on board had lost a baby through death, and it had been

---

* Ella later married Joe Dobrovolny and gave birth to eight children: Emmanuel, who died in infancy; LeRoy; Albena; Marie, who is the recorder of this account; Anton (Tony); Harold (Tom); John; Fred.

A precious possession that the Regals brought to America in 1877 was a statue of the Infant Jesus and His mother. Now in 1992 it is a prized possession of Mary (Ziska) Krysl, granddaughter of Martin and Victoria Regal. Below: Martin & Victoria Regal

buried at sea. I don't know if the child had died on that particular trip or on some previous voyage. However, the mother was still grieving and saw no beauty in the endless, rolling waves. I was at an age when I worried about other peoples problems and was preoccupied by the mother's grief and also by the idea that people who died on a ship were buried at sea.

Antonija (Elias) Dobrovolny
1860's and 70's

Antonija* Elias Dobrovolny's father was an energetic man. He had a garden an acre or so in size from which he sold vegetables. During winter he worked in the woods where he cut logs for lumber, and during spring he cut stone in a quarry.

Along with his summer gardening chores, he sometimes made trips on foot into Germany where he bought hogs or geese, drove them home, and sold them to villagers for meat.

Antonija remembered, as a child, running to meet her father when he was returning from these journeys and helping

---

*An'-ton-ee-uh. Only the first syllable is accented. The Czech J sounds like the English Y as in *yes*. *(Also spelled Antonia.)*

him pen the geese.

As a young woman, Antonija hired out to a neighbor as a milkmaid, a job for which she was paid thirty-five dollars a year. One of the articles which she bought with these earnings was a clothes iron which had a removable stone insert.

This clothes iron, brought to America by Antonija Dobrovolny and shown here by her grandson, Harold (Tom) Dobrovolny, is more than 120 years old.

The stone was heated in the hot coals in the firebox of the stove, retrieved with a hook, inserted in the metal jacket of the iron, and the tool was ready to do its job. Antonija brought the iron to the United States when they immigrated in 1878.*

Antonija had had the opportunity to hear some of the great orchestras in Europe. Sometimes her comments about the music of the American prairie lands were not complimentary. She would shrug and refer to it as "everyday street music."

"Someone picks up a violin and goes 'Fiddledy, fiddledy, fiddledy,' and folks think they have music. How would they know? They have never heard *real* music."

Antonija told of the impressive buildings and of the beautiful cathedrals in Europe. The small towns had churches, but on special occasions they might journey to a city and attend services in a cathedral.

It seems that once a year a large group of people walked a considerable distance, a trip that required a number of days, to attend some glad celebration. Her sons later could not ascertain

---

* Also, Judy Krysl, Antonija's great granddaughter, has a soup bowl that Antonija brought to America. Antonija gave it to her son Joe when (in 1911) he moved to the cabin on his South Place, thus beginning his ranch in Holt County.

whether it was a religious event or some secular holiday, but they supposed that it was held in Prague or Vienna. It must have been a joyous occasion, for Antonija spoke of it with such sad longing that tears would moisten her eyes.*

Antonija married Tom Dobrovolny in Radkovice, Czechoslovakia in the year 1877. It was a double wedding, for Tom's brother Anton was married to Karoline Texel at the same time. Tom and Antonija's first child, Frank, was born May 18, 1878. Soon after his birth, Tom's little family set out for America.

Anton and Karoline remained in Europe, living, at first, on the old Dobrovolny Estate at Radkovice. Soon, however, they sold the land and moved to a village called Dolni Vilimovice where they purchased another acreage.**

Hytreks in Europe
1880's

Johanna Hoffman first married a man whose last name was Sapok and who operated a tavern. He died young, leaving a little son named Roman who was the joy of his grandparent's life.

Johanna attempted to continue to operate the tavern, but it was difficult for a woman who was more interested in lifting her beautiful singing voice in a choir than in listening to the bawdy songs of the tavern.

After a few years, she remarried and her new husband, Gregor Hytrek, took over the operation of the business.

Gregor's older brother Fritz and his twin brother Stanislaus had gone to America, and their letters to Gregor describing the vast stretches of prairie land—free for the asking—turned Gregor's head westward. He decided to pack up his family and join them.

Roman's grandparents begged to keep Roman in Europe. They had lost their son in death, and felt they couldn't bear to lose his only child to the dangers of a distant, untamed land. Gregor and Johanna, by then, had two children of their own, Paul

---

* Anotnija's son Fred said she referred to this holiday with a term that sounded like "Pro-svets-thve."
**About 30 years after Tom came to America, two of Anton's sons (Joe and Anton, Jr.) immigrated to America. Unbeknownst to the Nebraska kinfolk, they settled near Ross, North Dakota.

and Stella. Would they not let the Sapoks raise Roman?

But Johanna could not give up her eldest child; after they journeyed to America, Gregor adopted Roman, and his name was changed from Sapok to Hytrek.

A Danish Story
as told by Astrid Willadsen*
1800's

In Denmark a few generations ago the eldest son always had the same name as his grandfather. If a man's name was Hans Willadsen, his eldest son would be named Willis Hansen (meaning *Han's son*). Willis' eldest son's name would switch back to that of his grandfather, Hans Willadsen (Willis' son). When this second Hans fathered a son, the child would be named—you guessed it—Willis Hansen. The two names flip-flopped back and forth as the generations rolled by.

Finally, because of the confusion generated by this practice, the government passed a law which stated that whatever last name a person had at that time should remain as the last name of his descendants. Astrid's grandfather bore the name Hans Villadsen which later was respelled *Willadsen*.

In the 1800's the military draft laws in Denmark were rigid. When a youth was called to appear, he must comply. Possibly, if he were later found to have a a serious defect, such as a bad heart or a missing leg, he might be sent home.

When Astrid's uncle (a brother to her father) was called, he was deathly ill with meningitis—so ill that he couldn't possibly get out of bed.

When he did not appear at the induction center, a sheriff was sent to bring him. Upon arriving at the Willadsen home, the sheriff found the youth dead.

A Farm in Denmark
1916

Astrid Willadsen's father, Andreas Willadsen, went to the county seat to sign the documents for buying a farm. He wore his every-day clothes, which, since he was a thrifty man,

---

* Eve Willadsen's grandmother who lives in Irwin, Iowa. Astrid's maiden name and her married name were the same, for she married a half-cousin. See appendix for genealogy.

were faded and patched.

The official reviewed the papers. "There are several mortgages on this property," he said. "Now, you understand that the first mortgage can be assumed by you as the new owner, but the second and third ones must be paid off. Have you contacted a bank and attempted to borrow the money?"

"Well, no, Sir," said Andreas to this unexpected question.

"Do you think you can borrow such a sum of money?"

"I don't know, Sir."

"Have you approached some person of means, then, in an attempt to raise this amount?"

The faded, patched figure stirred, somewhat bewildered by this line of inquiry.

"No, Sir. I haven't."

The official looked troubled. "This question of funds is the next matter which needs your attention," he said. "I can't proceed with the paperwork until the second and third mortgages are satisfied."

Andreas stood uncertainly for a moment.

Finally he spoke. "But won't you honor cash?" He drew a large wad of bills from his pocket and laid them in front of the official. It was an adequate amount of money to satisfy the mortgages.

Now, in 1992, Astrid's sister, Anna, lives on that farm in Denmark.

Christian & Astrid Willadsen

**Anyone who had a horse
to break could find plenty of wide open
space in which to do it!**

**Nick and Sarah Krysl
visiting the grave of their great uncle,
Roman Hytrek, who
died as a boy in the Blizzard of 1888.**

Chapter 3

The Great Blizzard and Indian Scares

Lost in a Blizzard
1888

Nothing in their European experiences nor in their one winter in America had prepared the Hytreks* for the suddenness and the ferocity of the Blizzard of 1888.

January 12th dawned clear and warm—a perfect day to send nine-year-old Roman on a couple of errands. First of all, he was to walk to the home of his uncle, Stanislaus Hytrek (several miles to the northeast), to return a knife they had borrowed for butchering and to ask Stanislaus to come and help shovel the deep drifts that had collected around the stable and shed. From there, Roman was to proceed a half mile south to the home of his uncle, Frank Frost,** to pick up some spices that Frank had purchased in town for them. The Hytreks needed the spices in order to process the meat they had butchered.

The boy, a small, slender child, set out, his little dog trotting at his heels. He was excited because of this rare chance to visit his kinfolk.

---

*Information obtained from Anna (Hytrek) Krysl, Roman's youngest sister, and Phillip Frost, Roman's cousin.
** Frank Frost had married Magdelena Hytrek, a sister to Gregor, Stanislaus, and Fritz.

When Roman passed the John Price place*, he waved to Mr. Price who was shoveling snow. A few minutes later, the violent storm advanced across the prairie, looking like an approaching, white wall, and instantly, the balmy weather was transformed into a frigid, breath-taking, roaring blizzard. Quickly, John Price mounted a horse and rode after the boy.

The storm was so forceful that John could see nothing—not even the head of the horse he was riding. There was no road nor fence to use as a guide, and he was immediately lost. Finally he loosened the reins, allowing the horse full freedom to go where he chose, and the animal, putting his nose to the ground, followed his own tracks back home. After stabling the horse, John headed for the soddy; however, the wind blew him off course, confused him, and nearly caused him to bypass the house. Finally, he was guided in by his wife who stood at the open door, banging on a tin dishpan with a large, iron spoon.

When the storm struck the Hytrek place,** Gregor immediately put on warm clothes. Since the blowing snow was so fine that it took a person's breath away, Johanna tied a piece of an old sheet over his face. It was his intention to hurry after the boy. However, as soon as he got out of the protection of the soddy, the wind blew him south. Not able to keep his balance against the force of the storm, he got on his knees and crept back to the shelter of the building. He hoped and prayed that the initial frenzy of the storm would pass. When it did not, he made several more attempts, but it was soon obvious to him that to proceed would result only in that he, too, would be lost.

The Henry Krobot family,*** who lived about a mile south of the Prices, heard a scratching at the door. They opened it and found a little animal encased in snow. After taking it inside, they thawed it out and gave it some warm broth from a pot that simmered on the back of the stove. Once the snow had melted from the creature, the Krobots recognized Roman's little dog. They wondered how he happened to arrive at their door, but the fury of the storm made investigation impossible.

The next morning after the blizzard had abated, numerous search parties were organized, but the child's body could not be found.

---

* John Price lived where Ray Krysl now lives. (1992)
** Where Andy and Nita Hytrek presently live.
*** Great-grandfather to Jim Krobot who occupies the same place.

Roman's mother was overwhelmed with grief, and the eerie sound of coyotes howling in the distance intensified the horror. Also, her tiny baby, Stencil, cried all the time. Finally, it was discovered that his grieving mother had lost her milk supply, thus starving the infant. After he was placed on cow's milk, he was satisfied.

In March, Jake Ripp and John Slaymaker were walking across the prairie on their way to a dance at the Castle place,* and they found Roman's coat. People can only wonder how he happened to lose it. One theory was that he unbuttoned it to tuck his little dog inside, and the raging winds tore it off; another was that, as his hands froze and drooped, the coat, heavy with collected snow, slid off his thin shoulders.

Louis Radcliffe organized another search party, and Roman's body was found about three quarters of a mile east of the Krobot place. He was leaning against the south side of the hill which is sometimes referred to as Schneider Hill.

It was decided that Johanna should not see the body of the child, and the coffin, made by Frank Frost, was nailed closed. The anguished mother implored, but those in charge stood firm. Roman was buried in St. Joseph's Cemetery in Atkinson, Nebraska. His grave is located south of the Seger monuments.

It can only be imagined how difficult it was to write the news of Roman's tragic death to the Sapok grandparents in Europe.

Fighting Grief
told by Rose Hoffman, a neighbor

Months came and went, and Johanna continued to grieve.

"If only I could have seen his body," she said over and over, "I think I could find some peace. As it is, I feel like something is yet to be finished. Others saw him—touched him—but I, his own mother, was not allowed to do so."

Being of deep faith she told herself that the child was with God, but her anguish would not abate.

She remembered what a gentle, obedient boy he was. One picture she held in her mind was of a morning when it was

---

*Ripps occupied the place where Bob Kaups now live, and Castles had settled on the quarter of land where Frank Gregers currently live.

Gregor Hytrek Family: Standing: Stencil, Paul, Stella, and John; seated: Mary, Johanna, Anna, and Gregor. (1897 photo)

time for him to go to school, and he had not said his morning prayers. She told him to say them on the way to school and launched him out the door.

Watching through the window, she saw him put the bail of his lunch bucket over one arm and remove his cap to tuck it under the other arm. She knew his hands were folded in front as he walked across the meadow. After a few minutes, he returned the cap to his head and began to jog toward school which was about two miles away. She knew that prayers had been completed.

When the second spring arrived, Johanna had a healing dream. She saw Roman romping in a green meadow which was dotted with flowers. His face was bright in the morning sun, and he was laughing. Finally, she could feel that the boy, wherever he was, was happy, and she noticed, too, that the sun in her own world was still shining also.*

---

* The location of the Gregor Hytrek homestead was: NE 1/4 of Sec. 17, Twp. 29, R.16 W. Andy and Nita Hytrek live there now in 1992.

Ella Brady and the Blizzard
1888

Early in the morning John Brady went downtown while his wife Ella* washed the clothes for their tiny baby Jessie** and hung them on the line. The blizzard hit with such blinding force that not only did the fine-blown snow make breathing impossible*** but also the battering winds whipped between buildings and knocked people off their feet. Even though the Bradys lived only a short distance south of the main square in Atkinson, John stayed downtown for the day-and-night duration of the storm.

Since Ella had only a few pieces of firewood in the house, she closed the doors between rooms and kept a fire only in the kitchen, using the wood sparingly. She hoped John would get home by the time it was gone. When he didn't come, the house quickly got cold. How much cold air did a tiny baby dare breathe?

Jessie had been born in Joliet, Illinois, and Ella and she had just arrived in Atkinson. After unpacking, John had cut up the packing crates for kindling and had stacked them on the back porch. Ella burned them next; since it was light, dry wood, it didn't last long.

Ella looked around the house for other burnable articles that could be sacrificed for warmth. She had an old chair, but now the heavy laundry tub of water sat on it. She dipped water from the tub, pouring it into the slop bucket until the bucket was full. Then she dragged the partially emptied tub to the floor

---

* Ella (Shaw) Brady, mother to Frank Brady.

** Jessie's tombstone says she was born Dec. 27, 1888. The person who gave the date must have thought that, since she was a tiny baby during the Blizzard of '88, she was born in '88. However, Jessie was born late in December of '87 and was sixteen days old on the day of the blizzard: Jan. 12, 1888.

*** Often an account of a blizzard includes the phrases "took my breath away" or "the snow was so fine I couldn't breathe." Rudy Dvorak said that it means exactly what it says. In 1949 he was in a storm of fine, blowing snow, and suddenly, he couldn't breathe at all. A mechanism in his throat blocked his airway— probably the same one which closes a person's throat at the onset of drowning. The fine snow in the air apparently produced enough moisture to trigger the valve and shut off his breath.

and used John's woodman's hatchet to demolish the chair.

John's decoy ducks were in a couple of apple crates. She dumped them out and chopped the boxes into pieces. She burned a piece of driftwood shaped like a goose that he had brought home as a novelty.

"All this was as nothing!" she later told her niece.

When the young mother could not find anything more to burn, she brought two feather quilts into the kitchen, one from their own bed and another from the guest bed, and spread them on the floor.

Already the house was bitterly cold. However, she decided to uncover the baby and change her diaper one last time, hurrying as fast as her stiff fingers would let her. Then wrapping the baby in a wool shawl, she crawled between the two feather quilts, huddling the infant to her own body. She, herself, was chilled from prowling through the freezing rooms looking for articles to burn, and the quilts from the bedrooms were cold. It took a long time, but she finally did warm up in spite of the ever-lowering temperature in the house.

The next day when John came home, he found that the slop bucket had frozen solid and had split down the seam, but that the wash tub—which had less water—had only bulged on the bottom. His wife and daughter were safe, snuggled between the featherbeds.

The baby clothes that were on the line had been blown away by the storm. The next summer a garment that was later recognized as Jessie's was found caught in a patch of weeds several miles south of Atkinson.

The Teacher in the Hay Pile

Etta Shattuck was teaching in School District 141, a country school south of Emmett. She had completed the fall term and decided to walk, on that particularly pleasant winter morning, to the home of a school board member where she intended to collect her pay. She had only recently left her boarding place when the blizzard hit. Repeatedly, the family shouted from the door, trying to guide her back to the house, but their voices were lost in the howling storm.

Etta was in a forty-acre enclosure and she reasoned correctly that she would be able to follow the fence until she eventually came back to the buildings. However, because the storm made movement difficult, she became confused. She thought she had followed the fence for miles. Finally, she crawled through it and drifted with the storm.

When she came to a hay pile, she decided to dig into it, but her hands were so cold that she couldn't make a large enough hole to shelter her entire body. Her legs, exposed at the opening in the hay, froze.

Three days later Daniel Murphy and his hired man came to that particular hay pile to get hay for the livestock. Etta called to them. They dug her out and took her home where Daniel and his wife did what they could to thaw her legs. After some days her parents were able to come with a team and sled to take her back to their home in Seward.

In an attempt to save her life, Etta's legs were amputated, but she died a couple of weeks later.*

Schaafs and the Blizzard

Joe and Rosa Schaaf's eldest son, ten-year-old Joseph, had been killed in a farm accident on January ninth and had been buried on the tenth.

After three days of grieving, the parents, of necessity, were making attempts to redirect their thoughts to tasks that were pressing for their attention. They had been waiting for a break in the bad weather, as they needed to butcher a hog.

We can imagine that, on the twelfth, Joe must have looked out the window and said words similar to these: "It looks like a nice day for a change. I'll get the fire going under the scalding barrel and you heat a boilerful of water on the stove. As soon as we've finished the chores, John can ride the pony to Goldfusses to see if someone from there can come to help butcher."

We can also imagine Rosa nodding, her face swollen from grieving. She knew that since John, at age seven, was now the oldest, he quickly would be flooded with new tasks, which in the past, Joseph would have done. Tears flooded her eyes: tears for Joseph, now dead, and tears for John, the little boy whose childhood was suddenly over.

"Well," she comforted herself, "at least, an errand to the neighbors is a pleasant chore. Better than last night's cold job when he had to struggle for an hour to draw water from the well

---

* Etta Shattuck taught Mary O'Donnel Gaughenbaugh, who became Nelle Gilg's mother.

to water the stock and then had to begin learning how to milk."

A few minutes after the boy departed, the blizzard with its fierce winds and plunging temperature engulfed the prairie.

Quickly, Joe hurried in the direction that Little John had gone. He must find him! The child had never been sent on an errand to the neighbors before, and in this storm, he would immediately be confused.

But Joe didn't find him; rather, he himself was soon lost, stumbling blindly in the storm and fighting to stay on his feet. It was his good fortune to bump into a hay pile, a circumstance about as likely as finding a diamond in road gravel! He dug into the hay and remained there until the storm abated —the next day.

We can only imagine the terror experienced by Rosa, waiting at home with her two younger children. So soon after the death of Joseph, now her second son and her husband were both lost in a howling storm.

Joe returned home the following day. As for Little John, the neighbors searched relentlessly for him. They must have passed over his body many times, for later it was found buried under the snow less than a mile from the place.

There is no record of what happened to the pony.

Fred Dobrovolny's Blizzard Stories

I was only three years old, but I remember the storm as if it were yesterday.

If the blizzard had come a day earlier, Frank [aged 9] would have been caught in it. We had had a lot of snow and everyone was short of supplies. When it cleared a little, Dad and some of the other men, including Mike Flakus, got together with teams, wagons, and shovels and went to town.

Since Dad hadn't come home when Mother thought he would, she sent Frank, on the morning of the eleventh, to the Flakuses to see if Mr. Flakus had come home. Frank just had a thin jacket, and it being a couple miles, he said he almost froze— and it wasn't even storming—just cold. Of course, he was afoot. If he'd have gone a day later, he'd have been caught in the blizzard for sure, but the way it was, he came back and said that Mr. Flakus wasn't home either.

---

* Location of Tom Dobrovolny's homestead: SE 1/4 of Sec. 18, Twp. 28, R 15 W; John's homestead: NW 1/4 of Sec. 29, Twp. 28, R15; Fred's: SW 1/4 of 25, Twp. 28, R 16.

The next day, the twelfth, started out as a nice day. Dad had returned during the night, and when he and mother did chores that morning, they let some of the animals out of the barn so that they could get some sun.

Dad had brought supplies from town, and some of them were still in the wagon. He was carrying them in and had the door open when the storm hit. It came all of a sudden, and Dad said that the fine snow blasted by the fierce wind actually shut off his breath. I remember that the door, which opened to the inside and faced east, was sucked shut with a loud bang.

We didn't have much in the house for fuel and Dad went to the crib to get some corn to burn. On the way back he was so blinded by the storm that he missed the soddy completely. Luckily, he ran into the clothesline post and then followed the wire line to the corner of the soddy.

The folks were worried about the livestock, but there wasn't anything they could do about the animals outside. You couldn't see a thing out there because the dense snow in the air shut out the light.

Presently, Mother heard a noise outside; it was made by three young pigs that had crowded into the wide door frame for protection. Dad brought them into the house. We saved those three—and two more that had dug into a pile of manure by the barn. Their backs stuck out of the snow and froze which caused the hide to come off. I remember Dad rubbing lard on their raw backs the next summer to keep the flies off.

We had two wagon loads of pigs ready to sell, but the weather had been so bad that Dad hadn't gotten them to market. We lost them all except for the two by the barn and the three that came to the house.

But getting back to the day of the storm—all that we owned was in our one-room soddy, and Mother and Dad watched those pigs all day and all night so that they wouldn't damage anything. Whenever I woke up in the night, the lamp was still burning—sitting there on the immigrant chest between the stove and the bed—and the folks were still watching those pigs.

In the morning, Joe and I sat on the wide window ledge in the soddy and watched the folks bring a half-frozen calf over the drifts and into the house. Her feet, ears, and tail were frozen, but we warmed her by the stove, and she lived. However, the hair never did grow on her hocks.

We had a steer calf the same age, but we didn't find him. He probably wandered with the storm and froze on the prairie.

Three days after the blizzard, Aunt Barbara gave birth to our cousin Mary. They lived about a mile and a half south over by the lake. Mother killed a chicken and made noodle soup to take to Aunt Barbara*. I can see her yet, struggling over the drifts with that pot of soup in one hand.

Fred Ziska said they strung a rope from their house to the barn because they couldn't see at all and needed something to guide themselves across the yard. He was about fourteen then.

Dora Backhaus** had gone to the well to get a bucket of water. She pulled the bucket up hand over hand, and was leaning forward to grasp it just as the blizzard hit. The wind almost knocked her down the well.

The snow completely covered Jeremiah Murphy's house. He had the shovel inside and he tunneled out. He had to throw the snow inside the soddy until he got to the top of the drift over the house.
Later someone came along looking for livestock that had been lost in the storm.
"Where do you live," they asked Jeremiah.
"Down there," he said, pointing to a spot below them.

John Bouska turned his cow out that morning. He said that he almost didn't make it from the barn to the house himself. He knew better than to look for the cow. He didn't find her for a long time because after she died, the drifts covered her. When the snow melted, he found that she had been frozen stiff while she was still standing.

Mrs. Hookstra was teaching in Schuyler. People managed to get their kids home from school; but when she started for her boarding place, the wind blew her down and she couldn't get up. She went home on hands and knees, following a row of young trees to keep her direction. Schuyler was settled

---

* It was a custom in those days to take chicken soup to anyone who was sick or injured. If they were very sick, they were fed only the broth; otherwise, they could have some of the chicken and noodles, too.
** A son, Billy, was born the following July, who in adulthood married Cecelia Fowler, sister to Hazel Fowler Freouf.

earlier than Holt County, and they already had some trees started. We didn't have trees here yet.

Fred finished his story: "Oh, that was some wind! Awful! I heard one fellow say that his cats were on the porch; and when that wind hit, it just swooped three cats up in the air. Awful force! And so desperately cold. Most anything out in it was soon dead. It was a fright!"

Barefoot Tracks in the Snow
as told by Joe Dobrovolny

When we were small, we were shut in the soddy when there was snow on the ground because, like a lot of kids then, we had no shoes until we went to school. We hated staying inside because there wasn't space to play. The one room was crowded with necessities—most all things that kids didn't dare touch.

Once when there had been quite a bit of snowy weather, Mother told Frank to shovel out a patch of ground south of the house and also to clear a path from it to the door. When he got finished, Mother let us go outside during the warmer parts of the day to run around on that patch of ground. We were supposed to stay off the snow, though.

One evening while the folks were doing chores, we went out to play. Frank was making hay twists from a haystack in the yard. The pile was almost used up, revealing the nests of the multitude of mice who were living under the hay. Suddenly, Frank yelled.

"Mouse! Mouse! Here Curly! Mouse!"

The dog had been playing with us, and when he ran, we followed—right over the snow in our bare feet.

We had a lot of fun dashing around chasing mice. We made sure we got to the house before the folks came in, but they saw our barefoot tracks in the snow and scolded us.

Thomas' Illness
Nov. 1888

When Thomas began to be troubled with failing health, his brothers noticed that something was amiss before their parents were aware of it. Thomas was a thin boy—slight, like Joe—but he had always been a gritty, strong lad. However, during this particular summer, he was quieter and less inclined to enter the wrestling matches and the general horseplay among the other children. Sometimes when the boys jogged across the prairie, he would be stricken with a sudden cramp and would be compelled to stop and double over until it passed. Finally, he gave up running completely.

"You fellows go on ahead," he would say. "I'll catch up later."

After Thomas became feverish and lost his appetite, his mother became concerned. She fed him castor oil, brewed teas for him, rubbed his abdomen with liniment, and encouraged him to drink hot milk. Nothing helped. By fall he was spending most of his time lying on a mat behind their little cook stove.

Tom and Antonija talked about summoning a doctor but decided against it. They had no faith in doctors. Earlier that same year the Balloons had taken their ailing son to a doctor and had brought him home dead.*

Antonija had been helping Tom pick corn, but finally decided she must stay home to care for Thomas. Tom, however, continued to go to the field.

One day Thomas had a particularly bad attack. He was crying out in pain and Antonija could do nothing to relieve him. Joe, aged five, was the oldest boy home. (Frank and Anton were herding cattle in the cornstalks of a field that had already been picked.) Antonija told Joe to hurry out to where Tom was working and tell him to come home.

Joe, wearing a pair of cloth moccasins that his mother had made for the older boys, ran across the frost-covered cornfield. He was afraid that his father would not listen to him, for children were taught not to make suggestions to adults.

"Thomas is in bad pain," Little Joe said in Czech. "Mother wants you to come home."

Joe was relieved when his father responded. The two of them rode home atop the half load of ear corn.

Thomas' abdomen was black, suggesting gangrene, and he was in excruciating pain. After some time, he quieted. It was thought that perhaps he had appendicitis and that, once his appendix burst, the intense pain receded.

---

* The Balloon boy was buried on the quarter northeast of Rosenberry Lake (now Wright's Lake).

Within a day (Mid-November, 1888) Thomas died. They laid him out on two chairs while the coffin, fashioned by a neighboring pioneer,* was constructed. Before the lid was closed prior to the trip to town, Mike Flakus lifted four-year-old Fred for a last look at his brother.

Fred was unaccustomed to being lifted. Since that action, he felt, was one reserved for babies, he made an embarrassed sound which people interpreted to be a giggle.

"He's too young to know what is going on," said Mike as he lowered the little boy to the floor.

A neighbor drove the team and wagon that carried Thomas' coffin. Tom and Antonija, as well as a number of neighbors, followed in additional wagons.

From the soddy window, four brothers watched the little procession as it slowly wound its way across the prairie. Now that all the adults had left the house, the boys felt no need to keep up pretenses. Their gritty exteriors melted away, and tears rolled down their faces. All—right down to the smallest of them— knew that the circle of five had been irrevocably reduced to four. Four it remained for eighty-two more years until another of them crossed over to the next world to again greet Thomas.

After Joe was grown, he and his wife and children were in St. Joseph's Cemetery in Atkinson on Memorial Day. As was customary, the children busied themselves at decorating the grave of a baby brother as well as the graves of other kinfolk nearby. They hardly noticed when their father selected a cluster of wild begonias and slipped away to visit Thomas' grave. Joe had, on occasions, commented that he should get a marker for it, but times were hard and he hadn't yet done so.

On this day when he returned, his family members snapped to attention when they heard his sad tones.

"They have changed the roads and the fences," he said. "I can't find Thomas' grave.

Now the children stood wide-eyed, suddenly experiencing a sense of unexplainable loss. They learned something about human nature that day: when an object always has been available, one is apt to give it scant attention; not until after it is gone does one realize its true significance.

---

* Joe and Fred thought it was made by Mr. Wondercheck, but Frank, who was older and probably knew, said it was made by Joe Kubart who also had made the casket for the Balloon boy.

This hotel in Stuart, Nebraska, was located east of the main square on the north side of the street. Now a flower shop and a house owned by Frank Murphy is on that location. The stone building west of it was a post office but now is vacant.

John Ziska Wedding
1888

From age fourteen until she was married, Mary Regal worked in the laundry of the Northwestern Hotel in Stuart. The bed sheets were washed by hand and were heated in "boilers," which were large containers placed on the tops of stoves.

Mary had to lift the steaming, cumbersome sheets, using a two-pronged stick called a clothes stick, out of the boilers and into the tubs. It was a dangerous job for an adult and doubly so for a girl in her early teens. Also, on summer days, it was a stifling one as well.

Effie Pacha Kubart was four years old when Mary Regal and John Ziska were married (November 20, 1888).

"It was a custom then," she said, "for those who were to be the attendants to travel through the countryside and invite people to the wedding. When they approached a farm, they pointed a gun skyward and shot three times to signal that a wedding invitation was arriving. People ran outside, laughing and cheering and joking.

Left: John and Mary (Regal) Ziska wedding, 1888.
Lower L: Joe and Antonia (Regal) Ziska Wedding, 1890
Lower R: Fred and Agnes Kramer wedding, 1901.

Notice the change from dark to light gowns. Also, Mary's dress, unlike later fashions, had a wire bustle under the back of the skirt.

"My mother helped frost the wedding cake. Folks didn't have any kind of egg beaters then. They put egg whites on a big platter and each worker held two forks in her hand and beat and beat and beat.

"The wood floor was scrubbed until it turned white. [Lye was probably used, as it tends to whiten wood.] They scattered straw on it during the preparation so they wouldn't get it dirty. When the wagon carrying the bride and groom was seen approaching, the straw was swept up.

"Some of the older kids were giving me a ride in a little wagon—sort of a hand cart. The women yelled, 'Bring the cart!'

"They pitched the straw into it. I remember how they hurried to have everything all cleaned up before the bride and groom arrived. We hauled the straw down by the barn.

"Everyone said how beautiful the bride was. She wore a wine-colored dress with white trim. The older girls said the gown was truly fashionable because it had a bustle in the back. Brides didn't wear veils then, but she had on a fluffy hat made of feathers. She let us touch it; we had never before felt anything so soft."*

The Candy Bucket
1889 or 1890

Because there was an abundant amount of forested land in some areas of the United States in early times, many products were sold in wooden containers. Hard candy was shipped to the stores in wooden buckets, after which it was weighed, packaged, and sold. One day Tom brought an empty candy bucket home to use for a water pail.

It didn't take the boys long to notice that there were still beads of candy deposited on the interior of the bucket. How could they fairly divide this prize--this unexpected sugar lode? After earnest discussion, a decision was made.

Using a pencil, they divided the inside of the bucket into fourths. Each boy's initials were penciled on the outside of the bucket, designating his fourth. Then they took turns sticking their heads into the bucket, each licking that part which was his share.

---

*Location of John Ziska's homestead: S 1/2 of NW 1/4 and N 1/2 of SW 1/4 of Sec. 10, Twp.28, R 15 W.

The Indianhead Calendar
about 1889

Tom had returned from town and had told Frank to carry the sack of flour into the house. When Frank climbed into the wagon to do so, he noticed a new calendar that someone had given Tom. There was a large picture of an Indian head on it.* Frank hid it by the corn crib.

Later, when he, his parents, and Anton went out to do chores, Frank slipped away and got the calendar. Creeping up to the soddy, he hid below the window. After making a noise in order to get the attention of the younger boys, Joe and Fred, who were inside, he slowly slid the picture up just as if an Indian were raising his head to peek into the window. Then quickly he slid it back down again.

He rolled the calendar into a cylinder, laid it by the hay twists on the south side of the house, and went back to the barn. Later when chores were finished, the group returned to the house. Joe and Fred had the door bolted, and had to be persuaded to unlock it.

"There was an Indian at the window!" said Fred.

"I hope not!" exclaimed Antonija.

"I don't think so," said Tom. "The animals are all calm, and we didn't see anything out there."

"But we saw him," said Joe. "He was lying below the window, and he lifted up and peeked in."

"Speaking of Indians," said Tom. "I got a new calendar in town. Did you see it when you unloaded the wagon, Frank?"

"Yes, I did. I laid it on the hay twists and forgot to bring it in. I'll get it."

By then it was completely dark outside. Frank was only about eleven, and the scare he had given his younger brothers bounced back and engulfed him. His spine tingled as he groped around for the calendar. An entire band of Indians seemed to be crouching in the dark, ready to spring on him. As soon as his hand located the calendar, he snatched it up, hurried inside, and handed it to his father.

When Tom presented the calendar to the family, Joe realized it was the figure they had seen at the window and was

---

* Fred and Anton said that in the 1880's and 1890's the most common picture on a calendar was that of an Indian Medicine Man.

afraid that Fred might say something which would get Frank in trouble. He signaled silently.
"Sh-h-h!"
Neither of them told.

Indian Scares in Green Valley
about 1890

The settlers and the Native Americans did not live in close proximity and had scant opportunity to understand each other's culture. They not only were separated by fear, distance, and custom, but also by language. The settlers, assuming that the Natives had adequate territory on the land reserved for them, and assuming, also, that they had willingly sold or traded their other lands to the U.S. Government, thought that the tribesmen had no reason to be restless and dissatisfied. The Natives, on the other hand, were understandably resentful because the newcomers had not only spread farther and farther across their hunting grounds, but also had killed off the buffalo which provided the main source of their food and shelter.

It was an enormous challenge for the settlers to attend to the tasks of eking a living from the raw prairie in this strange land. They had problems enough of their own to make it easy for them to fail to notice the plight of the bronze inhabitants then referred to as Indians. Newspapers, however, were full of stories of confrontations, both true and fictional, which resulted in making the pioneers fearful.

During and after the Indian "Ghost Dances" in South Dakota, the settlers were especially apprehensive. At that particular time there were several "Indian Scares" in Green Valley.

One day when Hattie Spence was teaching the school attended by the Dobrovolny boys (District Number 210) her father came galloping on horseback.

"There are Indians lurking in the neighborhood," he told her. "Send the children home to warn their parents. The people to the east should get away from the rushes around the lake. They can gather at Tom Dobrovolnys."

After Hattie instructed the older children to care for their smaller brothers and sisters and not to run ahead and leave the little ones behind, she dismissed school. Frank grasped the wrists of the two smaller boys, Joe and Fred, and ran like a frightened rabbit toward home which was nearly two miles away. Fred and Joe were soon gasping for breath and asked Frank to slow down, but Frank continued to drag them along at top speed. Later Fred said that he came far closer to dying from exhaustion that day than he ever did from an Indian attack.

When the boys finally bounded into the soddy and choked out the awful news to Antonija, she was terrified. Luckily, Balloons, bringing loaded guns, arrived at the Dobrovolny place and Tom came home soon thereafter.

He had been in Atkinson and said that there had been no reports in town and that he hadn't seen anything suspicious on the way home. He stood on the back of one of his horses and viewed the horizon.

"The trouble is," he said, "that we have only muskets, and the Indians might have Winchesters."

It was the first time that Fred had heard the term "Winchesters."

John Dobrovolny had no shot for his gun. Before taking his family to Tom's place, he cut nails into segments to use for shot.

When a neighbor named Teller heard the worrisome news, he shouldered his gun and walked to Whittlers. After learning where people were gathering he went on to Dobrovolnys. All this time his pigs had been trailing after him. John Balloon gave a shout when he saw the man, flanked by a group of pigs, arriving.

"We are saved! Here is General Teller with his loyal troops marching behind!"

The banter did little to lessen the tension. The group stayed on guard all night.

The next day details were fitted together which explained the source of the scare. Being great hunters, Joe and John Mlinar and the Dobias boys had hidden in a slough west of John Ziska's place and were "sneaking on geese." They covered themselves with blankets and stuck rushes in their hat bands in order to remain hidden from the geese.

Ike Millspaw came riding down the trail. The hunters lifted themselves a little to see who was passing by, and then ducked back into the rushes. Ike saw them. Indians!

As Ike hurried to alert the neighbors, he met George Spence and told him. George rode to warn the school that his daughter Hattie taught, while Ike took the news to School District 77 (the Ziska school).

John Ziska, the Regals, the Taslers, and the Pachas

gathered at the home of the Jan Ziska family. They, too, kept guard all night.

One Dark Night
about 1890
as told by Fred Dobrovolny

It must have been a winter or two after Thomas died, for we were churning that night, but mother wasn't crying. The first year after he died, she always cried when we churned because it was one of the jobs he was especially good at. He'd grab that old churn beater and really make that cream splash.

On this particular night, Dad had already gone to bed. He wanted to get some rest before he harnessed up in the middle of the night to take the butter to town. He had to get it there early in the morning to get it on the train.

People shipped cream and butter to Bennetts in Omaha, a store that was located where the Nebraska Furniture Store is now. We could ship butter in either five or ten pound cartons. We were trying to fill a ten-pound carton that night, and we stayed up late, churning.

We didn't have a cream separator yet—just skimmed the cream off the top of the milk by hand—and it sometimes took a long time to churn it. We took turns because our arms played out. When we weren't churning, we were supposed to be stripping feathers.

All at once the dogs outside started barking and someone yelled.

"Ho, there! Tom!"

Mother went to the door. The night was dark—black as a cellar with the door shut. It was the Ben Nehrs. They were on their way to Schwerings to a dance, and it was so dark that they wanted to borrow a light.

Lighting a lantern, Frank took it out. I trailed behind him, as kids sometimes do. The dim light from his lantern didn't reach far and all they could see of me were my feet moving on the sand.

When we got closer, a girl in the buggy laughed, and said to Frank, "Why, I thought that was a little dog following you!" At the time I thought she was teasing me, and I resented being referred to as a dog.

Later when Dad headed for town, he took the other lantern with him.

Toward morning, something frightened the horses, and they were galloping back and forth in the corral. The dogs were tearing around and barking like crazy. We were all scared, for we thought it might be Indians.

Later, Frank, who was about eleven or twelve, said he was glad both lanterns were gone because, since it was so dark, no one suggested he go to investigate.

We never knew what disturbed the horses—coyotes, maybe.

Sitting Bull
about 1890
as told by Maggie Simons Dobrovolny

When I was small, I saw Sitting Bull lots of times. He used to go past our place this side of Armour, South Dakota. The Indians would go from the Rosebud Reservation to Montana to see the Blackfeet Indians. The old chief of the Blackfeet and Sitting Bull would plan the Indian activities. We were always worried about Indian uprisings because the Indians seemed unsettled.

Sometimes if we were noisy at bedtime Mother would say, "Now, Sitting Bull went by today. If you hear anything tonight, don't make a sound. Be really quiet."

Boy! If you tell little tots something like that, they're scared! We would quiet down all right, but most likely we didn't sleep all night.

The Indians sometimes stopped for food. We were poor, but Mother always gave them some of what we had.

Frank Dobrovolny, Tom's eldest son, moved to Canada with the Rosenberrys in 1902 and homesteaded there.

Marguerite Simons was born at White Lake, South Dakota, on January 17, 1887. As a child she lived in South Dakota on an island in the Missouri River. She and her brothers later went to Canada to homestead.

Maggie married Frank Dobrovolny, son of Thomas and Antonija, in Lacombe, Alberta, Canada on November 22, 1903. Later they moved to Loon Lake, Washington, and [about 1909] to Holt County in Nebraska where they settled in the same community where Frank had lived as a boy.

Their six children: Mary (Schiffern), Henry, Jesse, Lawrence, Jay, and Dorothy (Kubart).

Desperate Search
1891
information from Dave Haumann*

Before the land in the Sandhills was fenced, traversing that region was dangerous, for there were virtually no landmarks to use as guides. This huge area of sand dunes is the largest such region in the Western Hemisphere, being roughly 150 miles wide and more than 200 miles long.

August Haumann, a German immigrant, and his older sons worked in the coal mines in Illinois. He heard of a place in the Nebraska Sandhills which, along with five cows, two horses, and some chickens, was for sale for the sum of $500. Wanting to get his sons out of the mines, he traveled to Thedford and bought the place, located six miles north of that town.

The family had no income except for the cream and butter from the five cows. The older children took jobs on nearby ranches, oftentimes working for only board and room. Thus it was that the oldest girl, Hannah, worked for a family named Gilson.

Usually on Sundays Hannah walked home to visit her parents and siblings. However, one Sunday in the spring, Mrs. Gilson requested that Hannah stay for the entire day because her husband was away and she didn't care to be alone. Two of the younger Haumann girls, eight-year-old Tillie and four-year-old Henrietta, were disappointed when they learned their sister wouldn't be making her usual visit, and they persuaded their mother to allow them to visit Hannah.

The ranches were about a mile and a half apart and were joined by a trail that meandered around and between the hills.

"Be sure to follow the path," said Mrs. Haumann, speaking in German.

"We will. We know the way," said Tillie.

"Start home at five o'clock," their mother directed. "You must be home before dark."

The two girls, happy to go calling by themselves on a Sunday afternoon, walked sedately down the path, hand in hand. The hills were greening and were dotted with a profusion of wild

---

Dave Haumann of Thedford is a nephew to Tillie and Henrietta. He wasn't able to converse with his grandmother because she never learned to speak English. However, his father and his uncles often talked about this tragic incident.

sweet peas. On the way home, the girls decided to surprise their mother by picking a bouquet for her. They became so engrossed in this task—bounding to and fro from flower to flower—that they lost the location of the trail.

The girls scanned the horizon. On every side they viewed a rim of inverted cones of sand, sparsely covered with last year's leftover grass. Upon climbing to the top of one of these cones, they saw more of the same sea of sandy mounds. They chose another hill, but when they reached its summit, they found an identical panorama.

When the children failed to arrive home by six o'clock, one of the boys was sent to meet them. Upon reaching the Gilson Ranch without finding them, he knew the awful truth—the girls had lost their way and were wandering in a vast region of many hundred thousand sandhills.

All night long members of the two families walked back and forth between the ranches, holding lanterns high and calling.

"Tillie! Henrietta!"

By morning their voices were mere croaks. Later in the day, the searchers found the footprints of the little girls. However, since there was a sparse scattering of old grass as well as some tender new blades, the trail was difficult to follow, and the rescue party, which included all the people of Thedford except the depot agent and the postmaster, moved slowly. A chuck wagon from the McMillan Ranch accompanied the group.

The footprints revealed more than direction: in some places the children's tracks were side by side, and in other places Tillie had obviously carried Henrietta. Depressions in the sand showed where they had rested.

When night came, the search party camped by the trail; at first light of day, they resumed their tedious task. A deeper gloom settled over the group when they came to a place where the trails separated.

Probably Henrietta had grown too tired to climb the hills and Tillie had directed her to rest in a valley while she herself climbed yet one more mound for a better view of the surroundings. Then, most likely, she had seen another hill that appeared to be even taller, and she had hurried to climb it before returning to the site where she had left her little sister. In the meantime, Henrietta had decided to go around the hill to meet Tillie. Thus the waves of dunes swallowed each of them—separately.

On the fourth day the searchers found Henrietta. She

was so dehydrated that she lay in a stupor. However, the doctor—who was in the search party—was able to revive her. In addition to dehydration, she was suffering from severe sunburn and was disoriented, but she recovered.

The search for Tillie continued.

Another rescue party was organized in Dunning, a town about thirty miles east of Thedford. It was this second team who, some days later, found the wasted, sun-scorched body of the plucky little girl.

The scene revealed her final actions. When she had reached a point where she could not struggle on, she had removed her apron, had spread it over some rose bushes to form a bit of shade, and had crawled under it.

There she had died.

When Henrietta grew to adulthood, she lived in Broken Bow, Nebraska.

Dog Fight
1890's
as told by Frank Dobrovolny

"One Sunday a bunch of us kids were out on the Balloon quarter playing: the Balloons, Boettchers, Nehrs and us—and probably some others, too. We were running around, playing with our dogs, and probably yelling and tussling like kids do.

"Our Fido always had been a fierce dog and was good with cattle. Boy, oh boy, he could keep those cows in line. They knew better than to head for a cornfield when he was along. Also, at one time or another he had whipped most of the dogs in the neighborhood, and usually they were wise enough to leave him alone.

"But on this particular day, there were just too many kids wrestling around the pasture which made the dogs edgy.

"They started growling and snapping, and the next thing we knew, there was one big tangle of dogs. Some of them gave up, but Fido got ahold of Balloons shepherd and we couldn't get him to let go. When one of the neighbors heard all the racket, he came riding up on a horse, pulled his revolver, and shot. He had to shoot Fido twice to make him loosen his grip.

"The shepherd ran for home, but his belly had been ripped open and his insides were exposed. He soon died."

"Fido had been shot once in the back and once in the shoulder. We boys and Mother nursed him carefully, and he lived, but he wasn't the same dog after that. He tried, but the cows soon discovered they could now outrun him, and we had a heck of a time keeping them out of the corn. People had grain fields here and there, and in those days, none of them were fenced."

First Trip to Town
1893

Early one morning Tom was getting ready to go to town to have two sacks of wheat ground into flour. Nine-year-old Fred, who was always an early riser, was the only one of the boys that was out of bed.

Tom said, "Fred has been so good about bringing me a drink every day out in the field that I think I'll take him along."

At first, Fred was disbelieving, He had *heard* about town, but he'd never been there.

When they drove across the Elkhorn bridge, Fred was amazed to see the tall cottonwoods along the river. He had seen pictures of trees, but had not supposed that *anything* could be so towering.

As Tom tied the horses at the water tower, Fred gazed around at the scattering of buildings in the center of town. The business section was referred to as "the four squares." Far to the west stood a tall building, the Catholic Church, isolated from the rest of the town by about four blocks of sand.

"Is that Malloy's Peak?" inquired Fred in surprise, as he pointed southwest. The famous peak was yet several miles beyond their own home.

"Yes, it is," said Tom. "And if you look carefully you can see our corncrib."

It was true. Tom had a sixteen-foot-high crib, and even though it was about fifteen miles away, they could see it pointing up from the treeless plain.

Tom lifted a box of eggs from the wagon. They were packed in oats to keep them from breaking as the wagon rumbled over the rough roads.

"You bring the kerosene jug," he told Fred.

They walked to Hart's Store where Mr. Hart removed the eggs from the oats and counted them. He filled the two-gallon jug with kerosene from a large barrel. (Other barrels held such staples as sugar, salt, vinegar, apples, coffee beans, and crackers. There were large buckets of candy, dried fruit, and poppy seed.)

After Mr. Hart had subtracted the price of the kerosene from the "egg money," there was a little left which he gave to Tom in the form of a few coins. Returning to the wagon, Tom fed the oats from the egg box to the horses.

They took the wheat to the mill south of town where the miller weighed it and figured out a certain percent for the grinding fee. For the remainder of the wheat he traded him an equal number of pounds of flour.

Tom visited with people around town, bought some harness rivets at the harness shop, and showed Fred the depot, the railroad tracks, the hotel, the Catholic Church, and the brewery located south of town.

"I was so awed by it all I hardly bothered to talk—just kept looking," said Fred years later.

It was night when they got home. Joe and Anton, though older than Fred, had never been to town and were wide-eyed at Fred's descriptions.

The following fall, Tom took Joe and Anton to Atkinson. On the way home they stopped at Joe Tomsik's place and stayed all night.

"When they got home the next day, they *really* had a lot to tell!" said Fred.

Stuck Wheelbarrow
1893

"Joe, you and Fred fill the barrel in the garden this morning before you go out to herd," ordered Tom.

The two boys put the large churn can into the wheelbarrow and rolled it to the well. Joe lifted the cover, and Fred tossed the wooden pail down the well.

Together, they struggled with the rope which lifted the heavy bucket of water to the top, and together they grabbed the pail's wire handle and poured the water into the churn can in the wheelbarrow. They repeated the process until the can was about two thirds full. It would be wasted effort to fill the can to the top because much of the water would then be sure to splash out on the journey to the garden.

Once they had pushed, tugged, and sweated until they had rolled the wheelbarrow through the sand to the garden, they dipped the water from the can to the fifty-gallon barrel. It took many trips to fill the barrel to the top. The sun would then warm the water, and Antonija would sprinkle her garden plants in the evening. She felt that warm water was better for them than was cold.

Each journey from the well to the garden loosened the sand in the trail a bit more until the boys had their load of water hopelessly stuck.

"Let's trade places," said Fred, taking the barrow handles from Joe. "You get in front and pull."

The two small boys didn't possess the strength to force the barrow forward and up out of the sand. One problem was that neither one of them was tall enough to lift the handles to a height that would properly balance the load.

Finally, Joe bent over and grasped the spokes on either side of the wheel hub.

He said, "When I count to three, I'll lift on the wheel while you push. Ready? One, two, three!"

Fred pushed with all his might, and when the barrow came up out of the sand, it lurched forward suddenly. One of Joe's hands caught between the spokes, and it was whipped around by the wheel, causing the hub to strike his arm sharply.

For a couple of weeks, Joe's arm was many colors.

"It was black and green and blue and purple," said Fred later. "It reminded me of an ear of smutty corn."*

Blackleg
1893

Much of the conversation among the men that day at the school picnic involved the current deadly epidemic among their calves—blackleg. At that time, there were no vaccines for the disease and no cure. Some of the settlers had lost more than half of their calves to the disease, but as yet, Tom's herd had been spared.

On the way home, Tom let the Boettcher children out of the wagon near their place, and he and his own family proceeded on. As they neared their corral, they saw one of the calves lying dead by a hay pile, and even though Tom knew the problem, he stopped to examine the animal. As he rubbed his hand over the calf, he found the tell-tale bubbles of fluid under the hide of one of the hind quarters. If he were to skin the animal, he knew that the flesh of that leg would be black with congested blood.

"I spoke too soon," Tom told the boys. "When I was

---

* Smut is a fungus plant disease which can grow on ears of corn.

saying that we hadn't been hit with the disease, this calf was dying from it."

Anton and Joe dug a hole near the calf while the others did the evening chores. It was after dark by the time the calf was buried. Then Tom pitched hay from the pile to the spot where the calf had lain and set it afire, hoping to kill the germs. The boys brought buckets of water and stayed on guard until the fire had burned itself out.

Blackleg was a disease that brought death quickly. One day a calf might refuse to eat and be feverish; within hours he would be painfully crippled; and the next day, probably, he would be dead.

The early-day cattlemen tried a number of preventative measures. It was thought that an infection in the body would gather germs to one area where impurities could be drained out, thus clearing a critter's bloodstream. One method of encouraging an infection was to cut a hole through the brisket and tie an old, much-used dish rag through it; another was to cut a hole in the hide of the animal and insert a piece of chewing tobacco.

Some people "bled in the feet" in the hope of preventing blackleg. To accomplish the task, they made a knife wound low on the calf's leg and let it bleed. The reasoning behind this act was that any poison in the leg would be carried out of the body. Actually, these measures encouraged rather than hampered the disease, for the blackleg bacteria could enter the body through the open wounds.

There were those who thought that a well-balanced diet would help build resistance to the disease; others thought that, since young calves were less likely to be stricken than were older ones, it was wiser to limit food so as to discourage growth. Some pampered their animals, trying to keep them stabled during disagreeable weather; others thought it better to "toughen up" their calves by exposing them to the elements.

"People tried everything they could think of," said Tom's son Fred many years later, "but until a vaccine was developed, nothing helped."

During that particular summer, nine of Tom's twelve calves succumbed to the disease.

**Fred Dobrovolny
showing a group of children
how he, as a boy in the
1880's and 1890's
made hay twists which were then used for fuel
for heating and cooking.**

Anton Ahle's Early-day Harness Shop in Atkinson, Nebraska.

Chapter 4

Fire and Drought

Fire of 1893
told by Fred Dobrovolny

Boy, that was a fire! It looked like the whole world was burning. Biggest fire I ever saw.

In those days, fires really spread fast because there were weeds and dry grass around, and stacks of hay or hay sheds here and there. People plowed fireguards and set backfires, but often the backfires would get away from them, too. The whole valley would burn!

Dad seemed to know the hay was in jeopardy. The two years before, the fires were bad, and he figured they could come again. We had put up six extra stacks of hay down on the creek, and we were hauling them home and putting them inside the fireguard along with the hay we had stacked closer to home.

I was only nine, but because the other boys were herding, I was the only one to help Dad haul it. We didn't have a rack—just a flatbed on a wagon. It took someone who was experienced in handing hay to arrange it so that it wouldn't slide off. Dad pitched it up onto the flatbed and I worked like crazy trying to stack it.

"Level it off!" he'd yell at me. "You're just like a chicken scratching around up there!"

On our homestead quarter we had a cornfield on the north and one on the southeast that were already picked, but the field on the west wasn't picked yet. When the fire came racing toward us from the southwest, Dad unhitched the horses from the wagon and hooked onto the plow to widen the fireguard.

"Let the animals out of the barn!" he yelled at me. "And draw what water you can to dampen the ground around the corn crib and the hay sheds!"

We had seen the smoke on the horizon that morning, and we boys had already filled all the buckets and cream cans with water.

Joe was herding cattle in the north cornstalks. As Dad plowed along the edge of the west field, he knocked down some of the cornstalks. He called Joe over from the north field.

"Pick up these downed stalks and lay them in the bottom of the furrows," he told Joe. "That way I can plow them under the next time I come around." The idea was to get everything off the plowed guard that might lead the fire across.

The wind was blowing at a good clip that day, and the fire came fast. As soon as it hit the southwest corner of the fireguard, we all grabbed buckets and sacks and went to make sure it didn't jump the guard. I tell you, the wind off the burning grass was stifling; it about seared your lungs. Whenever sparks came across the guard, we beat them out.

Boy, I never saw such a fire! Fire on every side as far as you could see. Some of Balloons hay stacks to the southeast of us were burning, and the flames on them were big fiery sheets flapping to the northeast.

John Balloon tried to save one of his stacks by burning the grass around it before the main blaze got to it, but once he got the fire started, it burned like crazy in the wind.

He fought like heck trying to get it out. He was whopping it with a sack which ignited, and as he flipped it up and down, a piece of the flaming sack flew on the haystack and set the top of the stack afire. First thing he knew, it was burning all over.

That was the trouble that day. Anyone who tried to backfire just set another fire. The wind was just too strong.

Well, we saved our place: the buildings, the cornfields, and the hay that was at home. The three stacks that were down by the creek burned, though.

But Uncle John lost everything. He was building a new frame barn that fall, and he hadn't gotten around to plowing his fireguards yet. When he saw the smoke rolling up in the sky, he harnessed a team and started plowing guards. Before he got the guards anywhere near wide enough, though, he could see the flames and knew the fire was coming fast. He disconnected the plow, cracked the whip over the horses, and ran for home.

Quickly, he tied the team to the corncrib and ran into the soddy to get Aunt Barbara and the children. He hurried them to Rosenberry's [Wright's] Lake which was west of the house. Once he got them safely situated in the lake, he meant to get all of the horses and bring them into the water, also; but the fire came so fast that he didn't have a chance to rescue any of the animals— not even the ones tied to the corncrib.

Uncle John told everyone to wet their heads because he was afraid that the flying sparks and the searing hot winds would set their hair afire. The flames came roaring and crackling out over the lake, burning the dry rushes that were sticking up out of the water.

The kids, Cousins Anna and Mary and Frank, were all small and were afraid they were going to burn up.

"I couldn't much blame them," said Uncle John. "The lake was weedy, and anything sticking out of the water was afire. It was strange and unreal, and it *did* seem almost like even the water was burning."

Uncle John's new barn burned and all the horses and the calves in it. The only stock he had left were the two horses tied to the corncrib. The fire came close enough to them to blister the hide on one side, but they both lived. Also, Uncle John lost all his cows in the fire.

The next day we boys were out surveying the damages to the countryside. Everything was black—burned to a crisp. On every side was scorched prairie sprinkled with old buffalo bones that glittered white against the burned grass.

We came to Schwerings who lived where Keith Jones lives now. Just like Uncle John, they had lost almost everything. Mrs. Schwering was lying under a wagon. Something sure was the matter with her, but I didn't know what. I thought she might be having fits or convulsions or something. On the way home, one of the other boys said something about her having cried so long and so hard that she had lost her voice. Then I realized that those heaving, croaking sounds were sobs. She had probably cried all night.

Why wouldn't she cry? They had lost everything, and like all of us, they hadn't had much to start with.

Rosenberrys, the three brothers—Sol, Mac, and Frank— who lived around the south, the west, and the northwest sides of

Rosenberry's Lake, lost all their hay. They bought some from Julius Jens who lived near Brown's Lake.

Balloon's hay was all gone. Later they bought hay for two dollars a ton from John Jonas who had a school section rented northwest of us. He had saved the hay on it by plowing fire guards and whipping out the flames that managed to jump the guard.

A man who lived a couple miles south of the present-day Vrooman place was blamed for the fire. Some people surmised that he had lost control when he was burning an area of his ranch that was contaminated with blackleg germs. Others thought he had set the fire in order to drive out his neighbors so that he could gain more grazing land for himself.

Frank Rosenberry was a leader in the community and he wrote a letter:

> "The people in this neighborhood do not tolerate folks who are careless with fire. Pack up and leave. We give you one week."

After most of the folks in the valley had signed the letter, it was delivered to the accused man. Within a few days, he was gone. None of us ever saw him again.

Nels Christenson, who was Ralph Ries' grandfather, was plowing fireguards and was going as fast as he and the horses could go. The plow handle broke, and the splintered stub stabbed him in the stomach. He had to pull it out himself. He was never well after that.

Maude Slaymaker, who was teaching school and was staying with Frank Frosts, died soon after fighting fire. She and Mrs. Frost whipped out the fire to save the house, and she got overheated and breathed too much smoke.

Shortly afterward diphtheria struck their family. With her scorched lungs, she didn't have a chance.

The Big Load of Hay
told by Fred Dobrovolny

I remember the last load of hay we brought home before the fire. A fellow from another neighborhood—Dad called him Throndick—was passing through and stopped at our place. He had collected some horses and had quite a bunch. His idea was to sell them and make a little money.

Already, some of the homesteaders were starving out and leaving their farms. It took a tough, plucky family to stick it out. Some families that left were going to look for town jobs, and they'd sometimes abandon their older horses. Throndick had caught up some of those strays.

When we pulled our wagon into the yard, old Throndick began to compliment us on our big load of hay. He had never seen such a load! And stacked by a little bit of a kid! He couldn't get through bragging us up.

He stopped at our place several times over the winter and stayed overnight. Every time he had a bunch of horses along, and all the while he was forking hay to them—our hay, of course—he was raving about what good quality feed it was and what great hay makers we were.

Young as I was, I learned a useful lesson from that man. I found out that whenever someone compliments you over and over on one of your possessions, you had better beware. He is probably after it—or something else you have that is of value.

Summer in Burwell
1894
told by Joe and Fred Dobrovolny

Tom's sons, Joe and Fred, agreed later that the family would have fared immensely better had they stayed in Holt County in 1894.

The year before, Tom had harvested a bountiful supply of hay, having by that time acquired (together with his brother Fred) a four-foot mower and an eight-foot rake. Tom had two teams and Frank's riding horse which doubled as a workhorse, and Fred had a team of horses and a pair of oxen.

For a hay sweep, Tom fashioned a plank with six teeth on it. A man stood on the teeth, made of 2" x 4" lumber, to hold them down firmly to the ground while he drove the horses who were hitched to the front. (After a few years, sweeps were made so that a horse was hitched on either side of the implement. Later still, the horses were placed behind the sweep.)

After the hay was mowed, sun-dried, and raked into long rows called windrows, it was then "bunched" with the sweep. Since as yet there was no stacker Tom pitched the bunches into stacks. Crude as this equipment seems to us now, it was a pronounced improvement over a scythe and cradle, and they harvested more hay that year than ever before. Having put most of it inside the fire guard, they had more hay than they needed.*

Tom gave hay to John to feed the team he had saved from the fire, and also gave Schwerings hay for their few surviving animals. Even then, he had hay left when spring arrived.

During the winter, John decided to move his family back to his eighty-acre farm north of Fremont.** Not only was he discouraged because of their losses in the fire, but also because their nearest neighbors, the Balloons, continued to resent them for settling on ground which they had been planning for their eldest son, Raymond. The ever-restless Tom, too, was looking over the horizon.

Tom's friend, Mike Flakus, had moved his family to a farm south of Burwell.*** Tom had visited him and decided that the firmer soil in that area was better farm ground.

The sandy fields on Tom's Holt County homestead had, at first, produced marvelously well, but nine years of corn-growing had begun to deplete the soil. Tom could notice that his crop yields were not as impressive as were earlier ones. When he expressed a desire to move to the Burwell area, Mike Flakus promised to watch for a place for him. In late winter, Flakus wrote Tom: a nearby quarter section of land was available for renting. Could Tom, he asked, come to examine it?

Tom and Frank drove a team and wagon to Valley County. (Burwell is in southern Garfield County. However, even though Burwell was the nearest town, Flakuses lived in the northern part of Valley County.) Tom rented the quarter which was six miles south of Burwell and one and a half miles northeast of the Boleszyn Country Church. Joe later reported that when they stood on high ground they could see the flag flying over Fort Hartsuff, located perhaps ten miles east of them.

---

* "Dad was good at cradling hay," said Joe many years later. "I remember that he took his scythe along when we went to Dora Lake. On the way home he always stopped at a little valley near Malloy's Peak. He'd let the horses graze while he cut a wagon load of hay to take home. He called that spot his "meadow."
** Now in 1992 John's grandson, John Soukup, lives there.
*** Before moving, Flakuses lived on the quarter across the road south of School District 210. Flakuses sold it to Frank Johnson.

Half of their new land was canyons, but the other half was reasonably level land.

Tom was anxious to begin plowing his fields, but his plow was in Holt County, and he didn't want to waste the energy of his horses to go after it. Rather, he bought a new plow in Ord and set Frank and the horses to work in the field. Then he, himself, walked the fifty-five miles home to get his old plow and more horses.

Tom rented his homestead quarter to John Morey for twenty dollars (to be paid in the fall) and traded him the left-over hay for a horse. After making plans with Antonija for the coming move, Tom returned to Burwell with his plow and all his other horses. With a total of six horses, he and Frank could each use a three-horse team.

The spring was ideal—full of clear, balmy days. They plowed all the arable ground (probably about eighty acres) and planted it to corn, completing the job by the end of April. Then they returned to Holt County with the wagons and horses in order to move the family and the livestock to their new home.

While Tom and Frank were in Valley County, John's family departed for Fremont. John secured an immigrant car and took the household goods and the surviving team in it. The next day, Sol Rosenberry drove John's wife Barbara and the children to Atkinson to board the passenger train. On the way to town, they stopped at Tom's place.

Since the boys were all herding, Antonija was home alone. Later, Barbara's daughter Anna told Joe that the parting between the two women was a sad one. Antonija, especially, cried bitterly. Barbara's parents lived in Fremont, which meant that, in a sense, Barbara was going back home. However, Antonija's only female relative and virtually her only friend on this side of the ocean was her sister-in-law, Barbara.

About the eighth of May, Tom's family started for Valley County. Frank rode his horse, and the three younger boys walked behind the cattle. Tom and Antonija each drove a wagon, and a neighbor drove a third wagon that held a crate of chickens, a box with four small pigs, and some bags of oats.

Each night they camped by a creek or pond. Later, Joe remembered that on one occasion he went to a slough with his father to get water. Tom dug a hole in the sandy ground near the

---

Tom's Valley County land seems to have been the SE 1/4 of Sec. 23, Twp. 29, Range 16 W.

slough and let the water filter through the sand into the hole. After dipping the water out of the hole, they carried it to camp where Antonija boiled it and made coffee.

The cows that were fresh were milked, and after saving enough milk to pour over the bread for their own meal, they fed the remainder to the calves, pigs, and chickens.

Years later when Joe and Fred were asked where they slept, neither could remember. "We were so used to bedding down anywhere that there was nothing unusual about sleeping out," said Joe. "I suppose Mother and Dad slept under one wagon and we boys slept under the other."

The cows were glad enough to lie down nearby, but one night something startled them and they bolted. Frank got on his horse, rounded them up, and brought them back to camp.

In the middle of the fourth day, the Dobrovolnys came to the two soddies on their new place. They moved the household items into the larger, and put the boys' husk mattresses into the smaller.

The corn was up when they arrived, but soon thereafter a killing frost nipped it off. Most of it did, however, sprout out again from the roots.

Antonija's first task was to plant the garden and to set out the cabbage and tomato plants that she had started in the house. Fred was kept busy carrying water to them. Since there had been no spring rains, the well was nearly dry. Fred almost wore the rope out, but in spite of his efforts, he could tease only about a third of a bucket of water from of the well each hour. Antonija was desperate to get enough moisture to the plants to save them until rain should come.

Water for household use as well as for the livestock had to be hauled from the neighbor's place.

As soon as it was apparent which corn plants were recovering from the frost, the boys were put to work at replanting. They carried sticks and bags of seed. Each boy walked down a long row, and wherever a plant was missing, he used his stick to poke a hole in the dry earth, dropped in a kernel of corn, and stepped on it, twisting his foot to cover it.

The expected rain never arrived, and the newly planted seeds lay dormant in the sun-baked ground. The plants that survived the frost slowly withered; their leaves turned to crisp ribbons which waved for a while in the hot winds before they broke off and blew away. When the well went completely dry, Antonija's garden plants bowed their heads and expired.

A year of no vegetables was an alarming situation. It meant no potatoes, carrots, nor turnips; no cabbage nor sauerkraut. After sixteen years of prairie living in which their circumstances had slowly improved, they now were stripped of all their resources. Dire need loomed ahead.

That summer, Joe herded cattle for the Parkas, a family who lived nearby. He was paid twenty-five cents a week which Tom collected and used for family needs. The Parkas were Polish, as were most of the people in the neighborhood, but the Czech and Polish languages are similar, and the children who played in the canyons or in the dry bed of Turkey Creek which crossed Dobrovolny land could understand each other.

A few times Tom and Antonija attended the little country church located to the southwest of them. The hills in the area were completely barren, and seemed to be made of something more like cement than of earth.

In August, Tom and Frank went on an exploratory trip to Holt County. Would it be better for the family to return there? After the fires the fall before, followed by the present dry summer, much of the formerly green valley was as bare as a tabletop.

Frank Rosenberry had paid forty dollars to rent six quarters of the old Gregg Ranch*, located where Jerry Gotschall now lives. He told Tom that he would give him half of any hay that he (Tom) gathered on the east part. Where the fire had gone through the year before, there was nothing but bare ground; but a few places had some old, brown grass that the flames had missed.

Tom and Frank, working in summer heat that reflected off the burning sand and that did not allow them a single breath of cool air, gathered what hay they could. They knew the year-old, sun-scorched grass held little or no nourishment, but felt that it would be better than nothing in an animals stomach.

Since John Morey was renting Tom's homestead, Tom could not move into his own soddy; but Tom's brother Fred had vacated his house in the spring and was now occupying John's soddy east of Rosenberry Lake. Thus Tom moved into the house of the older Fred,** located about three-quarters of a mile southwest of the District 210 schoolhouse.

---

* See next page for footnotes.

After Frank and Tom had gathered as much of the dead grass as possible, Tom returned to Burwell, taking all the horses along in order to move the family to Holt County.

A raw wind chilled the scantily-clad family on the fall day that they began their journey northward. Tom's friends insisted that he come over to visit them before leaving. He stayed all night and into the next morning which meant that

---

* Before land was homesteaded, the large cattle companies set up satellite ranches and herded their cattle on the "public domain" (unsettled lands). As settlers moved in to claim the land, the big ranches moved out. The <u>1885 Official State Atlas of Nebraska</u> shows six ranches in the southern part of Holt County. Even though the townships were not named, they were laid out and the sections numbered. A later Holt County map supplied the township names. The six ranch locations were:

    1. Russel's Ranch: 2 1/2 miles west of Stuart, Section 4 in Stuart Township. The Ranch site appears to be on the quarter west of the present Walt Kaup place.

    2. Housten's Ranch: On Section 32 in West Green Valley. Ranch site was just west of the 80 acres that Don Krysl sold to Bob Miksch.

    3. Gregg Ranch: Section 6 of Francis Township. Presently, it is Gotschall land.

    4. Hurlburl's Ranch: Section 17 in Fairview Township, 12 miles south and 2 1/2 miles west of Emmet.

    5. McClure's Ranch: Section 14 in McClure Township, 14 miles south and 2 1/2 east of O'Neill.

    6. West and Mark's Sheep Ranch: Section 23 in Ewing Township, three miles south of Ewing on Cache Creek.

One satellite ranch (located in southwest Holt County in the Boettcher area) co-existed with the homesteaders into the 1900's. It was called the Ditch Company, and was managed by a huge black man—a respected cowboy—whose only known name was Nigger Jim. He was sent here by one of the large Texas cow outfits. He herded in the Sandhills, for much of that land was not homesteaded until after the Kinkaid Law came into effect. That law allowed a settler 640 acres (a section) instead of a quarter section. Ora Whipple says that she heard, in later years, a sketch of that old cowboy's life on a television program, and it stated that he is buried near Minden.

** SW 1/4 of Sec. 25 of Holt Creek Township.

Antonija and the three young boys, ages ten, eleven, and thirteen, loaded the wagons without him. (Frank had stayed in Holt County where he was working for Rosenberrys.) When Tom had not yet returned by departure time, the exhausted Antonija directed the boys to head north with the cattle.

Since none of them was mounted, the boys wondered how they would manage the cows on a long drive while facing the chilling wind. However, they had no cause for worry, for Old Liz, the tall, red cow who as a yearling had lost her ears, tail, and the hair on her hocks during the Blizzard of 1888, apparently carried a vision of a green valley with fresh-water lakes, for she faced into the raw wind and led the herd unerringly toward Holt County. She had no way of knowing that Green Valley was as destitute as the area they were leaving.

Antonija, weighted with the knowledge of the ravages of the drought and the need her family faced, followed her walking sons. She drove one of the loaded wagons.

About noon the other two wagons, one driven by Tom and the other by two neighbors, overtook them. Deciding that there was no need for the entire group to be held back to the pace of the cows, Tom decided that the neighbors could go ahead. There was an unoccupied corner in their wagon, and Tom told Fred that he might ride. Joe and Anton could handle the cattle.

Fred, his heart flooded with both relief for himself and dismay for his thinly clad brothers who must yet face the bone-chilling wind, hopped into the wagon and snuggled down in the vacant corner. However, he soon discovered that sitting in a cramped position was no way to keep warm. After a few hours, he was a shivering ball of misery.

Fred tried to summon the courage to ask the men to let him out to run beside the wagon for a time in order to get his blood circulating, but he feared it would seem to them that he didn't appreciate the ride. Also, they were pleasantly conversing, bundled as they were in sheepskin coats and warm, Scotch caps. Since it was grossly impolite for a child to interrupt adults in conversation, Fred huddled in his thin jacket, and shuddered through the miserable hours.

There is no record of where or how the travelers spent the nights on the trip home, but the wagon in which Fred was riding arrived on the third day, while the cattle and the other wagons, both heavily loaded with tools, machinery, and household furnishings as well as crates of chickens and pigs, came at the end of the fourth day. Joe and Anton had completely worn out the cloth moccasins Antonija had made for them and their chapped feet, for the last half of the journey, had been wrapped in strips of gunny sacks.

The family moved into Fred Sr.'s cabin,* where they remained until about 1900 when Tom built a frame house (with two rooms and a loft) on a quarter section of land south of Holt Creek. It sits there yet, south of the Fred Dobrovolny II ranch yard on land which now belongs to Gordon Dvorak.

At the time that notes were being taken for this account, Fred and Joe were both reluctant to give a detailed account of the 1894-95 winter, saying that without experiencing it, a person could not possibly understand how bad it was. The comments they did make, follow.

"It was awful," said Fred. "The cows were all dry and the few hens we had didn't lay. After the fire and the drought, there was no wild game to be had. We lived on bread all winter. No milk. Not even any lard to spread on our bread. Just bread.

"Mother had some coffee essence that she used for coffee. We *called* it coffee. Coffee and dry bread made from either corn meal or from coarse-ground whole wheat—not bread like we have today.

"We all had colds the entire winter: we were coughing on the trip home from Burwell, and we coughed until spring.

"What did we burn? There weren't many cowchips. The older ones had all burned in the prairie fire, and the dry summer had produced no grass for grazing, which meant there were no new cowchips. No one raised corn, so there were no corncobs, and there was no grass for hay twists.

"We boys went along the creek almost daily, hunting for any brush not eaten by the cattle—maybe sticks the size of your thumb. Sometimes we might find a few old cornstalks sticking out of the field. Mother used whatever we found to bake the bread, and most of the the rest of the time the house was cold.

"We banked the building on the outside with dirt or whatever else we could find to keep the wind from blowing through the cracks, but it was a long, cold winter. Awful."

Joe said, "That was the seventeenth winter that the folks were in America, and it was the worst. We hadn't raised

---

* This little frame house had been vacated by a family named Deter, was bought by Fred Sr., and was moved to his land a few years before.

anything in Valley County, but the rent that Morey owed Dad saved us. We collected it—twenty dollars—and used it to buy flour. Cornmeal. Ground wheat. Like many families that winter, we lived on bread. For breakfast mother made cornmeal mush, but with neither milk nor sweetener, it was no more popular than the bread.

"If we ever said we were hungry mother would tell us, 'You can't be *too* hungry if you have bread.' She knew that it wouldn't help us any to feel sorry for ourselves.

"That winter the ground was so dry in most places that it didn't freeze solid like it usually does, and the sand drifted in the winter winds.

"There wasn't much food value in the little hay we had, and sometimes the stock would get so weak they couldn't get up. Dad made a cow-lift. It was kind of a tripod affair with a rope and a hand crank on it. Whenever a cow "got down", Dad and Frank would use that winch to crank her back up on her feet because a critter that "gets down" always bloats and dies. Then they'd feed her a nubbins or two of corn to try to give her a little strength. Sometimes she'd live and sometime she wouldn't."

"Dad and Frank went all over the country with the tripod that winter—cranking up cows.

"Where did you get the nubbins of corn?"

"Morey put most of the fields on Dad's old homestead into small grain which didn't mature, but he cut it for hay. One of the fields, though, he put into corn. It dried up and blew under, and he abandoned it. Mother would take a sack and go over there and dig around in the sand. She found little nubbins maybe two or three inches long. We saved them to give to the cows that got down.

"We boys were always on the look for game. If we'd see a rabbit anyplace, we'd tell Dad and he'd go after it. The prairie was completely bare except for the buffalo bones scattered in some places, and you could see a rabbit a half mile away. Trouble was, there rarely were any.

"A few times, though, Dad got one. Mother baked it and, oh, it was good! Mother was good at preparing meats!"

The small pigs that the family had hauled to Valley County didn't have much chance to grow because of the shortage of food and water. Tom sold the two larger ones in Burwell, and used the money to treat the neighbors who had furnished them with water over the summer. They hauled the two smaller pigs, who were hardly any bigger in the fall than they were in the spring, back to Holt County.

Schwerings had planted some corn on Old Fred's and it had blown under. The pigs rooted around and found enough old stalks to stay alive over the winter. In the spring, Tom butchered one for the little meat that was on it and saved the larger one to raise a litter of pigs.

In the spring of 1895, the neighbors assembled to consider a grave problem. They could not plant their fields because no one had raised any seed the year before, and they were all too destitute to buy it. Finally, the Rosenberrys made a suggestion: could they bond their township to acquire funds to purchase seed?

A committee was sent to O'Neill to look into the matter, and Francis Township (the area which now includes both Francis and Holt Creek townships) was bonded for the purpose of obtaining money to buy seed.

Coffee Essence
as told by Fred Dobrovolny

"When I was a kid, I didn't know you could make coffee without essence. Later, I realized it was a cheap coffee substitute which could be used to extend one's supply of coffee. It was manufactured in O'Neill from sugar beets which, at that time, people grew around there.

"Essence was dark brown and came in rolls nearly a foot long and about as big around as a broomstick. Mother sliced off an inch-long chunk and put it in the pot of boiling water. After a few minutes she set it on the reservoir of the stove to cool down a little. You daren't put the coffee in when it was too hot or it would foam up and boil all over the stove.

"Usually, one of us boys would grind a few coffee beans which Mother would drop into the pot. In a few minutes it was ready to drink.

"During '94 and '95 we didn't have any genuine coffee, but sometimes we had coffee essence. Dad complained about it being no good, but we boys thought it was great. We couldn't tell the difference. It was wonderful to have something to dip our bread into since we didn't have milk.

"Those were the days!" Fred chuckled ruefully, remembering. "They call them the Good Old Days." After a pause, he continued. "It was a time when all you had to do to turn dry bread into a good meal was to make a little counterfeit coffee to go with it."

Bumble Bee War
1895

Spring finally did arrive, and a few scattered bits of greenery were appearing on the prairie. Joe was herding cows for a neighbor when he found a bumble bee nest.*

Joe and his brother Fred were a champion team when it came to vanquishing a nest of bees. They each had a lath to use for a weapon, and after stirring up the bees, they stood back-to-back and whacked them with their slats. They had a pact: once they "declared war" on a nest of bees, they fought to a finish. Getting stung was not a cause for giving up; rather, it was a reason to fight harder.

At first, Joe planned to wait until he and Fred, who was herding their own cows, could both attack the bees, but he could not put down the vision of the light, sparkling honey that he knew was right there in the nest. His lunch, a thick slab of coarse bread that he carried in his pocket, would taste like it always did—about like sawdust. But with a generous spreading of honey, he would have a feast!

His mouth watering in anticipation, he decided that he, himself, would combat the bees. Removing his jacket, he draped it over his head like a bonnet and buttoned it under his chin.

He thumped the ground several times with his stick and jumped back as the bees came sliding out of the hole and burst noisily into the air.

Whack! Whack!

Joe flailed the stick back and forth, lashing at the enraged insects that dived at him like swallows after a prowling cat. The jacket, even though it was old and thin, protected his neck and shoulders; but there were other places for the bees to sting. Then several of the insects became entangled in his jacket and buzzed there angrily. He yanked the garment off his head, and shook it as he ran.

Twice Joe returned to fight and both times was forced to retreat; but war had been declared and surrender was an

---

* Bumble bees make their nests in holes in the ground. Their honey is a lighter color than that of the honey bee.

War had been declared and surrender was an unacceptable solution...

unacceptable solution. He had several matches in his pocket and could burn out the hive if he could collect enough bits of hay to make a fire.

The bee nest itself had some dry grass around it probably because the bees had, the year before, successfully defended their own bit of turf; but they also were defending it now so that he couldn't collect fuel in that area. He walked about, gathering bits of dried weed and old stubble. Laying those scraps on the piece of newspaper in which his bread had been wrapped, he crept toward the bee nest. He lit the paper around the little pile of fuel and shoved it into the tuft of grass, after which he ran back to a safe distance.

The fire spread from the weed scraps to the clump of grass around the nest. Joe jumped for joy! He had won! The honey was his! The fire would soon burn itself out, for the most of the prairie was, at that time, as bare as a desert.

Suddenly, Joe smelled burning cloth. Too late, he realized that the last time he had battled the bees, he had flailed them with his jacket, and when several had collected in it, he had dropped it there by the nest. Now it was going up in smoke.

The fact that it was a worn, hand-me-down gave him small comfort, for it was the only coat he had.

By the time the fire had burned down, Joe was too nauseated from the effects of the many stings he had received to enjoy the honey. He ate what he could and reburied the rest for the following day when he would be feeling better.

There were many chilly spring days, of course, when he could have used that old jacket!

Golden America
1895
told by Fred Dobrovolny

Charlie Balloon and I were herding near the Conklin place which was about a mile and a quarter east of the Midwest Ranch—where Jerry Gotschall's place is now. Charlie's brother Raymond was working for Conklin and was staying there.

After we had eaten our lunch—we each had a slab of bread—we stopped at Conklin's to see what Raymond might be doing. Mr. Conklin had gone to a little shed behind his house to get some cheese for their dinner. They made cheese, and there were shelves in the shed for curing it.

Boy, those loaves of cheese looked good, all wrapped in

cheese cloth and, I think, smeared with salty butter. They were lined up in a neat row and couldn't have looked any better to me if they'd have been made of pure gold.

And the smell! Wonderful! It made my stomach jump so high that for a minute I couldn't even breathe.

Conklin peeled back the cheese cloth from one of the loaves and began to slice it. Oh, those thick, smooth slices rolling off the knife! I can see them yet!

He gave Charlie and me each a piece. I ate mine fast until I got to the last bite which I kept in my mouth for a long time—as long as I could. I wanted for sure to be able to remember how it tasted, and I did.

After all these years—more than eighty years—I still remember.

When I got home that night, I told Mother about the cheese.

"It wasn't lumpy and white like cottage cheese," I said. "It was as smooth as cream and was a light, golden color."

She gazed out of the door—out across the bare prairie.

"*Zlaty Amerika*," she muttered. The phrase, which means "Golden America!" was used in Czechoslovakia to describe the wonderful opportunities which lay across the ocean.

It was a time in our lives when we didn't see any opportunity, but after this terrible setback, we started over and from then on our conditions steadily improved. Eventually, there *were* golden opportunities.

In her later years, Mother grew to like America.

"But," she told me, "during the hard times of the Nineties, if it wouldn't have been for the ocean, I'd have packed up you boys, and we'd have walked back to the Old Country!"

First Earnings

"I recall," said Fred's niece who was visiting him in his old age, "that Dad said that he remembered that as a boy you had a few coins in a tin can and that you liked to take them out and count them. In view of the fact that your father always collected your wages when you boys herded for the neighbors and that he used it for family needs, where did you get those coins?"

"Those coins were the first money I ever earned," mused the old man who, during his lifetime, had accumulated a sizable fortune. "My uncle wanted someone to help him clean out his hay sheds, and since all the other boys were herding cows for the neighbors, I went to do it. It was early in the spring, and there was a raw wind. My jacket was thin, and I didn't have any gloves. I thought I'd freeze to death before I got those sheds cleaned out, but I kept at it. Uncle said he'd give me ten cents a load, and I was excited to be earning real money. I think I worked about three days.

"I pitched the manure into a wagon, hauled it out to the field, and pitched it off again. By that time, Uncle owned a team of horses, and I used them rather than his oxen, which I couldn't handle very well.

"After I finished, he paid me. I think he gave me sixty cents, and I also had that nickel that I had gotten from the Polish man who took Curley, our dog. For some reason, Dad never asked me for that money. Sixty-five cents. All mine!"

For a time, his listener sat in deep thought. How would a boy who obviously needed even the most basic things in life use those hard-earned coins? Clothes? Food? Candy? A toy?

"You needed so many things," she muttered aloud. "What did you finally choose to buy with that hard-earned cash?"

She waited while an amused smile played on the old man's face. Finally he spoke:

"I never spent it," he said. "Still got it."

Runaway and Death
1894

One hot, August day Antone Tasler drove to Atkinson in a wagon pulled by a lively team. After completing his business around town, he went to the depot to get a buggy that he planned to tie behind the wagon and pull home. Laying the lines in the bottom of the wagon, he climbed out and took a piece of wire from behind the seat.

Approaching the depot was another wagon whose driver intended to unload a can of cream which was to be shipped on the freight train. Antone, knowing that his team was somewhat spirited, spoke to his horses and stepped to the wagon to get the lines. About that time, the team leaped forward which prompted Antone to dive for the lines. As he did so, one of his legs slipped between the spokes of the front wheel where it became entangled. By the time the running horses were halted, his mangled body, broken and beaten by the turning wheel, was lifeless.

Jacob Humpal volunteered to carry the awful news to Antone's family, and he and his son George raced out of town, driving a team and buggy.

After delivering the message, they decided to remain to do the evening chores for the bereaved family. They unhitched their panting horses and led them into the barn. As they were passing behind an untrained horse that was tied in a stall, the animal suddenly kicked at the newcomers, striking George. He was knocked senseless and remained so for more than an hour.

Antone & Josephine Tasler*

---

*   Antone (Jan. 16, 1832-Aug. 20, 1894) was a brother to Frances (Tasler) Ziska and a great-uncle to Ella (Ziska) Dobrovolny.   Antone was the father of A.A. Tasler, and the grandfather of Charley, Clarence, Tony, Bill, and Fred Tasler as well as Tillie Cearns. (Charley's grandson Charles was in the same high school class as Don Krysl Jr. who graduated in 1975. The two are fourth cousins.)

**One-Room, One-Teacher Country School
District 205**

Anna Hytrek Krysl and V.J. Krysl received their formal education in the late 1800's and early 1900's in this school. Three generations of Krysls and Hytreks attended there during the 101 years that it was open. In the picture are the last three pupils who worked and played there (Amanda and Amy Greger and Kitty Karo). In front are guests, Matt Serbousek and his mother, Mary Jo Krysl Serbousek. Mary Jo received her elementary education in the school, as did the teacher, Judy Krysl, who took this picture. The school closed after that term of 1987-1988. It also was Judy's last year of teaching since she planned to devote full time to Skyparlor Illustrations and her art work.

Chapter 5

Getting a Foothold

The Bologna Accident

Gregor Hytrek's first house in America consisted of one downstairs room and a loft upstairs. Downstairs, along with the kitchen and dining furniture, were two beds: the three girls (Stella, Mary and Anna) slept in one bed and the parents slept in the other.

The boys occupied the loft, and during the winter the family also hung their homemade sausages and bologna up there. In addition, a stone jar of sauerkraut and another of bacon-in-brine might be in the loft. One day when the Hytreks were working with meat, Gregor was removing some bologna from the smokehouse and putting it in baskets. Paul, who was about ten or eleven, was carrying it, a half-basket at a time, to the loft where his mother was hanging it from the rafters. The family had a little dog (probably the same one that was saved from the Blizzard of 1888) who went everywhere with Paul.

Paul was struggling up the ladder with a load of meat when the dog somehow got under his feet, causing him to fall down the stairs. Johanna heard the crash and ran to see what had happened. There at the foot of the steps was a scramble of boy, dog, and bologna.

Paul was not seriously hurt.

Tom's and Fred's Fancy Pipes

Both Tom Dobrovolny and his brother Fred had ornate pipes, the long stems of which swooped down to their laps in a cascade of metal scrolls and filigrees. A hand that rested on the arm of a chair was at a suitable height to support the bowl of the pipe situated on the end of the stem that was perhaps fifteen inches long.

Whenever they wished to light their pipes, they searched in the cob basket for a straw or sent some of the children outside to find one. The straw was inserted into the front of the stove through an opening which served as a draft hole. After it had ignited, the pipe was lit, and the straw was stuck back through the draft hole into the firebox. Since matches cost money, they were rarely used for lighting pipes.

To clean their pipes, they used the wing or tail feathers of a chicken.

The Birth of Ella May Ziska
1897

John Ziska had completed the hay harvest and was getting ready to thresh some stacked grain. He and his brother Joe owned a horse-powered thresher and did custom threshing. When his own fields had ripened, his machine was miles away from home, and he decided to stack the bundles of grain. Later, when the rush of the harvest season had passed, he could then thresh his own grain "from the stack."

One day R.O. Clifford who lived north of the Ziskas came to see them and knowing that John was a skilled bee-handler, asked him to harvest their honey. John decided he should help his neighbor before threshing, and so it was that John and Mary and their two small children, Freddie and Annie, went to Cliffords.

When the work with the bees and honey was completed, Mary said, "We'd better go home, John. I have some of those late plums that I want to pick yet this afternoon before we start

John and Joe Ziska's horse-powered thresher.

milking chores."

R.O.* remembered the remark, for Mary was heavy with child and had ridden to their place in a rumbling wagon, had helped with the honey, and now was talking about hurrying home to do more work.

About midnight the Cliffords were awakened by the rattling harnesses and the brisk trotting of John's mules as he hurried to get the midwife, his mother, Frances Ziska.** On September 26, 1897, Mary gave birth to their third child, Albena (Ella) May Ziska.

The following summer Joe Dobrovolny, aged fifteen, worked for the Ziskas and met Baby Ella who would later become his wife.

Bulls from England

By a stroke of good luck, soon after the Hytreks settled in Holt County, they discovered that they had access to purebred bulls imported from England. Frank Frost (who married Gregor Hytrek's sister) had been in the same German Army Unit as Lawrence Opp. The Opp brothers preceded the Hytreks to America and settled near Pony Lake which was perhaps fifteen miles southwest of the Hytrek homestead. The Opp Ranch was well-enough established to permit them to import breeding stock from England.

After they were finished with their bulls, they passed them on to other settlers, including the Frosts and the Hytreks. (The Frank Frost family lived a few miles northeast of the Hytreks.) The opportunity to up-grade their herds was a tremendous advantage to settlers, for much of the livestock in Nebraska had but recently descended from the rangy Texas Longhorns.

Probably the imported bulls were either Red Shorthorns or Herefords, as a popular practice was to first cross Texas cattle

---

* When R.O. Clifford lived on the Correction Line, he was married to Bertha West. After she died, he married Maude Henderson. Their children: Sylvia (Lemmer), Ferne (Coxbill), Florence (Boettcher), Melba (Dvorak), and Bob.

** In addition to being the midwife, Frances would probably be the one called to clean the wounds of a man gored by a bull or to instruct a mother concerning the use of a mustard plaster or a pack made of skunk grease and turpentine to treat a chest cold.

with Red Shorthorns and then use Hereford bulls after that.

A New Accordion
1897

When the Hytreks came to America, packing space for the family of five was at a premium, leaving no margin for frills. Thus Gregor's accordion was left behind.

Gregor was a man with a happy disposition and often sang as he worked. Johanna knew that he missed his accordion and sometimes suggested that they buy another one.

"Have you looked at the accordions in the Sears catalog? Which one do you like?"

Gregor would merely shrug and answer, "There are so many other things that we need!"

Secretly, Johanna began saving pennies and nickels.

One Sunday afternoon the Hytreks had a party for Gregor's birthday. Johanna had taught the children Polish songs and poems, and they presented a little program for their father. Lunch, consisting of the usual party menu of bologna, kolatches, and coffee, was served, after which it was time to present the gifts. The two youngest children were allowed to carry them.

First came Mary with a box of cigars. Gregor received them with profuse remarks of appreciation and with grand thank yous. Then he glanced toward little Anna who was waiting behind a corner of the cupboard with another gift. Of course, he was expecting it to be a second small package, perhaps a box of candy or a new necktie.

Johanna beckoned to Anna who came forward, tottering under the load of a heavy package—an accordian!

The guests called out for a tune, but Gregor said he was sure he would have to do some practicing first. However, when he put the strap over his shoulder and ran his fingers lightly over the keys, he suddenly knew that the music inside him was ready to burst forth. He "struck up a lively tune" and everyone danced, laughed, and clapped for the remainder of the afternoon.

Stencil soon began playing the accordion, and later Anna learned, also. After the family purchased a violin, Paul and Anna both began fiddling.

When Anna was about eleven, her parents bought her a Cornish organ, the bellows of which were powered by foot pedals. Gregor and Paul drove the wagon, loaded with the organ, into the yard, and Anna was speechless with surprise.

Many years later, when Anna and V.J.'s house was supplied with newer musical instruments which included a player piano, Anna's organ was moved to the machine shed. It was old enough to be out-of-style, but unfortunately was not yet old enough to be thought of as a precious antique. Eventually, Anna's son Don made an overnight stand from the wood in the organ, a piece of furniture now in the possession of Anna's grandson, Vincent Krysl.

The Home-made Bologna Press

Gregor Hytrek constructed his own bologna press. He began with a short section of stovepipe and fastened a funnel securely to one end of it. The casings were slipped on the spout of the funnel, and the ground, seasoned meat was placed in the stovepipe. A heavy cloth was laid over it, followed by a wooden plunger that was carved to fit the inside of the stovepipe. Gregor pushed the plunger with his abdomen, while using his hands to guide the casings as they filled with meat.

Since Gregor died at a relatively early age (when Anna was twelve) from stomach cancer, his wife wondered if the abdominal pressure required for "stuffing casings" could have caused the illness. He not only made large batches of bologna for their own family but made it for many of the neighbors, also.

Hytrek Choir
1890's

At first, the Hytreks belonged to the Atkinson St. Joseph's parish because the Stuart parish had not yet been established. Then for some time after the St. Boniface parish was organized in Stuart, they continued to attend church functions in Atkinson because they had made friends with other Polish-speaking people and also because church services were often conducted in Polish—or in Bohemian which was a language similar to Polish. (The Stuart parish was considered to be predominantly German, and quite often had German priests.)

Although a couple of the Hytreks probably stayed at home to do chores, the others usually went to Atkinson for Sunday mass, driving a team of mules on a buggy. Mules were a good choice, for they were lighter in weight and longer winded. Even though the Hytreks were on the road long before dawn, the team necessarily had to move along quite briskly if the family were to arrive at mass on time.

When Polish-speaking Father Clemenz was in Atkinson, Johanna Hytrek, who had a lovely singing voice, organized a Polish choir. Among others who belonged to the group were Magdalena (Hytrek) Frost and Mary Dlugosh. They enjoyed singing in their native tongue the old hymns that were popular in their European homeland.

Since Sunday was usually the only time they went to town, they marketed their cream and eggs and purchased grocery items.

The trip home was less hurried. They munched crackers and bologna while they chatted about tidbits of news heard in town. Also, it was a relaxed block of time when they could discuss the work agenda for the coming week.

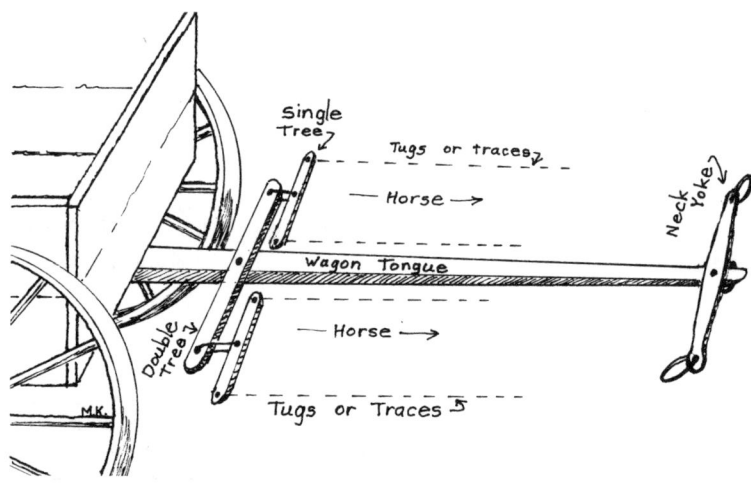

Hitch for two horses.

One end of the neck yoke fastens to the bottom of the horse collar of one horse; the other end fastens to the collar of the second horse. The neck yoke bears none of the weight of the load; rather it stabilizes the positions of the horses by yoking them together, and it holds the wagon tongue up. (The wagon tongue is used in turning, and also it keeps the wagon from rolling forward to bump the horses.) The weight of the load is born by the tugs (or traces), sturdy leather straps which lead from the sides of the horse collars to the single trees. The horses push into the collars which is the force that pulls the load.

Johanna and Gregor Hytrek's love for music has traveled down through the generations. Top: Their great grandson, Don Krysl Jr., with the Kearney High School Band which he directed for eleven years. Below, his children, Stephanie and Robert, with their instruments. about 1990.

Top: Don saying farewell to Kearney High before going back to college to become an optometrist. Below: Vincent Krysl Jr. on the drums and Vince Sr. playing the guitar. 1992.

Broken Neck Yoke

In the fall Gregor Hytrek hauled baled hay to town, using a wagon and four head of horses. One night when he was returning home, the neck yoke broke causing the wagon tongue to fall and stick into the ground.

The momentum of the moving team whipped the wagon to one side where it bumped the heels of one of the horses. Frightened and confused about what was happening in the dark, the animals jerked and plunged. They broke loose and ran away.

Gregor arrived home afoot early the next morning and found the horses grazing along the roadside near the barn.

Sorghum

Some people planted a patch of sorghum cane and made molasses from it. Using a stick, they knocked the leaves off the stalks, after which they cut them and hauled them to the horse-powered press. The sweet liquid squeezed from the stalks was then boiled all day and into the night in a huge vat. The fire had to be tended carefully, and the syrup needed to be stirred constantly, or it would stick to the bottom of the vat and scorch.

Once Johnny Erb and Dan Dierks made sorghum "on shares," and each got a barrel of the finished product. When John brought the sorghum from the Freouf place (Freoufs had a press and cooking vats) the Erb kids were wild with excitement.

"Can we have a taste? Can we have some for supper?"

Johnny had chores to do, and was in a hurry.

"We don't have a faucet yet, and we can't get the sorghum out until we get one," he told the children.

After chores, Johnny came in, carrying a long, slender stick. He opened the top bunghole of the barrel and inserted the stick into the thick molasses. When he pulled it out, it was covered with the bronze-colored sweetener. He scraped it off into a bowl, and repeated the process until he had about a cupful.

The family had sorghum along with their bread and milk that night.

Making a meal of bread and milk began with homemade bread which could be wheat, rye, or cornbread. The bread was broken into bite-sized pieces, placed in a bowl, and covered with milk. A sweetener, such as honey, sorghum, or sugar, could be added. It was eaten much as cold cereal is today.

The practice of eating bread and milk (or sometimes potatoes and milk) for the evening meal phased out in the early 1900's. However, a few of the "old-timers" continued to prefer this basic supper for many more years. For instance, John and Christina Krobot ate bread and milk every night until they moved to town in 1946. Henry Runte reported that when he was a child, their family habitually ate cornbread and milk for supper.

One day, John Dobrovolny said to his brother Tom: "I didn't get any sorghum planted this year. I don't know how my family will manage after last year's molasses is gone."

"Oh, don't worry," said Tom. "Just tell your kids what I tell mine. Sweets aren't good for you. Your teeth will rot."

Tom's family didn't plant sorghum until after the boys were half grown. However, having it made a huge difference in their lives, for thereafter they had pancakes and molasses for breakfast instead of corn meal mush, and for supper they had a sweetener for their bread and milk.

Tom's son Fred said that the home-made sorghum was sweeter and much more mild than the molasses one buys today.

Barrels of Sauerkraut
told by Ed Krysl

"Dad cut the cabbage, and Ma put it in a fifty-gallon vinegar barrel. She throwed in some salt 'n caraway seed, and beat it with a stomper that Dad had made from a block a' wood and a broom handle.

"Ma kept the kraut in the house where it was warm till it soured; then they moved it to the granary.

"Old man Kotetek was over one day. Dad made a rope sling on the barrel and put two stout sticks through the ropes on either side of the barrel. They grabbed a-holt of the sticks, an' carried it to the granary. Men were powerful in those days 'cause folks ate a lot of milk products which built strong bones, and they worked hard which built big muscles. But even then, they had to set it down and rest every few feet.

"Once Dad got a whiskey barrel. It was the same size as a vinegar barrel, but heavier wood. When he took the head off, he found a strip of chewin' tobacca nailed to the inside.

"I s'pose the idee was to make the whiskey stronger. Maybe they could water it down a little that way and add to their profits. It's a wonder they didn't kill someone those days!"

Fishing In Dora Lake

It was a rare occasion when Paul Dickau (Henry's father) found time to fish, but sometimes he did provide the family with a meal of bullheads.

Henry reported that they drove a team and wagon into Dora Lake and fished from the wagon.

"If the horses weren't used to it, they didn't like it," said Henry. "They'd paw in the water and scare the fish. My dad had to yank them around a little and cuss them out to get them to stand still."

Fred Dobrovolny said that his dad usually walked to Dora Lake. However, if some of his friends were going along, he took a team and wagon.

They, too, sometimes drove the wagon into the water so that they could fish from it. However, rather than to train their horses to stand still, they unhitched them and staked them out on the bank of the pond where they could graze.

Egg Shells
1890's

One day when the Kolena boys were herding farther northwest than was usual for them, they met the Frost boys (cousins to Anna Hytrek Krysl) who were also herding. Rudolph Kolena carried a can and a piece of tin which they used for cooking various items that might be found on the prairie.

"Not very many people will admit it," said Phillip Frost who was telling this story, "but when they were kids on the prairie, they ate a lot of different things—frog legs, black birds, and the like. During the eighteen-nineties, people didn't have much, and most kids carried only a chunk of bread for lunch. Like as not they'd be nibbling on it by mid forenoon, and it would soon be gone."

On that particular day, the boys found a nest of duck eggs. They used two piles of dirt clods to make the sides of the stove and laid the tin over the top. Gathering dry grass and cowchips for fuel, they built a fire under the tin and used the can to boil the eggs.

"Last Easter I ate twenty-seven Easter eggs," said Rudolph.

The other boys knew he was fibbing. In those days, each child was grateful for one egg. Twenty-seven was absurd.

"No one could eat twenty-seven eggs!" said Phillip. "That's impossible!"

"Oh, yes," said Rudolph. "The trick is—you have to eat the shells, too. The shells are an aid to digestion. They grind up the other foods just like the gravel in a chicken's gizzard. Just try it and see."

But the other boys could not be persuaded to eat the eggshells.

"When I was a child," said Anna Krysl, "Easter eggs were usually green. Many of the settlers grew a patch of rye. It was planted the year before, and it came up early in the spring. Mother would send us to get some of the green rye, and she'd boil it with the eggs to make them green.

"I remember once she soaked iron filings in water for a month or two and dyed some cloth a rusty red. We wanted to use some of the rusty water on the Easter eggs, but mother said that it might be poison. We had to be satisfied with green eggs."

Sour Milk and Sweet
late 1880's

Fred Dobrovolny told about the lunch they had one day when their mother was especially busy.

Antonija was making soap and was cooking it in the huge, iron soap kettle. This pot was about two feet in diameter and had three short legs. The legs lifted the kettle off the ground, thus allowing one to build a fire under it. The thick, boiling liquid in the kettle required constant care.

When noon arrived, Antonija called to Frank who was perhaps eight years old.

"There is a crock bowl of clabbered (sour) milk by the stove," she said. "You boys may eat it. Carry it to the table carefully. Don't drop it."

Frank did as he was told. He marked the congealed substance into five portions, and the boys, each with a spoon in hand, gathered around the bowl.

"Lets make a mountain," said Anton. "Lets eat from the outside rim, and leave the center standing."

The boys sculpted as they ate. Each one was responsible for shaping his portion of the mountain—which slowly changed to a hill—and finally disappeared.

Mary Disterhaupt Balloon said that frequently they had

clabbered milk with their bread at supper time. She hated sour milk and repeatedly begged her mother not to give her any.

"Just let me eat bread tonight," she implored.

"Bread isn't enough," her mother would say. "You need milk. Besides, you must learn to like it. When you get older and work for other people, it sometimes might be the only thing they serve. Miss Muffet ate curds and whey, you know."

It seems like Miss Muffet *did* like curds and whey, but Mary never developed a taste for it.

Ella Ziska remembered when their family was caring for Art Regal, her infant cousin whose mother, Emma, had died of child-bed fever (post-birth infection.) John tied an especially tame cow in the barn, and nine-year-old Annie was sent at intervals throughout the day to fill the baby's bottle with milk. (Since there was no refrigeration, it was difficult to keep milk fresh.)

"Once when Annie was busy kneading bread dough," Ella later said, "the baby was fussing. Mama told me to take the bottle and go out to the cow to see if I could get some milk. I was about five years old, and I had a hard time, but I did get some milk in the bottle." An examination of records reveals that Ella truly was only five.

When she was six, she was assigned a cow to milk night and morning. For thousands of days thereafter, night and morning, through her childhood, through her teens, and into her adulthood, the morning rising and the evening lowering of the sun signaled milking time. On her wedding day, she was excused from chores, but the following day—although the party continued in the barn loft—Ella helped with the milking.

The Noon Meal

Dinner, eaten at noon, was the main meal of the day, and might consist of vegetables, noodles or dumplings, and meat, eggs, or cottage cheese. During most years the settlers butchered a pig in the winter. Toward spring they "fried down" meat which would keep during the early summer. The well-fried meat was placed in a stone jar and hot lard was poured over it. The lard solidified and effectively sealed out the air. To use, one dug around in the lard and forked out the amount of meat needed for a meal.

The Miksches reported that they dried meat, and to keep

it from molding, stored it in shelled corn.

All the fat from a butchered animal was rendered and hoarded carefully, for it would be needed during the summer to fry any wild game the family might shoot. Rabbit, duck, prairie chicken, and pigeon might, on occasion, grace the pioneer table at noontime during the summer months.

In winter when there were no fresh vegetables, sauerkraut was served with the meat. Also, most people kept potatoes in hay-covered pits and might also have carrots, turnips, and squash stored the same way.

George Hytrek (the eldest of Paul's seventeen children) said that quite often their noonday meal consisted of fried potatoes (served on a plate) and clabbered milk (served in a cup.)

"It wasn't cottage cheese," he said. "Just thick, sour milk—something like plain yogurt. We liked it."

He reported that in later years they ate more meat, especially during the Depression of the Thirties when a farmer couldn't sell his animals because of the flooded market and couldn't keep them because there wasn't any feed.

Fruit Hungry

"Once in awhile Dad brought some apples home from town," said Fred Dobrovolny. "At such times, we boys could smell them before he got into the house with them. We were always hungry for fruit."

The only locally grown fruit were sandcherries which grew in the sandhills. During cherry season, people came to Dora Lake, and while the men fished, the women picked cherries from the nearby hillsides. Those who could afford sugar made sandcherry jelly, but others ate theirs fresh.

By the turn of the century, oranges were appearing as a holiday treat. A brightly colored apple or orange pulled from a Christmas stocking was ample cause for delighted shouts.

One year Barbara Dobrovolny planted muskmelons on a knoll near Rosenberry Lake and raised a number of large, juicy melons. On a fall day when Tom's boys were visiting, she cut some melons in fourths and gave each of them a piece.

"They were wonderful!" said Fred in his old age. "Being used to coarse foods, we didn't know that anything could taste so sweet and juicy and mellow. In my mind it seems as if they were huge melons—about twice the size of muskmelons we see today.

But I suppose, in comparison to the other fruit we had seen—like small apples or shriveled oranges—they *looked* big. Perhaps I remember them as being larger than they actually were."

School Subject: Rabbit Chasing
about 1899

When Paul Roth (who lived a few miles east of Atkinson) was a boy, the family dogs regularly followed the children to the rural school and waited outside for the happy excitement of recess, school dismissal, or better still, the passing of an unsuspecting bunny. Now these dogs had been well-trained by their young masters. They knew their jobs, one of which was to pursue rabbits. When a bunny appeared on the scene, the dozing hounds snapped awake and went to work, howling and chasing.

Surely you cannot believe that the boys would ignore the frantic call of the baying pack. Of course not! Every boy rose from his desk and raced out the door. The wild and noisy chase did little to teach the male pupils anything about multiplication tables or Columbus' route to America.

For some weeks the teacher did her best to tolerate the antics of the canine troublemakers and their young masters. Finally, however, she decided that it would be prudent to report the school interruptions to Paul's father, Henry Roth. She sent a message to Henry, asking him to stop at the school sometime soon.

On the evening after Henry's conversation with the teacher, all was calm at the Roth home. It seemed Henry was not at all upset about the activities of the unruly boys and their school-going pets. After all, Paul reasoned, his father had once been a boy himself!

However, the next day Henry appeared at the school, called Paul outside, and while the teacher and the other pupils looked on, gave him a severe whipping. Then and there, rabbit-chasing was permanently dropped from the school curriculum.

Another Prairie Fire
about 1898
told by Joe Dobrovolny

We'd seen pillars of smoke for several days, but mostly the entire horizon was hung with a smoky haze. On some days the smoke was heaviest one way and sometimes another—depending on the wind.

One morning we had just completed chores and were in the house for breakfast. Mother finished frying pancakes, and while we were still eating, she went out for a look.

"I can see the blaze. Its coming this way from the northwest," she told us when she came in.

We all hurried out.

"We'll backfire!" shouted Dad as he ran to the northwest corner of the fireguard.

After he had the backfire started, he told Anton to watch it as it traveled south along the fireguard, and Fred and me to watch it as it went east. (Frank wasn't home; he was working at Rosenberrys.) The head fire came in fast and hit before we were ready.

"Get the cattle and horses out!" Dad yelled when the fire jumped the guard on the north side.

We ran to the barn. Fred slid the halters off the horses—there were probably about six or eight of them—and turned them into the corral. I took out my pocketknife and cut the calf ropes. We were milking about twenty cows—which means there were twenty calves tied in the barn. We turned them outside, too. The horses were spooked by the fire and were galloping back and forth in the corral. Cows and calves were darting about and bawling, mostly along the west fence, for the main fire was on the east side of the buildings.

Fred and I got the harnesses out of the barn and piled them on bare ground near the milk house. We noticed that fire had crept up behind the house and was smoldering in the straw that was banked up on the north and west sides. (We were living on Uncle Fred's place then, which means it was a wood-frame cabin.) Anton and I used the backs of our scoop shovels to smother the fire near the house.

The hay was stacked behind the sheds, but it was April, and there wasn't a lot of hay—most of it had been fed over the winter.

The fall before Fred had dug a hole near the well and had filled it with water in order to keep fish. Now he jumped into it, soaked his clothes, and went to hold the fire away from the hay and the sheds. When Anton and I were satisfied that the house was safe, we went to help Fred.

The fire burned out the east side of the corrals, but we saved all the buildings.

The horses and cows were still in the enclosure, but the calves had gone through the fence and scattered. We had considerable difficulty rounding them up, but finally we had located them all except one. We looked everywhere for him. At last we found him curled up in the bottom of an empty potato pit. (Those days, we stored potatoes in straw-lined pits to keep them from freezing. The pits were maybe five feet deep.)

After the fire was over, we noticed Mother and Dad standing in the yard. Suddenly, we realized that we hadn't seen either of them after Dad told us to let the stock out. We never did know where they were while we were fighting the fire.

"Did you ever ask?" questioned his listener.
"No. Never asked. Young people were taught not to ask questions about things that didn't concern them. It wouldn't even have occurred to any of us to ask."

Tom Dobrovolny Family. Back: Joe*, Anton, Fred; Front: Frank, Antonija*, Tom*. About 1898.
* Direct ancestors of Steph, Robb, Vincent Jr, Adrienne, Renee.

Top: Joe and Ella Dobrovolny's children, from left: H.T. (Tom); LeRoy; A.D. (Tony); Fred; Albena; John; and Marie. The eldest, Emanuel, died as an infant. 1986 photo. Bottom: Donald Krysl and Marie Dobrovolny wedding. June 1, 1943.

Don & Marie Dobrovolny Krysl children: Judy (born 1946) feeding Lambo; Vince (born 1954) working in the hay field; Don Jr. (born 1957) using a home-made hack saw to cut iron for the construction of his dad's well-drilling machine.

John Ziska's Steam-Powered Threshing machine. About 1900, this machine replaced the horse-powered thresher.

Chapter 6

The Turn of the Century

Uncle Edd and the New Century
1900

There weren't many events to break the school routine in those days when the school house was a mere dot in the middle of endless prairie. However, District 77 could boast of numerous small installments of entertainment, for there was a jester in the neighborhood. His name was Edd Ziska, and he was the favorite uncle of Freddie, Annie, Ella, and Jim Ziska. In fact, so popular were his clown-like antics that all the pupils began referring to him as "Uncle Edd," and all watched for the times when he passed by the school.

Sometimes he came down the road with his jacket on backwards and his pipe held upside down in his teeth. Other times he put hats or scarves on his horses or fastened streamers in their tails. Once he tied deer horns to the head of his mule. He might ride backwards on his horse or on the wagon seat.

A pole fastened to the front of his buggy became a flagpole one day. The next day, it had a bed sheet attached to it, turning his vehicle into a boat. Also, he was fond of lying down in his wagon, giving the appearance that no one was driving the horses. Sometimes, he took his boots off and held the lines with his feet. He must have been a resourceful man, for it seemed there was no end to his tricks.

Ella remembered how each year he welcomed in the New Year, and was told that he greeted the New Century in the same way. She, herself, was a small child and slept through the dawning of the New Century.

At one minute before midnight, December 31, 1899, Edd opened the door, placed himself on the opposite side of the room, and waited. When the clock began to strike twelve, he bounded to the door, shouting: "Begone, all you eighteen hundreds! Leave this world forever and take all your heartaches and problems with you! Go!"

He swung his leg in a mighty kick to help the old century on its way.

"And what is this?" he asked in cajoling tones. "Why, it's a lovely, little child! Come right in. You must be the nineteen hundreds. We've been waiting for you. We mean to treat you right and know you'll do the same for us."

Then he presented the New Century to his giggling nieces and nephews.

Wrong Lunch Bucket
around 1900

Benbens, who lived near the place where Ray Krysl now resides, carried their lunches to school in syrup buckets.

One noon Victoria Benben opened her lunch pail and discovered she had accidentally picked up the wrong bucket and had brought syrup instead of sandwiches. Mary and Anna Hytrek shared their lunch with her.

A common lunch for them was bread spread with lard and sprinkled with either sugar or salt. Sometimes they had bread spread with syrup. After their orchard began to bear fruit, they might have an apple.

By the time Benbens moved to Elyria, a romance had budded between Victoria Benben and Paul Hytrek. Later they married and had seventeen children.

Stolen Hay
about 1900
as told by Phillip Frost

"Vaclav Krysl was a powerful man.

"I remember once when a neighbor put up some hay on a meadow that Uncle George [Gregor Hytrek] was renting and hauled it over to his own place. Uncle George went to Old Mr. Copp who was a Justice of the Peace and repossessed it.

"He and Vaclav went with a hayrack to get it. I can see

Vaclav yet. He was jabbing that fork in and out, and the way the hay was flying it looked about like a haystacker.

"And all the while he was yelling about sneaking thieves and no-good robbers and people so crooked that it was a wonder they could stand up straight. We weren't that close, but I think we heard every word. He had a voice like a freight train."

The Horse in the Well
early 1900's

In a corner of the barn, the Hytreks had a well which was fitted with a board cover. During the summer months, the horses drank outside in the wooden stock tank, but in the winter they often drank from the barn well which was outfitted with a hand pump and a tub.

One summer day after work, the horses went from the outside watering tank into the barn, and all except one followed the habitual procedure of going directly to their stalls where they waited to be unharnessed and grained. That one exception, a big, dark bay named Walnut, had a reputation for being snoopy. A grain sack was lying on top of the covered well, and he went to investigate. He began sniffing and pawing at it, undoubtedly hoping to find a few grains of oats.

Paul followed the horses inside but came running back to the door.

"Run and get Dad!" he shouted to Anna. "Walnut broke through the cover on the barn well and fell into it!"

Anna summoned Gregor. Walnut had fallen, front quarters first, into the well, and his neck was twisted back against the side of the casing, causing him to gasp for breath.

The family worked far into the night in an attempt to rescue the horse, but finally he died.

Eleven Fingers
1901

"You need to rest now. Try to sleep," Frances told Mary, John Ziska's wife.

"I'm waiting to see my baby," answered Mary who had just given birth to their fourth child.

"Barbara is washing him. It will take quite a while. You didn't get any rest last night; so relax and sleep now."

But Mary waited....

Two of Mary's sisters-in-law (probably Frances Ziska Freouf and Barbara Ziska) delivered the baby because their mother, who had been the neighborhood midwife, was ill.

When it was obvious that Mary would not sleep until she had seen her baby, Frances brought her the little bundle. She attempted to keep Mary from unwrapping the infant.

"Better keep him covered. There's a draft blowing through here."

"But its a hot day!" said Mary. Then she looked up in alarm. "What is the matter?"

Frances stepped back and chose her words carefully. "Well, he's a fine, healthy baby. Thank God that you have a strong, robust son."

By then, Mary had him unwrapped. His hands were hidden in a long-sleeved gown, but two straight legs were visible, and also two tiny feet, each with the correct number of toes lined up like peas in a pod. Then she turned her attention to extricating his hands and burst into tears.

John hurried to her. "Mary! Mary! Don't take on so. It will be all right. Don't cry. It isn't good for you."

John could hardly understand her words, for they came between sobs. "Other kids will make fun of him, like they did your sister Anna. Once they called her Pegleg because one of her legs was shorter, and she had hurt feelings for years."

"I know," said John. "But this problem with the tiny finger can be fixed."

But Mary wasn't listening. "In the Old Country one boy had a harelip. He cried when the other kids teased him. What—what—will they say about a boy with eleven fingers?"

"That extra finger—it can be removed," said John consolingly. "I examined it and I'm sure it has no bone in it."

Frances carried the baby back to the kitchen where she and Barbara again scrutinized the tiny finger.

"I think John is right. There is no bone in it," said Frances.

When Mary had quieted, John also returned to the kitchen and sent Barbara to sit with her.

He spoke to Frances: "We will take care of the problem now. It will be best for both Mary and the baby to have it over with. I will do it myself. If a person is quick about it, it shouldn't be too bad."

Frances nodded and faked a calm expression even though her insides had turned into a quavering mass.

"It will be best," she said. "Better than to leave it—like Mother did with Anna's leg."

As a girl, John's sister Anna had fallen and her leg had been twisted out of joint at the hip. Her mother would not permit anyone to pull it back into place. She was forever sorry because Anna, from then on, was handicapped.

So as not to disturb Mary, they took the supplies they needed and their tiny patient out to the top-buggy. John's three older children were in the yard. Ten-year-old Freddie was getting some ground corn and a pan of water for a hen who had hidden her nest and now had appeared with baby chicks.

"Put that pan down and take Annie and Ella into the house. Stay there until we come back in," directed John.

The operation was not as easily accomplished as they had hoped it would be, but at last it was finished. John wiped clean his razor, laid it down, and walked toward the orchard.

Frances now felt free to weep, and she did so as she tended the baby. She poured a generous amount of sugar on a bandage (a strip from an old bed sheet) and applied it to the tiny hand. The sugar would slow the bleeding and combat infection.

The wound healed, and the boy, just like everyone else, had five fingers on each hand—and only five.

This baby, born July 19, 1901, was christened Jacob Edward, but was known as Jim.

Pass the Bread
1902

Anna Hytrek,* whose family spoke Polish at home, learned both Bohemian and German words from her various classmates, and some of those words were remembered all her life. She was in about the fourth grade when Joe Krysl entered school. Joe had four older siblings who attended school also: Christina, Vencil, Anna, and Frank.

The Krysl children brought a loaf of bread to school, and when noon arrived, Christina, the eldest, sliced it, spread it with lard, and passed it to the various members of the family who sat with their respective classmates to chat during the lunch hour. Little Joe, however, hadn't yet learned to speak English, and he sat by himself on a low bench in the back. In order to avoid

---

* As an adult, Anna married V.J. Krysl and they became the parents of Leo, Amelia, Josephine, Christine, Don and Bill.

wastefulness, Christina gave Joe only a small portion of bread at a time.

Whenever he wanted more, he called out in his slow, Krysl drawl, "'Leh-eh—baw-aw-aw."

The Bohemian word for bread is actually *chleba*, pronounced kleb-aw, but Little Joe omitted the K sound at the beginning of the word.

One day after Anna had grown old and was crippled in her knees, she was using the handrail to laboriously pull herself up the church steps. Cecelia Miksch, a few years younger, came tripping along, spoke to Anna, and passed on up the steps.

Grinning to herself, Anna called in German: "Wait for me! Don't go so fast!"

Cecelia turned in surprise. "Anna! You're Polish! When did you learn to speak in German?"

"I learned that much from you when you were a little girl," explained Anna, laughing. "When we walked home from school together, we older girls would get ahead of you, and you'd call out in German for us to wait for you. You had just started school and couldn't talk English yet."

Anna remembered when Henry Miksch was in second grade and by that time could speak English well enough to recite a poem at the Christmas program. In his nervousness, he grasped the sides of his trousers and twisted them while he spoke. He rolled the r's the way German-speaking people do.

She even remembered his poem:

> They call on me to make a speech;
> I'm sure I don't know how.
> Perhaps it would be just as well
> If I only make a bow.

Chewing Tobacco
around 1900

Chewing tobacco arrived at the stores in long, one-pound strips, each of which cost fifty cents. If a customer wished, he could buy a six-pound box for three dollars.

If he wanted only one plug of tobacco, the store keeper, using a cutter with a long handle that lifted up like the handle of a paper cutter, sliced off a ten-cent plug.

Milk Gravy
about 1903
as told by Clarence Tasler

The family of Anton Tasler II lived near the Frank Ziskas. One day Clarence, one of the Tasler boys, was at the Ziska home. Frank and his wife Mary had gone to town to pick up some young fruit trees that they had ordered from a nursery, and the children were home alone.

Late in the forenoon, one of the children's uncles came. Lunch time approached and Lillian, the eldest Ziska child (about twelve years old), considered the bread and milk fare that was planned for the children's lunch. She wished she might offer her uncle a better meal.

Finally she said, "Uncle Hod, if you chop some wood so I can build a fire, I'll make milk gravy."

The man cut the wood, Lillian made a fire, and everyone had bread and gravy.

Frank and Mary Ziska later moved their family to Walla Walla, Washington. Before they left, Frank's nephew Freddie said: "Uncle Frank, I just don't see how you can move away and leave your beautiful orchard. You have put so much time and money into it."

"In Washington we will be able to have a much better one," answered the uncle. "There, fruit is a main crop."

General farming did not interest Frank as much as it did his brothers, but he had a well-groomed, productive orchard.

Deep Snow
early 1900's

One particular year the snow started falling in autumn, and storm followed storm all winter long. As the drifts piled higher, the Tasler boys were kept busy shoveling.

Finally, after the snow was so deep that it was difficult to make paths in it because they couldn't throw the snow up the sheer walls, they hit upon the idea of cutting stair steps from the house up to the top of the drifts. The steps were a grand invention, but whenever another storm came, the boys had a new carving job.

With the approach of spring, they looked forward to the end of snow-sculpting, but another problem arose.

Mary Ziska (Mrs. Frank) was tired of being virtually shut in all winter and longed for a little outside companionship. As the days warmed, she began making visits to the Taslers, their nearest neighbors.

Mary was not a small woman, nor was she especially nimble.

(Clarence Tasler, who remembered this story from his boyhood, would not, in those days of storks and cabbage patches, be aware that a summer baby would contribute—for some months in advance—to a woman's greater size and her lack of agility. However, such may have been the case.)

The spring weather was softening the snow, and every time the lonely Mary trudged across the drifts and floundered down the chiseled steps, the boys must get the shovels and reshape the stairway. They dreaded her visits.

Making Yeast Cakes
early 1900's

May Hanel told how her mother, Bertha Schindler, made yeast cakes. Because they must air-dry, she usually made them in the summer.

She used a purchased yeast cake as a starter. These cakes had a cornmeal base and came in a package of five.

To make yeast cakes:

Use 1 cup cornmeal. Cook it in water the way you would in making corn meal mush, except make it extra thick by using less water. Cool. (Heat will kill yeast cells.)

Mix 1 yeast cake into the cooked mush.

Add enough flour to make it hold together. The mixture should be very stiff. Drop by spoonfuls on slick paper or on cloth and pat thin.

Dry the cakes in a warm (not hot) place. It will require several days. Be certain they are *completely* dry before storing. By the time the cakes have dried, the yeast cells will have multiplied.

Store in a glass jar with a lid.

Each year Ed Schindler made two trips to town for supplies, bringing home always the same grocery items: sugar, coffee and dried fruit as well as a dozen fifty-pound sacks of flour. The family grew all other food staples—or did without.

Driving a Mule Team
early 1900's

Frank Teter* bought a huge overcoat to wear when he was driving the team and wagon on a cold day. If his wife and children accompanied him, they sat on straw in the bottom of the wagon and covered with quilts. Sometimes the children got out and ran along the side of the wagon in order to break the boredom of a long ride and to warm themselves.

The boys, one by one, grew to an age when they were allowed to drive the team. What a proud moment it was when a boy, for the first time, donned the great, long, sheepskin-lined coat and took his place on the wagon seat! A cap with earflaps and a pair of warm mittens completed the costume.

A generation later (probably in the early 1930's) Boyd Teter had a wonderful pair of mules named Tom and Jerry.

"Now, they were fast!" said Boyd. "There wasn't another team in the country that could keep up with them. They walked along at about five miles an hour."

One day he was driving home from Bartley, and his nephews, Eugene and Stanley, were along. Being accustomed to riding in a car, the boys thought the mules were slow.

When they were a few miles out of town, one of them said, "Uncle Boyd, these mules are too poky. Will you let me out to walk? When I get to your house, I'll tell everyone that you will be coming later."

After letting the boy out, Boyd drove off, the mules stepping along at their usual fast walk. The hiking lad fell behind and was forced to run.

After exhausting himself, he shouted, "Uncle Boyd! Wait! I want to ride."

Boyd stopped the team, and the panting boy climbed aboard. He made no more complaints about the mules being too slow.

Mounted Cowgirls
1903

While Anna and Mary Hytrek, with the help of their dog

---

* Frank was Shirley Teter Krysl's great-grandfather; Boyd is her great uncle.

named Grife, herded cattle, they whiled away some of the uneventful hours by breaking a couple of the milk cows to ride. Mary, being a year older than Anna, was the first to acquire the idea, and she chose the tamest cow, a shorthorn called Old Red, for her steed.

When Anna observed her sister's success, she began to tame and train a cow called Rocker. The name Rocker came from an old rocking-seven brand that she had on her ribs. Once the cows had been broken to ride, the girls put them to good use: whenever they came to a slough, instead of sloshing through the mud, they climbed onto their bovine steeds and rode grandly across.

One evening the young herders were bringing the cows home, and on approaching a marsh, each of the girls made a leap to mount her cow. Mary gained her coveted seat, but Anna slid off the back of fast-moving Rocker who was not quite as manageable as Old Red. Anna must now wade the marsh herself. Provoked because of her failure and Mary's success, Anna sent the dog after Mary's cow. "Sic 'em, Grife! Go get her! Go get her!" She pointed at Old Red.

When the barking dog vaulted at the hind legs of the cow, Old Red sprang forward, running and bucking. Mary fell off into the water.

Anna reported that when the mosquitoes were bad, they built smudges in the corral to discourage the insects from biting the cows and the people during milking. They set a few forksful of hay ablaze, after which they threw some damp hay or manure on the fire to make it smolder.

The cows soon learned that the smoke brought relief from the hungry insects, and they searched out a suitable location in its pathway. In those days, the cows were milked in the corral rather than being driven inside a building or locked into stanchions.

Expensive Wheelbarrow
about 1904

Mary and Anna Hytrek found a discarded wheel from a baby buggy in the junk pile and decided that they would make a wheelbarrow. A prune crate would function nicely for a box, but what could they use for handles? They searched the farmstead but located nothing suitable until they discovered the walking plow.

"Look here," said Anna. "These old plow handles would be perfect."

"Great!" answered Mary. "But how can we get them off?"

"Lets use the hacksaw," said Anna. "It works fine. I sawed a broomstick with it one day."

The girls brought the hacksaw from the tool shed and set to work. It was a more difficult job than they had supposed it would be, for the handles were made of hard wood, and the girls were far from experienced carpenters. However, they took turns and labored with determination.

When on the second day the last plow handle fell to the ground, the sweaty, red-faced, little girls grinned widely in spite of the painful blisters on their hands.

More problems loomed while they were attempting to fasten their creation together, for the wood in the handles was too hard to nail. Finally, they used wire to assemble their wonderful machine. The wobbly wheel and the loose-fitting construction were not obvious when the vehicle was stationary.

As soon as Gregor saw the wheelbarrow, he recognized his plow handles. Being a gentle man, he probably did not mete out much in the way of punishment, but the girls were stricken when they realized that the plow that had been parked behind a shed was not meant to be part of the "junk pile."

Noise at the Window

Several miles to the south on Holt Creek, John Ziska had a quarter section of hay meadow. One wet fall he had difficulty moving the hay from it to the farmstead. After days of laborious trips with his hayrack, he decided to ease his task by waiting for snow and for colder weather, after which he could use a hay sled.

Suitable conditions arrived in early January: the ground was frozen, eight or ten inches of snow provided an adequate base for using the hay sled, and the sky was clear. John and his trusty mules, Jenny and Gin along with two younger mules, went each day to the creek land and returned with a sled load of hay. John, always one to watch the weather signals, was anticipating a "January thaw." He wanted to have his hay home before such a time arrived.

It was a lovely day when he and the mules set off on the final trip. In fact, it was too lovely, for by the time John had loaded the hay, the bright sun had begun to reduce the snow. Several times the sled runners sliced through to hit earth, but John was able to keep the load moving. He snaked back and forth, avoiding the bare patches of ground that were beginning to appear. However, one spot he could not avoid, for he must use the creek crossing. Upon approaching it, he stopped.

While he rested his team in preparation for the hard pull ahead, John climbed down from the load. He examined the trail that dipped to the frozen creek, passed over it, and wound up on the other side. The ice on the stream was firm, but the earth on either side of it was beginning to soften. No part of the crossing looked promising, but John decided that his best chance was to crowd to the far right where there was a narrow rim of untrampled snow.

When he reclaimed his seat in the hay and urged the team forward, the left runners cut through the slush, stalling the sled.

The team was willing and pulled valiantly. John used every trick he knew to lift the load out of the rut, and each time he tried a new strategy, the mules put their heads down, laid low in their harnesses, and, inch by inch, struggled forward. They finally pulled clear of the crossing.

From there, he was able to avoid locations where the earth was peeking through the snow, and eventually reached home without additional problems.

Mary and the older children had the milking chores nearly finished. After John unhitched the team, the mules hurried to the watering tank for a drink before entering the barn. John slid the harnesses off their backs and let them out into the barnyard where they shook their hides vigorously and proceeded to the feed rack.

After supper a noise at the window startled the family. They all looked up, but in the dim yellow light from the kerosene lamp, they could not discern who—or what—was on the other side of the pane.

Suddenly there was a loud, long, agonizing bray, a thud against the side of the house, and then silence.

John quickly lit the lantern and went out the door. Through the window, Mary could see, as her husband tipped the lantern and leaned forward, that one of the mules lay on the ground.

"It's Jenny!" she said.

John's hand moved over the mule, exploring. Finally, he looked up, shook his head, and blew out the lantern.

Mary knew from the stricken expression on his face, that Jenny was dead. She knew, too, that John had extinguished the light in order to have some private time with the animal who, along with Gin, had carried him repeatedly across the prairie and had worked faithfully for him during the many years since.

Later, John said that he supposed that Jenny, while pulling resolutely on the stalled hay sled, had injured a blood vessel which finally had ruptured and had caused her death. When she sensed that all was not well, she had gone to summon the master who usually supplied her needs. But this time he couldn't help.

Eventually, John sold the quarter on the creek. It is now owned by Garwoods, who came to the area in 1919 and live about a mile east of Wright's Lake.

Sunbonnet

Ella Ziska could hardly wait to wear her new pink and gray sunbonnet. Her Aunt Anna had made several of them that winter and had given one to each of her nieces.

"Let's wear our new bonnets to school," said Ella on a clear, spring day.

"Oh, it isn't warm enough yet. They are for us to wear in the hot summertime," said Annie.

Ella looked out the window. "The sun is shining. Mama, isn't it warm enough for us to wear our bonnets today?"

Mary smiled indulgently and helped the child tie the calico strings under her chin.

However, the warm morning was not a reliable weather forecaster, for after lunch, a raw wind swept over the valley, bringing dense clouds and a sleet storm.

Bill Blackburn hitched a team to the wagon and drove to school to pick up his children as well as the Ziska youngsters. Little Ella, huddled down in her coat and wearing that pink bonnet, came out of the schoolhouse and into the pelting sleet storm. Bill teased her as he lifted her into the wagon.

"Oh, I see that it is sunbonnet weather!" he exclaimed. "I hadn't realized it was such a warm day, or I wouldn't have bothered to come to get you." He grinned at her as he pulled the brim of the bonnet forward a little. "We don't want you to get sunburned."

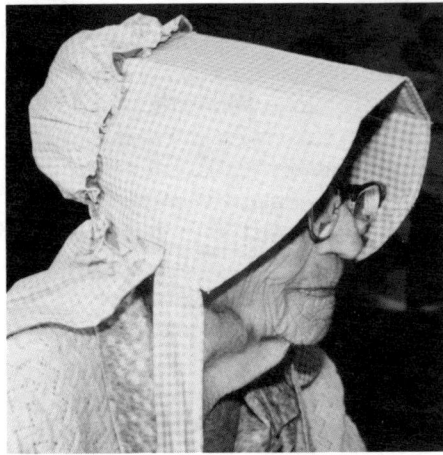

Sunbonnets went out of style by the 1930's. However, some people have continued to wear them to this day. This picture shows Mary Laible, grandmother to Kevin, Mary Jo, Tom and Chuck Krysl, in a new sunbonnet that she had made. 1986 photo.

Another Sugar Treatment
1903

Bill and Clarence Tasler, at ages ten and eight, clung tightly to the bushel basket as they headed for the granary where a pile of cobs was temporarily stored.

"Is this a tornado?" yelled Clarence, shouting to be heard above the roar of the wind.

"No," said Bill. "A tornado blows in a circle. This is a wind storm."

At first, opening the door and, at the same time, holding onto the basket seemed impossible. However, Bill finally set the flimsy container on the ground and stood inside of it to keep it from blowing away. Then the boys both tugged at the door. Once it was open, Clarence braced himself to hold it while Bill leaped out of the basket and tossed it into the building. Then the two boys managed to get themselves inside.

Once the container had been filled, a new problem confronted them.

"How're we going to keep the door open long enough to get these cobs out?" asked Clarence.

"Well, help me get it open, and then maybe you can hold it while I lift the basket out," said Bill.

Once the flimsy portal was forced open against the gale, Bill helped support it until his brother got a secure hold. Clarence held the edge of the door with one hand, reached across it to plant his other hand firmly against the framework on the hinge side, and braced himself.

"All right. I think I got it!" he gasped.

Bill let go and dived inside to get the cobs. But the gale was master!

Slam!

A scream from Clarence joined the wail of the wind. The tip of his thumb was caught in the hinge side of the door.

Bill shouldered the door open and bounced outside. By then, Clarence had pulled his thumb free and was bent over in pain.

"Let me see it!" said Bill. "Is it hurt bad?"

Clarence was already stumbling toward the house, the wind pushing him along. Bill ran ahead, calling for help.

Cora, their mother, took one look at the injury and sent Bill to ask a neighbor, Mary (Mrs. Frank Ziska), to come and help. The fleshy end of the child's thumb was pinched flat and was torn back from under the tip of the nail, exposing the underside of the bone.

Cora dipped water from the bucket into a pan and plunged the boys hand into it. She sent one of the younger children (probably Charlie) to the well for colder water. Of course, Clarence was screaming with pain.

The wound was still bleeding profusely when Mary Ziska arrived. As painful as it was to the boy, it was necessary to pull the loose flap of flesh forward to reform the tip of the thumb.

"Luckily," said Cora, "the thumb nail seems to be all right. But how can we stop the bleeding? Wrap it snugly?"

"Frank's mother would put it in sugar," said Mary. "She said that it stops bleeding and also it helps prevent infection."

Since Cora was holding the injured boy, she sent Bill to dip a cup of sugar from the sack. When he had brought it, she looked from the thumb to the cup and back again.

"Bill, bring another cup—an empty one," she commanded.

Cora inserted the thumb in the empty cup after which she added the sugar.

Eventually, the bleeding slowed. The women removed the saturated sugar and replaced it with fresh. This time they bandaged his hand, including the cup.

They laid the boy on the bed, and in order to reduce the throbbing pain, they propped high the cupful of sugar-and-thumb. The treatment was successful; the wound eventually healed.

Looking to Oregon for Greener Pastures
about 1902-1904
as told by Dale Masters, Claude's son.

Since money was difficult to obtain during pioneer years, Squire Winfield Masters decided to move his family from Nebraska to Oregon where, he had heard, a man could earn some cash by working in the lumber camps. He sold all his property except for four horses which he loaded in a livestock car on the train. He, his second wife, Lulu Prudence (La Porte), and their four children, the eldest of whom was eight-year-old Claude, were passengers on the train.*

In the livestock car along with the horses, was a large box which contained grain for the animals. Originally, the box had been a packing crate for a piano, but Squire had put a partition in it, making two compartments. The upper one contained the horse feed, and the lower one became a hiding place for two half-grown boys, sons of Squire and his first wife. By hiding the boys, one of whom was named LaVerne, Squire hoped to save a bit more of his cash in order to have it available to begin their new life in Oregon.

When the train was in motion, the boys crept out of hiding and sometimes sat in the doorway of the car. Whenever they slowed for a stop in a town, they secured themselves in the secret compartment. Sometimes the conductor saw the boys in the doorway, but searches during subsequent stops failed to reveal their hiding place. Finally, the conductor spoke to Squire:

"I've seen some extra boys in the boxcar with your horses. You'll have to pay fare for them."

"Pay fare for *what* boys?" asked Squire. "You'll have to produce them before suggesting that anyone pay fare for them."

When the family, now including all six of the children, left the depot in Oregon, they saw the conductor across the street. La Verne waved impishly.

There *were* work opportunities in the lumber camps, and Squire, a sturdy man, was soon employed.

Lulu raised a huge garden, and the money they had brought with them took care of their needs until the vegetables

---

* Margie Masters Dobrovolny, wife of Henry Dobrovolny, was the third youngest of Squire's second family. There were seven or eight children in his first family. After his wife died, Squire remarried and fathered nine more children.

matured. All would have gone well except that the man who had hired Squire kept insisting that, as yet, he was not making any money, and that Squire would have to wait for his wages.

After two years, the Masters family was penniless and in need. Finally, Squire decided he *would* get some of the hard-earned cash that his boss owed him, and he, with Claude trailing behind, went to confront him. Claude's dog, the hungry pet of a destitute family, brought up the rear.

The man lived in a one-room house with nothing but a patch of earth for a floor. In the middle of this cabin was a small stove that was used for both heating and cooking. A pot of beans simmered on its flat top.

"I've come for my pay," Squire told his boss. "You owe me for two years of work—twenty-four months!"

"I know I owe you, but I can't pay. I'm flat broke."

"I've got to have it. My family is in need."

"I'd give it to you if I could, but money is one thing that I don't have."

"You seem to come up with the cash when you want new saws or repairs or horse feed. Now, its time to come up with my wages. I earned them."

"I told you, I'm broke. You've heard the old saying: you can't get blood out of a turnip."

The muscled arms of the lumberman shot out and grabbed the boss. He lifted him in the air and set him down firmly on the top of the stove. The pot of beans crashed to the dirt floor. As Squire hustled his startled son out of the cabin, the boy saw his dog leap forward and begin to lick gingerly at the hot beans that were scattered about.

Having no money to pay for train fare, the Masters family returned, a distance of a couple thousand miles, by team and wagon. Lulu had given birth to a fifth child while in Oregon, and, along with the two sons from Squire's first family, there was now a total of nine people.

Once, while coming through the mountains, they had to pass over a narrow, curving ledge that was too dangerous to drive across. Squire unhitched the horses and led them over the ledge, one at a time. He removed the wagon tongue and used it to brace the vehicle in order to prevent it from falling down the precipice as they shoved it around the narrow curve. In Colorado they stopped to earn money to pay for food for themselves and the horses.

The weary family finally arrived in Bancroft, Nebraska.

The next year they moved to South Dakota where Squire took a homestead. The older boys, using a four-ox team, hired out to plow virgin prairie. They received fifty cents per acre.

The As Perry Railroad
1901

When word came to Fred Dobrovolny that his brother Joe had returned from Wyoming to Holt County and was working on the As Perry Railroad which proceeded north from Atkinson, Fred decided that he would like to get a job there, too. His parents were against it, however.

"Those men live in camps, and the days are already cold," said Tom, his father. "They put in long hours, from before dawn until after dark, no matter what the weather. Since Joe has been roughing it in Wyoming, he's used to that kind of rugged life."

Fred insisted that if Joe could get used to that rough way of living, so could he. At age seventeen, he was a sturdy fellow while Joe, even though he was a year older, was smaller and finer-boned. Fred was sure he could stand it, and he desperately wanted to earn some money of his own. His mother, seeing that he was determined to take the job, helped him pack his few belongings and supplied him with a pillow and quilt.

When Tom drove him to Atkinson, the weather was raw and cold. The twenty-two mile wagon ride took a good part of the day, and both men were well-chilled by the time they arrived. Tom grumbled, telling Fred that he didn't realize what hardships awaited him.

"You won't last a week. That kind of work is for fellows who haven't any other way to make a living. You'll find out. The cold—day and night—day and night—will get old mighty fast."

Mostly, Fred didn't answer. The one thought to which he clung was that he could do it if Joe could. Of course, riding in an open wagon was cold, but if a person were working, he would be in a better position to handle the freezing temperatures.

Fred wasn't on the job long before he was ready to admit that his parents were right. The workday began before dawn and continued until nightfall. He ached from strained muscles, he ached from exhaustion, and most of all, he ached from the grinding cold.

When night came, the men returned to camp where there

was a shed that was hardly more than a shell in which they slept. Since it housed about sixty or seventy men, it was as big as a cattle shed. The walls were full of cracks which allowed the frigid winds to blow through.

At one end of the shed there was a wood stove. They built a roaring blaze in it, and gathered around to try to soak up some of its warmth. Even though they fired up until it glowed as red as a foundry, it heated only the immediate space and did little to warm their chilled bones. After they crawled into bed, a wooden bunk with no mattress and only their own blanket or quilt for warmth, the fire went out. A few hours later Fred awoke, stiff and cold. He supposed that some night he would actually freeze to death, but he was resigned to it. He would not quit and go home, thus giving his father the opportunity to chuckle and say, "I told you so."

The men were roused long before daybreak for they must feed and harness their horses, eat their breakfast, take care of their personal needs, and be at the work site ready to begin at first light. The stars were still shining when they started work in the morning—and the stars were again shining in the evening when they quit.

Some of the men were set to plowing, while others, including Joe and Fred, manned the scrapers which moved the loosened soil to the grade being constructed for the railroad. There were about seventy scrapers, with a team to each scraper, and a long string of plows. A number of work rings made up the site. Each ring went up to the bluffs, and then around and down where the fill was being made.

After a brief stop for lunch and for changing to fresh teams, the work continued on and on into the endless afternoon. The bone chilling temperatures numbed their hands and stiffened their joints.

Meals were cold, and the menus unvaried, for at both dinner and supper they were served cold, canned salmon and bread. The women cooks baked bread all day in order to keep up with the appetites of the crowd of hungry men. Joe got so tired of salmon that he disliked it for the rest of his life.

Finally, one day the foreman, Fred Spears, came out to the work site and called the men together.

"I'm sorry to have to bring you bad news," he told them, "but the job is over. Get your belongings and go home."

Go home? Fred could scarcely hide his joy! It didn't take him long to be ready. He and Joe caught rides to Atkinson with Bill Timberly; from there they rode with Dustall as far as the Collins place; the remaining eight miles, they walked.

The way Joe later explained it, the reason for the sudden halt of the project was that another company was building a railroad north from Norfolk. They wanted to stop the Perry railroad because they feared the competition, and they tried to buy Perry out. When he wouldn't sell, they managed to buy enough stock in the Perry road to get a controlling interest, after which they shut it down.

"That Norfolk company never knew," said Fred, "what a favor they did me. Why, they saved my life!"

Perhaps Joe had warmer bedding. In his version of the story, he didn't comment about the cold weather.

Sleeping Sickness
about 1904
as told by Fred Dobrovolny

"Dad was looking for some mules to buy. We were getting more machinery and needed another team. Some parts of the country were bad hit with sleeping sickness among horses, and Dad thought mules might be less likely to get it.

"Kutroba* who lived near Miksches planned to leave the country. He had a sharp-looking team of black mules for sale, but he wanted a big price—more than Dad wanted to pay.

"Then some of our horses came down with sleeping sickness. After an animal took sick, he probably lasted only three or four days. Once in a while a horse might survive the disease, but even if he did, he sometimes had brain damage and would be stupid or crazy.

"Well, we tried everything on our sick animals: fed them flax—made them gruel out of ground feed and warm water—used Dad's old tripod and sling and winched them up on their feet—we even bled them in the mouth.

"The idea of bleeding them was an ancient practice—it was done in Europe in the Old Days. You were to bleed the animal in the area where the injury or disease was located. For instance, if a horse had an infection in the leg, you could bleed him from the foot. Supposedly, it would carry off the poison, and the body would replace it with healthy blood.

To bleed a horse for sleeping sickness, you pried his

---
* Kutroba lived on what was later the Don Krysl place.

The house in the background is that of Tom Dobrovolny. It was built south of Holt Creek in 1900. Tom's granddaughter is pointing her toe at a cowchip and thinking that she is glad that she does not have to pick it up to cook her dinner. 1991 photo.

jaws open, and using a sharp knife, cut a slit in the roof of his mouth. At our place, after I was old enough, I was the one that had to do it. It was kind of a touchy job. When Johnny Erb was bleeding his horse, the animal swung his head and got a really bad cut in the mouth. You had to be careful."

[Clinically, the practice of bleeding was obsolete, but it was carried on as a home treatment for many more years.]

"Then, quite by chance, we had a new idea to try. Out in his pasture, Harry McShane found one of his mares lying by the windmill where the cold water that was draining out of the tank-overflow fell directly onto her head. Harry tried to get her up, but she was too far gone, and when darkness came on, he went home.

"The next morning Harry returned. He took his gun in case the horse was still alive and suffering, but he figured she'd be dead. When he got there, he was surprised to see her standing on her feet. He assumed the cold water on her head was what cured her.

"After that, all of us with sick horses went to the John Dobias ice house for ice. We hoped that cold packs would be the magic cure.

""Nothing helped. Most of our horses died.

"Dad went back to Kutroba and gave him his price for the black mules, Jack and Ginny. They were a good team, and we worked them for years.

"After we bought his mules, Kutroba headed for South America, and no one ever heard of him again. Dad always wondered if he had met with foul play."

Floating Bridge
early 1900's

One wet year the Elkhorn River was badly flooded, preventing the people south of the river from getting to and from town. Finally, Gregor Hytrek, Frank Frost, Martin Miksch, and Egnatz Hamik decided to pool their resources in an effort to get their hogs to market.

First, they hauled their pigs to the river and penned them at a nearby farmstead. Some of the men tied their wagon boxes to the running gears in order to keep the boxes from floating away in the deep water, and managed to take their wagons across the river. Then the two groups of men set to work building a bridge that was partially floating and partially suspended. They tied two parallel pieces of rope across the river, after which they fastened floating planks securely to the two ropes.

The details of how they managed to get the pigs over this unstable bridge are not available, but it is said that the men did get them to market.

Snipped Yarn
about 1905

While Libbie Mlinar was crocheting mittens, her small son Charlie picked up the scissors, slipped around her chair, and quietly cut the yarn. Coming to the end of the severed yarn, Libbie assumed it was a flaw in the skein; she fastened it and proceeded.

Charlie put his scissors to work again. The second time Libbie came to the clipped end, she was dismayed. It was unusual for a bundle of yarn to have two such defects. What a nuisance!

A third loose end made her indignant, and she checked the brand of yarn. Fleecy Strands? Well, she wouldn't buy *that* kind again!

Charlie should have had the good sense to quit when he was ahead and choose someone else to harass, but where could he find another game that would give this much delight?

After another snip, Libbie realized what was happening.

The teller of this story did not reveal how the annoyed mother solved the problem, but you can believe that the remainder of the skein of yarn was all in one piece.*

Commotion Upstairs
early 1900's

In pioneer days it was considered a sin for a woman to wear short sleeves in public. The human body, male or female, was properly clad only if it were covered from throat to ankle. Thus, Charlie Mlinar's startling experience while clad only in his underwear was one he remembered all his life.

Fall was a busy time of the year with the push to get work done before stormy weather arrived. Charlie Mlinar (who told this story) and Hi Nightengale were doing road work in Green Valley, and they were staying overnight for a few weeks at the John Ziska home. Also, a baling crew was headquartering there, making a total of eleven men—most of them in their late teens or early twenties.

After supper this group of young laborers filed out of the crowded house, partly because of their respect for the overworked Mary who needed space to do her house chores and partly out of their own need for enough space to engage in the kinds of revelry young folks enjoy. However, they all knew that another day of hard work lay ahead, and they soon subdued their voices, pulled in their elbows, and trailed through the little house and up the stairs.

All eleven of them, as well as the older Ziska boy, slept in the one upstairs room. A half-dozen husk mattresses were strewn on the floor, and each would sleep two people. After pants and shirts were pulled off and laid at the foot of these make-shift beds, the lantern which hung from the ceiling was blown out. Husks rattled as the men settled down for the night.

Soon thereafter, a couple of men rode into the yard. John Ziska answered the door.

"Is Charlie Mlinar staying here?"

"That he is," said John.

"Could we talk to him? We have a message for him."

John lit a lantern and took the two upstairs. Mary was busy cooking apple jam to be served on the pancakes the next

---

* Libbie was a sister to Theodore Kubart; an aunt to Father Frank Kubart; and the wife of Joe Mlinar.

morning. She had glanced up as the visitors passed through the room, but she hadn't recognized them in the dim lamplight.

Upstairs, John held the lantern high in order to widen the circle where it cast its hazy light. He peered at the figures that covered the floor.

"Charlie? Where are you? You've got company."

"I'm over here," called Charlie.

He sat up and reached for his trousers. However, Charlie's bed partner, feeling mischievous, grabbed Charlie's pants away from him; when the two began to scuffle, the other men jumped to their feet.

Downstairs, Mary was startled by the sudden noise. Who were the two men who had arrived? Had they attacked someone up there? She hurried to the stairway door, intending to call to John to ask what was happening.

In the meantime, the trouser-snatcher pulled away from Charlie, bounded to the other end of the room, and threw the garment down the stairway. Charlie followed him and ran down the steps to retrieve his pants. Just then, Mary opened the door.

The John Ziska Family about 1902. Back: Freddie, John, Mary, Annie; front: Jim, Ella. Years later, when looking at this picture, Ella said, "Notice the strained look on Mama's face. She was so overworked at that time that she nearly had a nervous breakdown. Papa had to stop inviting other work crews to stay at our house until we girls got older."

She came face to face with Charlie who was clad only in his underwear shorts. In a flash, both faces flamed raspberry red as the two startled people fled in opposite directions.

Years later Charlie still wore an embarrassed smile as he told the story.

Pacha Barn Dance and the Mack Children
told by Effie (Pacha) Kubart

"When folks first settled, they had to get along however they could with makeshift shelters for their animals. They made sheds of hay or of sod and built chicken coops out of packing crates. But by the early 1900's the big barns with hay lofts were appearing. We built ours in 1905.

"My, but folks were proud of their barns!

"There wasn't much space for dancing in the small, crowded houses, but now the spacious hay lofts made wonderful ballrooms. When a dance was planned, some postcard invitations were sent, but mostly news traveled by word-of-mouth. Then, on the day of the dance, a signal flag was tied to the top of the windmill. Folks came from far and near—even drove out from town. Everyone was welcome!

"The Macks came to one of our dances. They had small children and put them to bed in a place we had fixed along the side in the haymow for kids to sleep whenever they got tired. We had some loose hay there, and spread blankets over it.

"I don't know just how it happened, but when the Macks went home, they forgot to load up their sleeping children. I can imagine that each was talking with friends, and that while the father was hooking up the horses, the mother went down to rearrange the quilts in the back of the wagon. However, since she was reluctant to carry the children down the steep loft steps, she decided that her husband should do it. But while he was hitching the horses, he saw her fixing blankets in the wagon, and he thought that she had brought the kids down.

"Then, when they were finally able to tear themselves away from their friends, they started home. They were a couple of miles down the road before they realized their mistake.

"They, of course, were embarrassed to have to come back and admit they'd left the kids. I always remembered it because I could see how it could happen—just like when my folks forgot me when we were coming from Iowa in the covered wagons."

Baseball in Green Valley
early 1900's

One Monday morning when Frank Krysl went to the barn to hay the horses, he discovered that he couldn't get into the haymow.

Even though there was no ladder, the long-legged Krysls usually had no trouble getting into the mow. First, they climbed to the top of the horse manger; next, they stepped to a cleat nailed to the wall; and from there they pulled themselves up onto the second floor.

On this particular morning, however, Frank was stiff from the Sunday afternoon baseball game and couldn't climb into the mow. His younger brother had to hay the horses.

Baseball was a popular Sunday afternoon sport. Bases made of sandbags were laid out in various pastures, forming the ball diamonds, and people in the community came to cheer their favorite team.

The Hytreks, Krysls, and Frosts made up the West Green Valley team. V.J. Krysl pitched and claimed, years later, that they usually won their games.

On the last day of V.J.'s life (1951), he seemed to be awake but did not speak nor focus his eyes on those of us around him. He was propped up with pillows to assist his breathing.

His eyes would slowly survey the bedspread and stop at a certain spot. In slow motion he'd reach to that spot, pick up an invisible object, bring it far back over his head, and hurl it forward with his long, loose-jointed arm.

We all hope he was striking out the opposing team members, one after another, that day.

The Ziska barn, built in 1910 and destroyed by a tornado in 1970, was the site of many barn dances.

John Ziska's children Annie, Freddie, and Ella, taken about 1900.

**The Ridgeway Shearing Crew
early 1900's
Joe Dobrovolny is the second man
from the left.**

Chapter 7

Working on the Open Range

Rawhide Creek
Lusk, Wyoming

When Joe Dobrovolny told this story, he spoke as if the mode of travel involved was a railroad train. Modern Lusk residents tell a similar tale, but assume that it was a wagon train. However, it is repeated here in much the same way that Joe, on many occasions, related it to his children.

Two railroad passengers were conversing.
"If that young whelp don't shut his mouth pretty quick, I'm a goin' to stuff it full of his own fist," said a tall Westerner. "Ever since I got on the train at Chicago, I've listened to nothing but his big brag about what he's planning to do when he gets out to Wyoming Territory. It's disgustin'!"
"Shore is!" answered his companion. "He says he's gonna' rope himself some wild horses and start up a horse ranch. Gonna' keep spreadin' till he owns the whole territory."
"Fat chance!"
"Last night he told how he planned to paper his parlor with rattlesnake hides. At first it was funny to listen to his blow, but I'm tired of it."
"Everyone is. When he said how he intends to shoot the first Indian he sees, that old fellow by the window warned him he'd better not and explained to him that we'd soon be in Indian country, and that the railroad has the right to pass through, but that is all."

"Well, it's a good thing someone is patient enough to try to set him straight."

The train clacked down the tracks which wrapped over and around the hills that rolled across the miles of Nebraska prairie, and all the while the young Easterner in his bright, new Western garb talked about his expected adventures in the rough, wild Wyoming Territory.

When the train neared the Nebraska-Wyoming line, the Easterner stood at the window, watching expectantly. A ridge of pines wound across the countryside, appearing here, disappearing there. The engine slowed when the terrain became rougher, and bluffs appeared on the horizon. As the train curved around a hill, several young Indian women could be seen washing clothes in a stream.

The Easterner whipped out his gun and before anyone could stop him, fired, killing one of the Indian maids. The others fled to the nearby camp and spread the word: the chief's daughter had been shot!

The train's stop at the next station was long enough to provide time for the angry braves to get into position. They barricaded the track, forced the engine to a halt, and demanded that the murderer be relinquished to them. Otherwise, they vowed to slaughter and scalp everyone on the train.

The railroad officials met briefly with a group of the passengers, and the decision was made that the one guilty person be given over to the Indians rather than that the lives of the innocent be jeopardized. The young fellow, who by now had lost all his bravado, was slid out a door and into the waiting hands of the tribesmen.

The train was not immediately released—not until after the execution which was not easy to watch and was worse to hear.

The Indians tied the prisoner to a pine tree and, beginning at his armpits, proceeded to remove his skin. They got all the way to his knees before he died.

Once dead, his body was tossed into a nearby creek. Ever since, that stream has been called Rawhide Creek. It is located near Lusk, Wyoming.

The Ill Sheepherder
1902 near Manville, Wyoming

Joe Dobrovolny awoke in the middle of the night,

feeling unusually hot. He slid out of his high bunk and walked across the floor to fling open the door. It was only four steps, and yet it was the length of his dining-living area as well as his kitchen, for he lived in a sheep wagon.

He laid a hand on the tiny stove by the door and found it cold. The fire he had used to make his bacon and biscuits the night before had long since burned out. Why was he hot? Usually these spring nights near the mountains were bone-chilling.

As he opened the door, a cool breeze washed over his face. He peeled off his undershirt to let the air flood his body as he looked out over the sea of 1800 sheep bedded down around the wagon. The ever-watchful shepherd dog, Muggins, stood up in expectation but relaxed when no commands were given. Joe, leaving his door open, went back to his bed, grateful that his blanket had cooled.

Sleeping fitfully for the remainder of the night, he had to force himself to crawl out of bed when dawn neared, for he knew that the sheep would begin to wander out to graze as soon as night grayed into morning. His brow was hot, his head ached, and his throat was parched. He drank two cups of water from the water keg; then sat on the wagon tongue, head in hands. With no appetite and no energy, breakfast was not a consideration.

After drinking from the nearby creek, the flock began to drift out, and Joe sent the dog to keep them together while he followed in their wake. When they reached the feeding grounds, Joe spent a good part of the time lying on the cold earth, for he felt too dizzy and weak to stay on his feet. Every little while, he raised his head to view the grazing band and directed Muggins to bring back any wandering sheep.

It was a long day, and Joe was relieved when it ended. He and the loyal dog had managed to keep the sheep together and had gotten them back to the bed grounds around the wagon. Supperless, he fell onto the lumpy mattress, a wool bag* stuffed with hay, that softened his bunk.

His second day of illness was a repeat of the first except that now his whole body ached. One moment he was weak and hot with fever, and the next he shivered with chills. He wondered if lying on the cold ground was making him worse, but he was too exhausted to do otherwise.

After the sheep were bedded down for the night, Joe

---

* A large bag in which wool was packed at shearing time.

This picture of a sheep wagon hangs on the wall in Billy Green's house in Ludlow, South Dakota. Before Billy began his own ranch operation, he lived in a sheep wagon and herded sheep.

Billy's visitor asked, "With those flimsy, canvas walls, how did you stay warm in winter?"

"You weren't supposed to be warm," answered Billy. "Most of the time it was the same temperature inside as it was out!"

The door of the wagon is off-center because the tiny stove and cupboard are located on the right side of it.

knew he should build a fire and cook some food, but the thought of carrying in wood and carrying out ashes dissuaded him. Once he had lifted himself onto the wagon tongue and then up into the wagon, he went to bed.

On the third day, a raw wind was blowing, and the sky was overcast. Joe shivered through the forenoon, wondering why he was so ill. The cold ground was a poor excuse for a sick bed, but lying down conserved what little energy he had.

When he, John Husak, and Joe Balloon (J. B.) had

This tiny stove and cupboard are inside a sheep wagon. The door is at the right. The high bunk (not shown) is across the opposite end. A board slides from beneath the bunk to make a table. The photographer sat in the far corner of the bunk to take this picture.*

arrived in Wyoming a few weeks before, they found there was an epidemic of measles in the area. J.B. and John had both been exposed when they visited the Hitschew Ranch** to watch some of the hands break a horse one Sunday afternoon. Joe had not gone, as his boss, Sam Joss (pronounced Jose to rhyme with dose) was taking him to the herder's camp that afternoon.

Joe had worked for Sam the previous summer, and Sam felt confident enough about Joe's work to trust him with a band of 1800 yearling sheep. Having been out on the prairie all this time, Joe felt sure that he hadn't been exposed to the measles. Besides, he felt too sick for it to be measles, and he had no red rash. He wondered if he could hold out another two days until the camp tender came to bring the week's supplies. Could he manage to take care of the sheep that much longer? He decided he *had to*, since there seemed to be no alternative.

Late in the afternoon, Joe raised his head to survey the band, and observing that a yearling was wandering away from the flock, he sent Muggins to turn it back. The dog completed the

---

* This wagon has been preserved by Dick Butler who lived with his parents in it until he was a year old. Floor: 8 1/2' X 3'8".
** Sam Joss' wife's parents.

task, returned to the herder, and playfully leaped up, landing with his forepaws in the middle of Joe's back. Startled, the sick man sat up. He was in no mood for play, but it would not have been necessary to have used such scalding remarks to make that point clear to the gentle dog. The next time Joe looked up, Muggins was gone.

Mentally, the herder rebuked himself for having scolded the faithful animal. Thinking back over the last three days, he knew he hadn't eaten anything himself and thus hadn't fed the dog either. No wonder the shepherd, a breed noted for being sensitive, had felt abused and had abandoned him.

When evening came, it was with great difficulty that Joe got the yearlings back to the wagon which was about a mile and a half away. Perhaps he tried to end the day too soon, for the animals were contrary and paid no attention to his attempts to drive them. As the flock spread in an ever widening circle in spite of his efforts, he feared that the band might split into separate groups. Weak and unsteady, he caught his foot on a rock and fell. For a brief moment he lay there, worrying, while his body gathered energy.

When he stood up, he noticed several sheep off to one side, facing in the direction of the wagon. Could he *pretend* to want them to turn back to the flock, letting them in their stubbornness slip by him, so that they would start the band back to camp? The ruse worked: the contrary animals refused to be turned, trotting briskly around him. Other sheep in the area followed them, and within minutes the entire band was a vast wool blanket, rippling toward camp. Once started, they moved easily, possibly because in each of the one thousand eight hundred woolly heads was a thirsty tongue and a vision of the cool water in the creek near the wagon.

After the sheep had finished drinking, Joe bunched them around the wagon as best he could. With no dog to send out to bring back nighttime stragglers or to bark at the approach of a coyote, he was uneasy. The animals, too, seemed restless. Numbly, the bone-weary herder walked around them, waiting—waiting—for them to settle for the night.

Once the animals had bedded down, he climbed into his bunk where he spent a miserable night. Frequently, he walked to the doorway to view the sheep, knowing all the while that he probably was powerless even if he had observed a danger to the band. Before dawn, he arose unrested and watched them closely while he wired several tomato cans together to make a tin dog, a contrivance used as a noise-maker to help drive sheep. When the animals began to move out, he managed to guide them in the direction of Headquarters, the Lost Spring Ranch, located about four miles away. With the aid of the tin dog, he kept them rippling along in spite of the fact that the blackness that pressed in around him repeatedly caused him to stumble.

About a half mile from the ranch, Joe sighted another band of sheep on the horizon. He let his own band stop to graze and, fighting dizziness and a chill which danced up and down his spine, he managed to work himself around them, grateful that he could do so, for it placed him between the two flocks. It was imperative that the yearlings not mix with the others, which happened to be a band of "droppin' ewes," a term applied to ewes that were giving birth.

The depth of Joe's relief is difficult to describe, for of the many dangers which could have befallen the flock, none had. Now he would soon be relieved of his responsibility for them, so that he, himself, could lie down somewhere and get the rest he needed.

The other herder, an older man named Turk, was mounted on a horse. This circumstance Joe regarded as fortunate, for it would not take him long to ride to the ranch for a replacement. However, once Joe reached him and explained the situation, Turk refused to help. Because Joe looked younger than his nineteen years, the older man assumed he was a kid who was tired of a tedious job and wanted to quit.

"You go!" Joe demanded in a voice hoarse from his inflamed throat. "I can't herd any longer, I tell you!" Then he returned to his own band and sat down.

He was angry—furious, in fact. The sheep were spreading out, but having no dog and having no energy himself, he knew he couldn't possibly hold them together. Oh, but he was sick: exhausted, weak and *sick*. Dark thoughts ran through his head as he looked at the mounted man silhouetted against the sky. He wished he had a rifle to shoot over the head of the insolent fellow, an action which he felt sure would produce some activity. He had put every resource he possessed into getting word of his condition to someone else, and what good did it do?

However, Joe's good fortune had not yet abandoned him, for Sam Joss's young brother-in-law, a lad about twelve years old, came riding out on a pony. Turk told him to ride to the ranch and tell Sam that Joe had brought the yearlings to Turk and was quitting. The boy did so, and in just a few minutes Sam came galloping across the prairie like a roll of thunder.

"Get those yearlings back!" he shouted. "They'll get mixed up with the ewes! What gives you the right to change their feeding grounds?" He interspersed these remarks with some considerably stronger phrases. When he paused for breath, Joe spoke, croaking hoarsely.

"I've been sick for several days, and I just can't follow them any longer. There they are."

Sam eyed the herder closely for a moment and then said, "I guess you *are* sick. Stay here with the sheep while I get someone to take your place, and then you can come to headquarters."

In a short time, J.B. came out to relieve Joe who then walked to the main ranch.

Clara, Sam's wife, took one look at Joe and said, "You have the measles."

"I don't think so," said Joe. "I'm just too weak and sick for it to be the measles. Besides, I don't have any rash at all and I've been ailing for four days."

"It's no wonder—being outside in this cold weather, you couldn't possibly break out. Dr. Sparling has been called to Manville several times to treat the measles. Mrs. Baghn is awful sick—and the Rossman kids, too.* As for you, it's a wonder you didn't die out there in the cold a-runnin' around after those sheep. Probably woulda' if you weren't so ornery! This is serious! Now, you get to bed, and we'll get you warmed up."

Clara picked some mountain herbs, scalded them, and made tea. She said it would lower his fever and make him break out. The warm bed, the rest, and the tea brought results, and by evening the rash appeared. The following morning, Joe, being completely covered with measles, looked as if he had been sculpted from raw hamburger.

Since it was lambing season, Sam was short handed. When he went to Lusk for supplies, he inquired in the stores and the taverns, hoping he might find some "box-car tourists," (a local term used in referring to railroad bums) that he might hire, but he was unsuccessful. On the third afternoon that Joe was in the house, Sam came in and asked him if he would care to go out and sleep with a band of ewes and lambs. Since Joe was feeling better, he went.

The next morning before dawn, Sam rode out to the

---

* Later, Rossman's two-year-old daughter died of the measles.

wagon and awakened him. It was snowing and blowing. He told Joe to move the band down into the sage brush where someone else would take over, and then to come back to the wagon and make his own breakfast. While Joe was eating, Sam returned and told him to go to a big hill about a mile and a half away where another herder, Ralph, was holding a large bunch of ewes and lambs. The plan was to keep the animals bunched against the hill for protection against the storm.

The brisk wind and the wet, clinging snow continued to chill the herders and their flock most of the day. Toward evening the snow let up, and Joe and Ralph decided to move the band to the camp area around the sheep wagon where there were pens in which to hold the sheep overnight. Movement was slower than they had anticipated, for the hungry ewes were interested in spreading out to graze, and the lambs stumbled along in the wet, spring snow. When it became clear that they could not reach the camp by nightfall, they selected a protected area to hold the sheep.

The two men looked at each other ruefully, for both knew that the rigorous day could not end for them; it would rather slide into an even more rigorous night.

"I have a suggestion," said Ralph. "There isn't any reason why we both have to stay up all night. Rather, one of us can walk to camp and sleep for half the night, and then come back to stay with the sheep while the other one goes to camp for the second half of the night."

"I'll sure agree with that plan," said Joe. "But the trouble is that, since this is the first day I've been up since I was sick, I'm awfully tired. Once I get to bed and get warmed up, I doubt that I will wake up before morning."

"I think I can get up all right. I usually wake up a time or two each night," said Ralph.

"That means that you go to camp first. Come back about midnight, and then I'll go to camp."

Joe stayed with the flock all night. From the scattered pines in the area, he gathered wood and made a fire. Alternately, he sat by the fire and circled the sheep which were restless because of their hunger. Joe's feet were wet, and he was chilled to the bone. He began to feel weak and wondered if his illness were returning or if he were merely tired and hungry. Time dragged the first half of the night. Surely, Ralph would return by midnight, but it seemed to the miserable herder that midnight would never come. But it did come—and it went—and the expectant herder's hopes turned into grim resignation. The frigid hours until dawn seemed endless.

As soon as it was light enough, he drove the band to camp and awakened the apologetic Ralph. Exhausted, Joe wiggled his wet feet out of his boots and crawled onto the bunk.

After Ralph built a fire in the tiny stove and began to fry the bacon, he noticed that some of the sheep were wandering away, and he called to Joe and asked if he would rather take over the cooking or round up the sheep. Joe decided that it seemed more efficient for Ralph to proceed with the breakfast, and he chose the sheep. However, when he attempted to pull on his wet boots, he discovered that his chilled, puffed feet would not wiggle into them, and he went without them. Already, his feet were so cold that the snow couldn't make them much colder, he thought disgustedly.

Rocks were visible under the blanket of snow, and Joe attempted to avoid the cactus by leaping from rock to rock. Whenever he got close enough to a wayward ewe, he picked up a rock about the size of a duck egg and fired it in front of her. The noise of the bleating band covered the sound of the galloping horse so that Joe didn't see the boss until he came pounding up behind him.

"Here, here!" Sam shouted. "Don't throw rocks, or you'll break their legs!"

"Well, right now, I don't much care," answered the disgruntled herder, as he turned to face his boss.

Sam's voice softened when he saw Joe's face which was still rough with rash and red from the cold. "Oh, now, Joe, you know you don't mean that." Then he noticed the bare feet. "Where are your boots?"

"I been up all night, and my feet are so puffed that I can't get them on."

"Where's Ralph?"

"Making breakfast," Joe said. "We haven't eaten since yesterday morning."

"Go back inside," said Sam, gruffly. "I'll ride around the sheep now, and then Ralph can take over after he's eaten."

After a few more days, Joe's rash receded, and his outer skin fell off in sheets. "I shed my skin just like a snake," he said.

(Later, in telling this story, Joe always said, "Sam was a good fellow. He had somewhat of a nervous nature, but he was a good guy. He and Joe Balloon never did get along, though.")

In about a week, the men on Sam's Lost Spring Ranch began shearing. J.B. sacked wool and Joe learned to shear. After that, he sheared every spring, in a total of seven different states, for eleven years—up until, and including, 1912.

By the time the wool was harvested that year, J.B. was anxious to quit and persuaded Joe that they should move to Casper. When Joe went in to draw his pay, Sam said, "I figured you'd decide to go with J.B., but I want to tell you something. Even though you travel together, don't ever take a job again at the same place he does."

"Why not?"

"Well, because if he doesn't get along, then there are two of you who don't get along."

Joe and J.B. walked about a hundred miles west, carrying their bedrolls. They took a job harvesting alfalfa for the Dennick and Wright Ranch located about twenty-five miles southwest of Casper. Joe swept, using a team of mules.

After a couple of months, Joe realized that Sam's advice had proven to be sound, and he decided to move on by himself. He bought a four-year-old horse named Slate from the foreman of the sheep camp tenders. The horse was a tall, slender, pale black animal and was Joe's first head of livestock. He rode Slate through the Laramie Mountains and on into the plains.

At Medicine Bow he worked at a sheep-dipping vat for a few weeks before riding on to Laramie.

First View of an Automobile
1902

There was a crowd gathered at the corner of the Laramie Livery Stable when Joe rode up, and from his higher perch on the back of his horse, he could see that they were scrutinizing one of those new machines referred to as a horseless carriage. After stabling his horse, he joined the group.

This modern conveyance, invented by Henry Ford just ten years previously, was little more than a seat mounted on narrow-rimmed wheels with wire spokes. It had no top and since it was guided by a lever, no steering wheel.

Clustered around the little vehicle were a number of intensely interested fellows who were completely engrossed in examining it. The outer ring of men and boys looked on with curiosity as well as humor, for this contraption didn't look very promising to them.

"Grass 'n oats grow out of the good earth," said one of the men sagely. "Mother Nature supplies. But gas—that's a different thing. Gas you gotta' buy. It'd bankrupt a guy!"

"How yuh gonna' cross the creek? Yuh'll have to take a team along to pull that thing through," scoffed another.

"It ain't got no head ner heart. Can't hear gee nor haw nor even giddap. You have to guide it every step of the way. Why, the only time a person ever gits to relax is when your team is a-takin' yuh home. This thing 'ud plum wear you out."

"It's a city wagon, that's for sure. If a fellow went outside of town with it, he'd be hung up in the first rut, or else on a rock somewhere."

"Well, we gotta' have some better roads."

"Better roads! Who can afford 'em? Taxes are too high already. Country'd go broke buildin' roads. But this little machine 'ud be nice in town—no horses to harness—no manure."

"Well, I don't think they should allow them in town. Did you ever hear one of them go poppin' and rattlin' along? Horses go plumb crazy when they see one of the durn things. We'd have horses a-runnin' and a-tearin' every direction. Someone 'ull be killed."

A small boy asked, "What is it?"

An older boy answered, "It's one of them gas-leen buggies. You know—it goes by itself. Don't need horses. It's called a otter-merbeel."

"Auto-mobile," corrected a still older boy, enunciating carefully. He spelled it, using a hyphen.

[The derogatory remarks about the automobile were typical of those made at the turn of the century. When Joe, as an old man, told this story, his brother Anton was present. The two of them together smilingly recalled these comments.]

In the town of Laramie, Joe worked in a livery stable until Jake McGill,* the owner of the Kite Ranch, rode into town looking for ranch hands. Joe hired out to him.

It was there on the edge of the Laramie Plains that Joe spent the worst winter of his entire life.

---

*   John (Jake) McGill was born in Scotland in 1846. He immigrated to Canada at age 20, and a few months later, to Wyoming where he lived out his life as a prominent rancher and also, for many years, as a state senator. He died in 1918.

Early Winter in the Mountains
1902-1903

When Joe arrived at Jake McGill's Kite Ranch, located near the northeast corner of Wheatland Reservoir No. II on the edge of the Laramie Plains, he was assigned a team and slip scraper. He then joined a crew that first dug a long irrigation ditch and then constructed a dam. The year before, the government had replaced Jake's private dam on the Laramie River with the huge one that formed Wheatland Reservoir No. II. Because of the fact that Jake's dam was ruined by the new construction, his Kite Ranch received tremendous water advantages: it got first water rights from the reservoir. Now Jake was building ditches and dams on his ranch in order to make full use of those coveted water rights.

The crew worked long, grueling hours, for they were racing with approaching winter. The men, who bedded in a cabin during the construction of the ditch and on the ground in a tent during work on the dam, were roused from sleep long before dawn. Breakfast must be completed, horses harnessed, and teams driven to the work site in time for action to begin when the first rays of light emerged.

The soil to be moved was turned over with a plow; then once loosened, the scrapers scooped up the coarse, earthen fragments, the horses struggled up the incline, and the load was dumped on the bank. The young, agile men sometimes leaped on the frames of the scrapers and rode them to the floor of the canal where they were turned upright and refilled.

Around went the endless parade: the teams hurrying down to the bottom of the ditch, then laboring with the heavy load up the incline, both horses and men struggling for footing in the disturbed earth. Down—around, up—around, hour in and hour out, through the numbing cold of the morning, the brief warmth of the day, and the chill of the evening As the days shortened, the midday warmth disappeared, leaving twenty-four hours of penetrating cold.

Meals were prepared at a cook wagon and eaten outdoors, which meant that constantly the men were at the mercy of the elements. On some mornings the top soil was crusted with frost or blanketed with snow, but work went on until well into November at which time Old Man Winter struck with force enough to shut them down.

From there, Joe rode Slate to Rock River and found a job

with a man who baled hay and harvested ice. After the bone-stiffening nights in a tent, Joe was elated when he was directed to put his bedroll in the bunkhouse. His high spirits soon came back to earth, however, for when he reached the shack, he found that it had "cracks in the walls that were wide enough in places to throw a cat through." The wind could sail in with such freedom that it didn't even have to whistle.

The hay was baled by a horse-powered baler, the horses walking in a circle to operate the machinery that pressed the hay into solid bales. The ice on a lake was sawed by hand, loaded with tongs, and unloaded into ice houses where it was packed in sawdust. Joe worked there until February, after which he took a job hauling mail.

Carrying Mail

Up until this time, the winter had been grueling, and Joe was tired of being forever cold. His new job would afford him the luxury of warming up overnight.

The mail route was forty-five miles one way. On alternate days, it began at Rock River and angled northeast to McGill's Kite Ranch where Joe ate the noonday meal and changed horses. In the afternoon, the trail proceeded northward to Garrett where he spent the night. The next day he made the return trip. If there were no packages, Joe rode horseback, using mail pouches that straddled the back of the saddle. When there were packages, he drove a team and wagon.

Forty-five miles a day is a long, hard ride, but Joe's young body adapted quickly. The road was a winding, well-packed trail through old snow, and he took pride in delivering the mail on time. He preferred the job to sawing ice or pitching hay into a baler all day, particularly since his nights were now spent in a furnished room.

Then one morning he awoke to find snow falling, thick and fast. The cook who gave him breakfast shook his ancient head.

"It's no good out there," he said. "You better not go. It's bitter cold and gettin' colder. If snow keeps fallin' at this rate, you won't get through even if it doesn't blow. It's pilin' up fast."

Joe grinned. "I don't think it will be that bad. It's too cold for the snow to amount to a whole lot. And you know the old saying: 'The mail must go through!'"

"Yep," growled the cook, nodding his shaggy head. "I

Top: Old Rock River Post Office (It is now used for storage.)

Middle: McGill Kite ranch house where Joe ate lunch and changed horses.

Bottom, left: Garrett P.O. attached to the back of the Garrett Ranch house, now occupied by Roger Garrett (below) and his wife. His grandmother, Mary Agnes Garrett, was the postmistress in 1903. 1989 photos.

heerd them words before. Heerd them too many times. Heerd my own cousin spoutin" 'em—big and bold and brave-like. About thirty years ago there was an Indian uprising. We told him not to go on the mail route that day, but he wouldn't listen. He died with an arrow in his back."

At first, Joe didn't answer but thought to himself, "No wonder the old fellow is spooked. He lost a cousin deliverin' mail." Aloud, he said, "Well, nowadays we don't have to worry about Indians, and as for snow and cold—I've been battlin' *that* all winter."

The cook went into the kitchen and came back with a muffler. "Better take this," he said as he tucked it into the pocket of Joe's coat which hung on a nail in the wall.

When Joe went to the livery barn for his horse, he was again warned about the weather. However, he picked up the mail bags and, full of the bold assurance of youth, headed northeastward down the trail. The storm, coming in from the northwest, was hitting him at an angle that allowed him to turn his face to avoid the worst of the raw breeze. Eventually, though, the biting cold prompted him to pull the cook's scarf from his pocket, even though he already had his own muffler around his neck. This second one he tied over the lower part of his face and around the back of his Scotch cap.

The horse was slowed a little by the collecting snow, but when Joe reached the Kite Ranch, he found he was only about a half hour later than usual. He ate lunch quickly, swung his saddle and the mailbags onto a horse named Juggler, and in spite of more grim predictions, this time from the ranch cook, rode north toward Garrett.

For the first hour the horse made good time, but as the snow deepened, he plodded along more slowly. The temperature had lowered, and periodically, Joe beat his hands on his thighs to enhance circulation. He pulled the scarf up to cover the lower part of his nose and wiggled his toes inside his boots.

Sometimes across the trail there were snow-filled hollows that had to be circumnavigated, and Juggler floundered around them. After these obstacles were conquered, Joe, blinded by the thick snowfall, trusted the animal to help him relocate the trail. By now, nagging doubts were beginning to creep into his mind; he was ready to admit that he should have stayed in Rock River, for the amount of snow that was falling in spite of the extreme cold was surprising. There was a raw breeze which was causing some drifting, and Joe knew that it would take only a little more wind to put the thick blanket of snow back up into the air, in which case, he would not survive. It was a sobering thought.

Familiar landmarks were now either invisible because of the churning flakes or else changed by the accumulation of snow. Joe hardly recognized the broken pine that he figured was the halfway mark between the Kite Ranch and Garrett. He had named it The Indian Chief because the half-severed top lay back in such a way as to resemble a feathered headdress. Now as they passed it, the fronds were bent low by the collection of snow. He was relieved to know they were halfway between the ranch and Garrett and was thankful that the horse's instincts were still guiding them correctly.

Suddenly, the numbed man noticed that the wind was changing directions. Perplexed, he strained his eyes forward to see through the swirling storm. Then on the ground before him, he could discern the half-covered tracks of a horse. Someone else—someone equally thick-headed and unwise—was out in the storm, also. But who? In this weather, tracks would be erased by snow and breeze in a very short time, which meant this fellow traveler couldn't be very far ahead of them. Juggler moved faster down the half-broken trail while Joe squinted his eyes for better vision—and pondered.

Then out of the storm appeared the broken tree—the Indian Chief. Hadn't they already passed that tree? But now it was on the wrong side of the trail. Momentarily, Joe was confused; then in a flash, realization flooded him. The horse had circled around and was doubling back on their own trail. No wonder it had seemed as if the wind were changing!

Irritated that the trusted animal had tricked him, Joe automatically turned him back to the north. The instincts of a good horse are invaluable in helping a rider reach a destination; however, Joe thought stubbornly, it is the rider, not the horse, that should determine that destination! He just wasn't going to let the animal get away with reversing directions even though it might be the most intelligent option in this particular situation.

This resolution, however, did nothing to keep the threads of concern from weaving back and forth through his mind. Was the horse right? Should they have turned and put the storm to their backs even though they were equidistant between the ranch and Garrett? The snow had gotten deeper and deeper and would continue to do so. Could they get through the rougher country ahead?

Darkness fell early, hastened by the gloom of the storm. More and more often, the horse staggered in the bulky drifts and his breath came in gasps. Joe dismounted, hoping to give the horse relief from carrying the extra weight and, at the same time, improve his own circulation. He couldn't walk ahead to help break the trail because the horse often lunged in the deep snow, and being ahead of him was unsafe. Thus he struggled beside the animal, wallowing through the snow on feet that were so numb that they could have been made from wood.

Tired as Juggler was, his longer legs made more progress in the snow than did those of the man. Finally, Joe remounted, loosened the reins, and gave the animal complete freedom to determine the way. He knew that his life depended on Juggler's ability to find shelter, and he was finally willing to accept any choice that the horse made.

Sometimes the animal bogged down and completely stopped, lowering his head and breathing hard. Joe let him rest before urging him on. Now that Joe was free from making decisions, he raised the scarf to cover more of his numb face. His feet and hands had been void of any feeling for some time.

The man, completely closed in by the dark night and the storm, lost all sense of time. Juggler continued to hunt his way, wading through the ever deepening snow; his progress became more halting—more labored—more sluggish. Several times when he stumbled, Joe was gripped with the fear that the exhausted animal was going to let himself drop into the snow and give up, but each time he regained his footing and labored on. Finally, he completely stopped and this time no amount of urging would coax him forward. Then he swung his head, and a bridle ring clacked against something. It was the Garrett barn!

Flooded with relief, Joe struggled—and struggled again—to dismount. Man and horse were both encrusted in snow and actually frozen together. Finally, Joe tore himself free and slid to the ground where he groped about—with hands as stiff and clumsy as a pair of fence posts—for the barn door. Luckily the mountain behind had given enough protection to keep the snow from drifting around the barn, but the snow on the level was deep enough to keep the barn door from opening.

"Actually, I don't know," Joe said afterward, "how I got that door open, frozen stiff like I was. I remember fighting around in an attempt to lift the latch. I couldn't leave the horse standing outside. He had saved us both—actually, *just barely* saved us, for he couldn't have gone much farther."

Once the horse was inside, the man turned toward the house and was relieved to see a dim, yellow glow in a kitchen window. He stumbled toward it—waddled—stumbled—waddled some more. What if his numb legs wouldn't get him there? He had heard of people freezing in their own yards!

But he did reach the door—only to be confronted by another obstacle: his hands were too stiff to grasp the knob. He bumped the door with his knee, with his arm, and finally with his shoulder. He tried to call out, but the cooks scarf, frozen securely around his face, formed an effective gag.

Suddenly the door came open, and there stood Mary Agnes Garrett, ranch wife and postmistress.

"Mercy on us!" she exclaimed, as she viewed the mummy-like figure in front of her. "Whoever you are, get in here!" She turned and called to her husband. "Sewell!"

Sewell Garrett, his trousers hastily pulled on over his long winter underwear, soon came into the kitchen and both set to work to rescue the person inside the snowy shell.

Once the scarf was peeled away and his coat unbuttoned, Joe tried to unshoulder the garment.

"Hold still and let us do it," said Sewell. "No need to be embarrassed about accepting a little help. Everyone has to have an experience like this before he understands this country."

They peeled off his outer clothes, and Sewell set them in a corner where, since they were so well frozen, they stood by themselves.

Joe's face was board stiff and at first he couldn't talk intelligibly, but finally the Garretts got his message: the horse was in the barn, loose, with saddle and bridle still on; the mail was in the saddle bags.

"Forget the horse and the mail," said Sewell. "I'll look after them."

Mrs. Garrett dipped cold water from a bucket into two pans to soak Joe's hands and feet.

"Get the fire going," she told Sewell. "We need to get some coffee inside him." She looked at Joe chidingly, "I hope you know, young man, how lucky you are to be sitting here."

Joe smiled sheepishly—anyway, smiled as best he could with an inflexible face.

"I know," he grunted.

Joe had frozen the bridge of his nose, his left cheek, and the two outside toes on his left foot. However, he continued to carry mail until it was time for the ranchers to take on more men for the commencement of spring work, at which time he gave up the mail route.

When the new mail carrier arrived at the Kite Ranch, Tom McGill, Jake's son, asked about Joe.

"He quit. He's looking for ranch work," said the carrier.

"When you get back to Rock River, tell Joe to ride out here. We'll put him to work," said Tom.

At this point, Joe had no way of knowing that the winter storms would spill into spring, and that another desperate situation lay ahead.

The Invalid Band of Sheep
1903

This story is told in Joe's own words, just as he narrated it about sixty years later.

Tom McGill put me to work on a ranch out in the foothills, a place where Tom Dodge was the foreman. Both of them, Tom McGill and Tom Dodge, were about the same age, maybe 25 or 26, and were nice fellows—pleasant to be around. Old Jake McGill (his name was John, but he mostly went by Jake) was a stern fellow, a man of iron will. Now don't get me wrong. He was a good, honest person, respected and all, and had a good head for business, but he had no time for small talk—everyone's attention was supposed to be set on the job at hand. However, at the time, Jake wasn't home; he was a state senator, and he was in Cheyenne taking care of legislative affairs.

The first few weeks I was there, it was nice weather, the snow melted, and some of the soreness began to go out of the frozen patches on my face, even though I had big scabs over my cheekbone and the bridge of my nose. I did the ordinary ranch work: fed a few cattle and some sheep, helped build a sheep wagon, repaired corrals, and the like.

Then one day Tom Dodge came in and said that Quintin, the sheep herder who was in charge of the invalid band, was sick and had requested a replacement. Tom asked if I'd care to herd for a few days until he got someone else. He took me out there—it was around March 17. We put my bedroll in the cabin, a tiny little shack that was maybe eight foot by ten and fitted up something like a sheep wagon, and then went on out to where the sheep were grazing. Quintin's dog stayed with me, and Quintin went home with Tom.

It was a gray, foggy day, and by the time night came and I got the sheep to camp and corralled them, it was snowing. This camp was in a wide basin and was reserved for spring grazing because the snow was too deep in it in the winter. The way it turned out, they'd brought the sheep into it a little too soon, for by morning we had eighteen inches of snow.

As I said before, it was an invalid band. Most of them— and there were about 2,400 in all—were old ewes that ordinarily would have been sold in the fall. However, prices were so low that the whole critter would hardly bring any more than their hides were worth and Jake decided to keep them in the hope that prices would go up. The ones that couldn't make the winter would be skinned out for their pelts. We had some young sheep in the band, too—ones that had been born so late in the season that they required special care over the winter.

The corrals were butted up against a bluff and so were somewhat protected and got less snow. I managed to get the sheep on their feet, and as they moved around, they packed the snow underfoot, after which I climbed up high enough on the bluff to get a count of the animals. To count a big band, you count the black sheep and multiply by fifty. Most sheep are white, but about one in fifty is black. Anyway, I found that almost all of the sheep were up and about. I did locate a few that had been smothered and skinned them out.

But my big problem was how to feed them. It being a spring camp, there wasn't any hay. There were some pine trees and some sagebrush up on the sloping sides of the basin, and I'd heard that in a tight spot, sheep could live quite awhile on sagebrush. So I floundered my way up to a pine tree, chopped it down, and managed to drag it down to the corral. I meant to drag it to the sagebrush and make a path for the sheep. Trouble was, though, I couldn't pull it uphill—it was too heavy.

So I climbed back up and cut down a smaller tree. I was able to handle it better, but it didn't leave too good of a trail. The sheep would follow it because they were hungry, and they liked the pine needles, but they kept getting stuck in the snow. The stronger ones would crowd the others out of the pathway, and I'd soon have a hundred or so of them stranded in the snow.

Every little while, I'd make a trip down one side of the path and up the other, turning the stuck sheep around so that they were facing the trail. Then I'd go back and drag the pine higher toward the sagebrush. After I got the band fairly well strung out, I chopped more trees and dragged them over to the sheep. They were crazy for those pine needles—ate them like honey. Every time a tree went down, the sheep would push that direction and be hung up in the snow. They wore themselves out struggling, and I tell you, I was just as exhausted from fighting with them to get them out and turned around.

Late afternoon, I started them back to the corral, but it was a battle. Some of them were too hungry to want to go back, and the others were bogged down in the snow. By the time I got them corralled, I was so wore out and bone sore that I didn't even care to start a fire and make supper. I ate something, though—maybe some dried prunes and a can of tomatoes—and went to bed.

I did my best to feed the sheep this way for about three or four days, and then Quintin came walking out. It was about a four mile walk—maybe five. Seems Old Jake had come back from Cheyenne, and Quintin figured that if he wanted to keep his job, he'd better not lay around headquarters any longer. Well, Quintin said that we were to take the sheep to another camp that was several miles away because there was a haystack there. He said not to bother taking our bedrolls or food or anything because Tom Dodge would bring out supplies to the other camp that evening.

I couldn't imagine how we could move them, but I figured that if the boss said to move them, we'd better try. (Later, I asked Tom Dodge if he had said that we should take them to the other camp. He answered, "Well, Quintin made the suggestion to me; and I told him that it would be a good idea except that I thought you wouldn't be able to get them out of the basin.")

Next morning after bacon and biscuits, we started out. We struggled all day—it was a heck of a mess! We drug a tree ahead to break a path, but all along the way, those hungry ewes would see some sagebrush and try to get over to it. Wasn't long till half of them was stuck in the snow. We turned them around and headed them back down their own path to the trail, and by then the other half was hung up. We were plumb wore out!

When night came, we'd made only about three-quarters of a mile. The snow was just too deep. We didn't even have them up out of the basin. We bunched the sheep the best we could so that we could guard them from wolves and the like, and they bedded down. They were as exhausted as we were.

There wasn't any sleep for us. No thought of it. I had an ax along—the one I was using to cut trees—and I slivered the butt of a fallen tree, put some pine boughs around it, and managed to set it afire. It was a cold night and a long one. We froze one side while we baked the other, and then turned around and did it the other way. Once I got too close to the fire and scorched the top of one of my boots so bad that it never was the same again. I had just gotten new boots—a little bigger than I ordinarily wore because of my puffed-up, frost-bitten toes.

To make matters worse, Quintin got to complaining. He grumbled around, saying that it was foolish for us to freeze and starve ourselves for the sake of sheep that were worth as much dead as they were on the hoof. Let them die, he said, and we could skin them out. He was an Italian, and had come west from Chicago. He wasn't used to this kind of rough life.

We did agree on one thing, and that was the fact that we couldn't possibly get the sheep up over the rim of the basin. The next morning we turned them down the trail toward the old camp. My idea was to give them time to eat the sagebrush on the way down. I cut a tree and did what I could to break a path to the clumps of sage. I told Quintin that he could go down and make us some breakfast, and after he'd eaten, he could come back to be with the sheep while I went down to eat. He went, and I did what I could to spread the sheep out toward the sage.

I knew it would take Quintin quite awhile to get to camp, build a fire, make biscuits, and all. He wasn't too handy at such things. I was plenty busy, but time sure did go slow—wore out like I was, and hungry and cold. We hadn't eaten since breakfast the day before.

Well, Quintin didn't come—and he *didn't* come—. It was noon before he showed up. I figure after he'd eaten, he curled up by the stove and took a nap.

When I got down to camp, I was expecting to find some breakfast. My stomach was growling about like a freight train. But whatever Quintin had made, he also had eaten, and he'd burned all the wood, too. When I went back outside, ax in hand, to cut more wood, I saw the sheep coming down the broken trail with Quintin behind, a-doggin' heck out of them. I yelled at him to stop, but he didn't pay any attention. The trail skirted the upper edge of a wash-out, and coming at that speed, I knew they'd never make the curve. They'd go over the edge and pile up. I signaled to him to stop pushing them, and to bring the dog around to help head them away from the ravine, but he pretended not to see me. I cut through the band, swinging my ax.

"You ornery son of a gun!" I yelled. "You get down

here and help turn these sheep or I'm going to chop your stubborn head off."

He *noticed* me then, and he *came*. The two of us and the dog got the band turned to follow the trail around the washout and down into the corral. Then right there in the pen, we had a quarrel, both of us as mad as a pair of fighting bulls.

He said that we were supposed to *herd* the sheep, but that didn't include sitting out in a snow bank with them day and night. He made some cracks about *some* people being willing to freeze to death, but that he sure wasn't one of them. My face had scabs from when I froze it on the mail route, and he said that my scabby face was enough to tell him what kind of guy I was— someone too dumb to come in out of a storm.

I fired right back. Most of what we said you wouldn't care to write down.

Finally, I walked away and went up on the hillside to cut a tree. After I got several down, I drug them over by the trail, and then let the sheep out. I went back to choppin' even though I was worried about what the boss would think about me cutting all those trees down. I had been raised in treeless country where any tree, big or small, was practically considered sacred. But getting those pines down was the only way to feed the sheep,

Agnes Turney and Owen McGill are the children of Tom McGill and the grandchildren of Jake. Also, they are the niece and nephew of Tom Dodge, for he eventually married one of Jake's daughters. Agnes now (1992) lives in Wheatland, Wyoming; Owen and his wife Henri live south of Wheatland and raise Longhorn cattle on Squaw Mountain.

particularly after Quintin had rushed them past the sagebrush.

Eventually, he came up and sat on a stump, but I didn't pay any attention. I just had no more use for him. About that time, Tom Dodge arrived on horseback. I sure was relieved when he approved of what I was doing. (Later, he said that he'd expected to find half the band dead. We'd lost some, but not very many.)

"You'll just have to keep cutting pines for them for a few days," he said. "We can't get them to the other camp until this snow goes down. As soon as it looks like we can, we'll come and help you move them. In the meantime, do the best you can for them; we have our hands full at the main ranch."

"All right," I said. "I'm willing to try. But you'd better get that fool of a Quintin out of here or I'm liable to clobber him. We can't seem to agree on anything."

"I asked him to walk out here," Tom said, "and I hate to ask him to walk back. But I'll send Milton Gildersleeve out here horseback tomorrow. He can bring a second ax, and a file to sharpen the axes. Quintin can ride the horse back to the ranch."

When Tom left, I felt more settled. I knew I had to get something into my stomach—by now it was late afternoon. After I cut some wood, I went in and made a meal. I was careful not to overeat so that I wouldn't get sick when I went back out to work. I ate biscuits, a few raisins, and a little bacon, and put some beans on the stove. They'd cook part way as long as the fire held, and then we could finish cooking them in the evening.

The next day Milton came and Quintin left. I got along fine with Milton. I was wore out when he came, and he being fresh, I had to work like crazy to keep up with him. He was a good hand with an ax—a little faster than I was, so that he cut on the side that we wanted the tree to fall. Since I was from prairie country, I hadn't had much experience with chopping wood. I picked up some know-how from him and got better at it.

The sheep, hungry like they were, went to work on the trees the minute they hit the ground. One sheep rushed in just as a tree fell and got caught by a leg in the crotch of two branches. The tree rolled half over before it settled, and the sheep was lifted six or seven feet into the air. He just hung there and began to eat on the branches around him. We cut off the one that was holding him in order to get him down.

We fed the sheep the best we could for seven grueling days. It takes a lot of feed for a couple thousand sheep; and, hard as we worked—from dawn to sunset—you can be sure that not one of them got overfed. We still had to stop every hour or so and pull those old feeble ewes out of the snow. There were too many sheep for them all to get around the trees we cut, and some of them tried to get across to the sagebrush. There they'd be, hung up in the drifts again. Both Milton and I were wore out before the day was half over.

Milton stood it a little better than I did. He was a bigger fellow, and like I said before, he started fresh at a time when I was already exhausted. I really needed more nourishment, but I didn't dare eat much or it would come back up. Every bone ached from slamming those axes against wood all day. My elbows were about shot, and I was spitting blood. Our hands were callused, but we got blisters under the calluses. That was seven days that I sure wouldn't care to repeat.

During the week, I slept in Quintin's bed, and after the first night, I discovered it was full of graybacks (body lice). I didn't get rid of them until I went back to the main ranch.

Finally, Jake McGill and Tom Dodge came with a four-horse team and a wagon to move the sheep to the camp where there was some hay. Even with the four of us working at it, we didn't get the sheep up out of the basin until the second day.

On the four-day trip, I started to go snow-blind. I never could stand bright lights, and usually I kept a pair of sunglasses on hand to wear when the sun was bright on the snow, but I had gotten them broken.* I was helping an old ewe, and she flopped around, knocked my glasses off, and stepped on them. Now, on the trip, the sun was bright, and my eyes burned like fire. I kept them closed as much as I could—just peeked out enough to get my bearings—but they kept getting worse.

We killed and skinned the sheep that played out, threw the pelts into the wagon, and left the rest for the coyotes. However, most of the sheep made it to the new camp.

Since my eyes were bad, Tom Dodge did the cooking over the campfire each night and morning. We slept on the ground in our tarps: Jake and Tom paired up, and Milton and I slept together which meant that Milton got the graybacks, too.

After we got to camp, Tom poulticed my eyes with used tea leaves before we went to bed, and it took some of the inflammation out. The camp was on higher ground, and there

---

* My "sunglasses" weren't made of glass. Rather, they had wooden "lenses" with narrow slits in them so that a person could peek out, but which strained out most of the sun's rays.

were patches of earth sticking up out of the snow which helped to reduce the glare.

The next day, Jake and Tom went back to headquarters, and after a few days, they sent out a regular herder to take my place. I went back to the main ranch, too, and after supper, I took a bath and boiled my clothes to get rid of the graybacks.

I stayed there at the Kite Ranch until we finished shearing, after which I went to Rock River where I applied for a job on a shearing crew. The boss said that they had an opening, but that another fellow was arriving in three days to fill it.

"You look like a kid to me," he said gruffly. "How old are you? Sixteen?"

"Twenty last January," I answered. I wasn't very big, and was skinny at the time. Lots of places where I worked I got called "The Kid" because I looked younger than I was.

He asked me how many sheep I could shear, and when I told him seventy-five a day, he said that I could work for the three days. However, when the other man came, the boss sent him on and kept me instead.

After Joe, in his old age, finished telling about this worst of winters, he sat lost in thought for awhile. Finally, he spoke:

"I shouldna' told you anything!"

His listener looked up, surprised. "Why do you say that? This is a wonderful story!"

"But it isn't all there. Words can't tell how bad it was. And even if I could find words to tell, you wouldn't believe me— and neither would anyone who read what you wrote. They'd think I was making it up. And since I can't tell how really bad it was, I shouldn't have said anything!"

Dark Shed
1903
as told by Joe

We had some excitement that first year that I sheared at the Kite Ranch. The big log shed we were working in didn't have any windows and was just too dark. Since we couldn't see well enough, we were doing a rough job and also we kept nicking the sheep, mostly running into an ear or an udder or gouging a flank. The men were disgusted, and tempers were flaring. Shearing is a tedious enough job in daylight, let alone in a dark, dusty shed.

It seems the building, which was constructed a year or so before, was light enough for shearing the previous season because there were cracks between the logs that let in plenty of light. Over the winter, though, the shed was used to shelter the animals that were close around the ranch—the horses and some of the weaker stock that needed special care. Trouble was, the cold wind and snow sailed in through the cracks.

One day the stable boy—he was an old fellow but was referred to as the stable boy—got ahold of an old trowel. He laid it on a rafter in the shed, and every morning he used it to smooth the fresh piles of cow dung into the cracks. By spring, the shed was warm and tight—all caulked with cow manure—but too durned dark for shearing.

So there we were, bent double over the sheep to get a closer look at our work, blinkin' and starin' like a bunch of owls—but still cutting up the sheep. Our backs ached, our eyes burned, and worst of all, we were doing a lousy job. The air was thick with cuss words.

Finally one of the fellows—we called him Quirt because of the snappy way he talked—raised up from his work.

"I'm going to get us some light into this con-sarned shed!" he vowed.

He walked over to a corner where the pitchforks and other tools leaned, grabbed an ax, and out he went.

At first, we didn't know what the deuce he was up to, but in a little while we heard a heck of a racket up on the roof. It wasn't too long before the ax head broke through, and with it, a shaft of light. Quirt never let up on whacking away at the roof

Ruins of the Shearing Shed at the Kite Ranch

until there was a big, yawning hole that let in a brightness that made us feel like the sun had just come up. We all let out a whoop and went back to work.

Since the shed was only a few hundred yards from the ranch house, it wasn't long before Jake heard about the mangled roof, and he came stomping across the corrals, all sprawled out and red as a turkey gobbler. He glanced just once at the jagged hole in the roof.

"Quirt!" he roared. "Quirt Evans! Get out here!"

Quirt went outside.

Jake scalded him with the worst tongue lashing I had ever heard. He overhauled him with all the abusive terms he knew and then made up a few more on the spot. The longer Jake hollered the madder he got until he finally drew his six-gun and ordered Quirt off the place.

At the sight of the gun, Quirt took a couple startled steps backwards.

"Get moving! Now!" As Jake spat the words out, he fired a shot in front of Quirt's toes.

Pop-eyed, Quirt turned and ran. More bullets hit the ground behind him and kept him running at top speed until he disappeared over a rise. He had a long walk—maybe twenty-five miles to the nearest town.

The next day Jake directed one of the hands to load Quirt's bedroll and belongings and haul them to town. As for the shed, the hole remained until fall. Then Jake had it repaired and also had window panes installed in the sloping roof to let in light.

Eighty-five years later when Joe's daughter visited the

McGill descendants, Jake's grandson Owen chuckled and said: "Dad (Tom McGill) said that if the hired man had known what a poor shot Grandpa was, he wouldn't have had to run so fast. Grandpa couldn't hit anything, even when he aimed right at it."

The Ambush of Willie Nickell
1901-1903

The conflict between the cattlemen and the homesteaders accelerated during the years that Joe was in Wyoming. Since the ranchers were organized into an association, they had the upper hand and insisted that the sheep of the many settlers were overgrazing the land. Also, the ranchers suspected the wool growers of cattle rustling.

Certain public lands were posted by the members of the Stock Growers Association and were proclaimed off-limits to sheep. Gunmen were hired to enforce the cattlemen's demands, with the results that sheepherders were sometimes shot and flocks were scattered. A gunman named Tom Horn was one of those boundary patrollers. He was suspected of killing several homesteaders, but there was not enough evidence to prove it.

Joe Dobrovolny was working for Sam Joss of Manville, Wyoming, when Willie Nickell, a thirteen-year-old boy who lived in the Laramie Mountains, was ambushed. Supposedly, Willie was mistaken for his father, Kels Nickell, who had trailed sheep into a section of the Laramie Mountains which had been proclaimed cattle range by the stockmen. One rainy morning in July, 1901, Kels sent Willie on an errand. Willie was riding his father's horse and also was wearing his father's slicker and hat. In the misty dawn, he was mistaken for his father and was gunned down.

The following winter, Tom Horn, who had been tricked into implicating himself while intoxicated, was arrested for Willie's murder. Since several of the best lawyers in the state defended him, one can suppose that someone with considerable financial clout was backing him. Interest in the gunman's fate ran high on the McGill Ranch because both Tom Dodge and Tom McGill were acquainted with Tom Horn.

The gunman was convicted and in the fall of 1903, he was hanged.

Friction between the Wyoming homesteaders and the cattlemen, often called the Range Wars, continued for most of the decade.

Teddy Roosevelt Rides By
1902

Another historic event which transpired while Joe was at the McGill Ranch was President Theodore Roosevelt's horseback trip from Laramie to Cheyenne. It was a segment of his 1903 tour of the western states.

The President was one of the first environmentalists and was a great outdoorsman, spending considerable time in the Dakotas and also, after the termination of his presidency, on big game hunts in Africa.

The horseback cavalcade through southeastern Wyoming was widely publicized and caused a great deal of excitement among the cowboys in the area.

"That is the closest *I'll* ever come to a President of the United States," said Joe in telling about it.

Some of the men on the McGill Ranch rode to a high bluff in order to watch the long procession of horsebackers pass by, but the caravan was too distant for them to discern which one of the riders was President Roosevelt.

In 1904, after migrating with the Ridgeway Shearing crew across Wyoming, Montana, the Dakotas, and into Iowa, Joe returned to Wyoming, picked up Slate, and rode north.

In 1971 Joe had been relating his Montana and South Dakota experiences, telling, in general, how cattle were trailed and how a roundup was handled. This writer was waiting for him to recover from eye surgery before asking him to fill in the details that would make his story more complete. (What problems did they encounter crossing rivers? Who was the wagon boss of the roundup in which he participated? Which horse was his favorite? Why? Etc. Such questions would have brought forth interesting personal experiences comparable to Joe's Wyoming stories.

However, Joe sickened and died that summer; thus, we must be satisfied with a less detailed story.

Trailing Cattle across Montana and the Dakotas
early 1900's

One season Joe worked as a trail hand, moving cattle from Montana across Dakota to Evarts, which was the location of the rail-head (Chicago, Milwaukee, & St. Paul Railroad) on the Missouri River. The first part of the drive was bossed by a great cattleman, Bird Rose; later, one of his foremen took over.

The last eighty miles of the drive were on the six-mile-wide strip along the north edge of the Cheyenne River Indian Reservation. It was a long row of townships leased from the Cheyennes by the railroad, and its purpose was to provide a trailway for western cattlemen to drive their herds to the rail head. The Standing Rock Reservation lay north of this "Strip."

The Strip ended at the Missouri River near Evarts which was about a dozen miles down river from present-day Mobridge. The cattle were driven across the river on a pontoon bridge to the Evarts stockyards.

Bird Rose required that all men and horses on the drive be calm-mannered. He wouldn't tolerate a skittish horse, nor even one that carried his head high in a spirited fashion, for such actions distracted the cattle and made them nervous. When Bird Rose bossed a trail drive, the words *trail drive* were misleading for the cattle weren't driven; rather they were allowed to graze at their own speed while the cowboys merely kept them pointed in the right direction.

Ambling slowly is not natural for a group of well-mounted young fellows; but if a man couldn't learn to be patient, Bird didn't want him around. When the riders were relieved of duty so that they could go to camp for a meal, Joe reported that they walked their horses over a couple of hills until they were out of the sight and hearing of the herd, after which they spurred their horses and raced to camp.

In order to be near the herd, the camp was moved twice a day. It seems that under other trail bosses, the night stop was beside a creek or watering hole near which the cattle were bedded for the night. A second stop was made between watering facilities where the noonday meal was eaten.

However, Bird usually did it the other way around: he stopped at the watering place during the day and chose high, dry ground for bedding the herd at night. The advantages were that there were fewer mosquitoes on high ground; that the cattle, who instinctively prefer to bed on a rise where they can see the area around them, were more satisfied; and that the drive was not locked into covering a specific distance each day. A disadvantage was that often the cattle (and the cook) had access to water only once a day instead of at both night and morning.

The watering sources were sometimes natural and

sometimes man-made, the latter having been constructed by the railroad. They were planned to be about twelve or thirteen miles apart, a distance considered to be a day's drive. Since the cattle were unhurried, they actually gained weight along the way.

The cowboys slept under the stars in a "tarp," a type of sleeping bag that, if folded correctly, shed water even in a drenching rain. For purposes of drainage, Joe preferred to make his bed on a slope. Before unrolling his tarp, he made two depressions in the ground, one for his hip and the other for his shoulder. However, the long day in the saddle, coupled with the fact that the brief night would be interrupted by a two-hour stint of night-herding, made the hours in bed a luxury under almost any circumstance.

"In the morning, we rolled our tarps securely," said Joe, because space was at a premium. If you did a sloppy job, the nighthawk left your bedroll lying on the prairie and come night, you'd have to ride back to the last night camp to get it."

"The nighthawk? Who was the nighthawk?"

"He was the one that herded the horses at night. In the morning he put them in the rope corral so that the cowhands could choose their mounts for the day. After breakfast he helped the cook break camp, and then tore down the corral. He loaded it—the ropes and stakes—into the bedwagon and tossed the bedrolls on top. After he drove to the next camp, he could sleep for the rest of the day.

"The horse wrangler took care of the extra horses during the day. There was quite a bunch of them, for each rider had a string of about eight or ten.

"The last shift of night riders went off duty at four o'clock. One of their responsibilities was to ride into camp at 3:30 a.m. and awaken the cook. The other cowboys were roused at 4:00 a.m., for they must have their beds rolled, gear packed, horse saddled, and breakfast eaten by the time the first light in the east brought the herd to its feet. If there was water in the area, the animals first were driven to it, after which they were pointed east and allowed to spread out for grazing.

"Contrary to what you might think, a trail drive is monotonous—all day loafing along with the grazing herd. The only time there was any excitement was during such events as river crossings or sudden storms. Once lightning started a prairie fire, but luckily the wind was in our favor, and it went the other direction."

When asked if the cattle ever stampeded, Joe answered:

"No—not like stampedes I've heard about—at least, not to the point where they got away from us. Once, though, they had a good run—all because of an old buffalo bull.

"At that time there weren't many buffalo left—just a few surly loners—but they could be a nuisance. If one of them decided to stand at a crossing, you just as well re-route because he sure wouldn't be the one to change *his* plans.

"One day when the herd was pretty well strung out, a buffalo bull ambled up out of a draw, straight toward the middle of the herd. He let out a low, rasping grumble, deep in his throat. Like a flash, the front half of the herd sprang ahead, horns clacking and hooves pounding the ground like a roll of thunder. The other half swung back, arched out behind the buffalo, and ran forward, also. They ran about a half mile or so, but we were able to contain them so that they didn't scatter. You couldn't really call it a stampede.

"Some of the boys kidded me that I was the one that had startled the cattle. We had been having dark, rainy weather, but that day the sky cleared and the sun came out bright. The boss told me to ride ahead to the next night camp and unroll some of the beds to sun them. They were inclined to get musty during wet weather. The nighthawk was awake, and he helped me with the beds. Afterward, I took off my shirt and put it in a bucket of water to soak, intending to wash it come night. I put on the extra one that I kept in my bedroll.

"I got back to the herd just before the buffalo appeared. The boys said that what *really* spooked the cattle was not the buffalo—rather it was me in my clean shirt. Those steers were so used to seeing clothes the color of Dakota soil, they said, that a clean shirt was cause for a stampede. They threatened to take me down and mud me up a little. I was a little uneasy, but I tried not to show it. They were a good bunch of fellows, but a couple of weeks before, I'd seen them pile onto a guy—a man we called Mac—and I wasn't anxious to have them get after me.

"Mac was a guy with a vile tongue, something cowhands don't tolerate. Even though they were an isolated group, they took pride in living a clean, respectable life. They had their own code of ethics, with specific penalties for breaking the various rules. Now ordinary cussing was acceptable, but obscene remarks were an offense—especially if they referred to what we called the "fairer sex". The other hands told Mac that he should clean up his language, and they made sure that he was aware of the penalty—an action called chapping.

"He didn't take the warning seriously and continued his foul remarks. After all, who among the good-natured group would carry out the threatened punishment?

"One day after Mac gave forth with a smutty term, two of the cowboys looked up, their eyes meeting. When they leaped to their feet and grabbed him, the other cowboys jumped up to help. They stripped off his pants and bent him over a pile of bed rolls. One hefty fellow began to swing a pair of leather chaps, and when he got through, Mac's backside was as red as a newly-painted barn.

"It took just that one lesson. His conversation was overly respectful after that."

Mostly, socializing was confined to evening campfire gatherings where the cowboys swapped yarns. Some were stories that had made the rounds of the many campfires in the West River Country, being told and retold hundreds of times. Infrequently, a rider might be met along the way—perhaps a trapper, a message bearer, or a cattleman in search of lost livestock. This newcomer quite possibly stayed the night, providing an opportunity for the drovers to hear new stories. He, in turn, picked up *their* "oft told tales" and carried them to other camps. An unusual happening would most certainly develop into a tale that would bounce from camp to camp, oftentimes being repeated verbatim. Many of those stories became legends, traveling not only across country, but also down through the years where they might unexpectedly resurface.

For instance, decades later (after Joe had begun ranching in Nebraska, had married, and had a family) Joe's wife wished to persuade her children not to play with snakes and told them that a severed snake head could bite a person. To prove her point, she told them one of Joe's South Dakota stories.

This tale was about a fellow who, thinking himself a master snake handler, was fond of boasting that he could pick up a rattlesnake by the tail and, in a motion similar to that used in cracking a whip, could pop the snake's head off. Once, in performing this trick, the severed head flew back, struck the fellow on the arm, and bit him.

After about five *more* decades (1986) Joe's daughter and a South Dakota rancher, Billy Green, were viewing Little Rattlesnake Butte, the place where Joe, during the time that he had worked for Jim Mitchell, had begun collecting rattlesnake hides with the idea that he would cover his saddle with them. Billy, having a rapt audience of one, was telling snake stories. He began with a modern one:

"A neighbor boy, Raydell Sperle, was riding to the pasture on his motorcycle one day," said Billy. "For some reason he shut the motor off, and just as he did so, he heard a rattle. He had the front wheel on a big rattler. He figured the snake could reach his feet, and he was pretty scared. He was going to slide off the back of the motorcycle, but then noticed that there were about six snakes coiled around the back wheel. Then he *really* was full of fright! I'm not sure how he got off of them, but I think that he kicked the kick-starter. The one that was pinned by the front wheel was injured, and he was able to kill it, but by then the others had escaped."

Billy continued with another story.

"Once I had a rattler get ahold of me right in the pant leg. I had my Levi's cuffed, and there were so many thicknesses that she couldn't get through, but she got her fangs caught in the material. I bolted! You can move pretty fast when a rattlesnake is holding onto you! She was a big one—like three or four feet.

"After I got loose from her, I took a forked buffalo berry stick and got her tangled in it by wrapping her 'round and 'round on the prongs. I carried her to the sheep wagon to take a picture of her. The wagon was close, maybe two or three hundred yards. When I got there, I laid my hat down to keep her attention and ran inside to get my camera. Oh, she was mad! She'd strike at the hat and also at me, but I got the picture.

"Afterward, I cut her head off and performed a Cesarean. Then I had seventeen more snakes, each of which was in a little plastic-like sack. When I was cutting open the third sack, the first little snake was already striking at me. They were only a few inches long, but the fight was born right in them. I killed them all, of course."

Billy's third story really startled his listener.

"One time a young fellow about twenty-two was going to show how he could catch a rattlesnake by the tail and snap his head off. Well, he did it all right, but the severed head flew back and bit him on the arm."

Joe's daughter imagined that this was the same tale that her father had brought from Dakota more than eighty years before—or do South Dakotans regularly indulge in the practice of snapping snake heads off?

Another of Joe's stories involved Corbin Morse who lived northwest of the South Dakota Badlands and had, so the tale went, ten thousand cattle which had recently been brought up from Texas. He had borrowed heavily to obtain them, but figured there was money to be made in the cattle business, and this was his chance.

One night when it was blizzarding outside so that the weather was "not fit for man nor beast," Corbin was sitting in a local restaurant eating his supper. Some time before, he had sent several cowboys to check on his herd which he knew was drifting southeast with the storm—directly toward the Badlands. The cowboys were to haze them away lest they tumble over the wall and pile up.

While Corbin was eating, a snow-plastered figure entered, which turned out to be one of the rancher's cowboys. He walked over to his boss.

"I hate to be the one chosen to tell you this," he said. "But your entire herd went over the wall. There wasn't a thing we could do to stop them."

There was dead silence in the room, for everyone present knew that the rancher had poured all of his resources into getting those cattle. Corbin continued to eat, his expression unchanged. Finally he looked up at the cowboy.

"Well—" he said softly. "Easy come, easy go." He finished his meal.

Is this story about Corbin true? Joe said that it had been retold by more than one source in almost the same words. Research reveals that there was a Corbin Morse who lived out his life as a rancher in the area east of Rapid City. An acquaintance of his said that Corbin had lost some cattle in the Badlands in early days, but that it was thought to have been a lesser number—perhaps 3000 head.

When the trail drive reached The Strip and entered Indian territory, the stories were then inclined to be sprinkled with Indian tales. Often, they were about every-day differences between the cultures of the Redmen and the Whites. One of the tales which could be counted upon to hold the interest of the cowboys around the campfires as well as Joe's children who heard it many years later follows:

Even though reservation lands were leased to the big cattlemen, the Indians who lived there retained special free-grazing rights. Any white man who married an Indian received the benefit of these rights through his mate.

A certain Frenchman with an Indian wife had built up a fair-sized cattle company. However, he died prematurely, leaving the ranch operation to his mate. She retained the non-Indian foreman who had worked for her husband, but she and the foreman, being of different cultures, often disagreed. Sometimes she got so angry when they were tending ranch affairs that she threw herself on the ground and refused to move. There was nothing for the foreman to do but wait until she decided to get up and resume the day's activities.

One day a cowboy came upon the foreman sitting quietly in the wagon while on the prairie beside him was a lump of pouting humanity about the size of a sleeping buffalo. The Indian woman was a large person, both in height and width, and when she flopped down, it made a considerable heap.

"What's the problem?" asked the cowboy, even though he was well aware of the woman's habits.

"Oh, a little disagreement," said the foreman.

The two men chatted for awhile. Finally, the cowboy winked at the foreman and said, "Well, if I were you, I wouldn't put up with that woman's stubborn habits. Here you sit in the hot sun, a-wastin' your time because of a mule-headed woman. Why don't you put a bullet in her and leave her to the coyotes?"

"Then I *would* be in trouble," said the foreman.

"I don't know why. I sure wouldn't tell anybody. Probably no one will come through these parts until roundup time, and that is four months away. The coyotes will have her all cleaned up by then..."

"Well, there are enough coyotes around here, that's for sure," said the foreman in an attempt to walk around the subject.

"Why don't you just grab your six-shooter and do it? I won't tell a soul. I swear it." The heap moved a little. The cowboy pulled out his own weapon. "Here," he offered. "It might be better if you used my gun."

The mound on the ground unfolded, and the woman stood up. After she climbed into the wagon, the foreman clucked to the horses, and they went on their way.

When the drovers reached the Missouri River with their herd of plump steers, they met with the men representing the buyers and strung the herd out for counting. Next it was necessary to cross the river, using the pontoon bridge. The cattle were driven into a broad, fenced lane that narrowed gradually until its two sides joined with the sides of the bridge. This bridge, along with its side railings, was built on a compact series of boat-like structures.

A horseman led the way onto the bridge, and the cattle, pushed from behind down the lane, were on the swaying span before they realized it. After twenty cattle were on the bridge, the overseer yelled, "Cowboy!" and a rider slid from the sideline onto the bridge. After another twenty cattle were on the bridge, another cowboy took his place behind them. The idea was to space the cattle evenly and thus to avoid the possibility of having them pile up on any one part of the bridge. The pattern of cattle and cowboys, winding like a giant snake across the river, was an impressive sight.

When all were across and the cattle were penned in the railroad stockyards at Evarts, it was time for the cowboys to relinquish their horses. The farmers east of the river paid good prices for horses that had come from a trail drive because they knew that they were well-trained. Thus the animals were sold rather than returned to the ranch from which they had come. For the cowboys, this farewell was the most difficult part of the entire drive, for they had become attached to their faithful mounts—their trusted partners. Joe said that never was there a time before or since when parting with animals was so difficult.

When Joe, in his advanced years, was telling his daughter these stories, his brother Fred was present. Fred also had a Dakota Indian story. He related it to them. It follows:

"After the hide hunters had swept down from Canada and had slaughtered the buffalo," said Fred, "the Indians lost their main source of food. One day an Indian couple and their tiny baby stopped at a soddy. They indicated that they needed food and were taken inside. However, before they entered, the mother set the cradle with the baby against the outside wall.

"When the Indian couple emerged from the soddy, the papoose and cradle were gone. Naturally, the Indians were frantic, and the settlers, in addition to their concern for the baby, were apprehensive lest the Indians think *they* had something to do with the baby's disappearance."A quick search of the little farmstead, however, revealed the culprit—and the horrible, chilling story. A big sow had carried the cradle away and had devoured the baby.

There was no way for the settlers to make restitution to the grief-stricken parents, but they did kill the pig and bury it."

Going Home

Joe spent parts of 1904 and 1905 working for Jim Mitchell who lived near Ludlow, South Dakota.

After the fall roundup Joe's boss, Jim Mitchell, laid off his extra hands, including Joe. Joe hired out to a neighboring rancher and took up residence in a sheep wagon.

Since Joe had informed his boss that he wished to vote, another herder arrived early on election day, and Joe rode Slate to the voting place. There he met Jim Mitchell who commented that his family was planning a trip to Bel Fourche for supplies.

Bel Fourche! A railroad town! Suddenly Joe, who had not seen—nor heard from—his family for three and a half years, had a sudden desire to go home. Within the next few days he quit his job, made arrangements to ride along with the Mitchells, and sold the horse that had carried him twice across Wyoming, through Montana, and finally into the Dakotas.

The Mitchell ranch was located in the extreme northwest corner of South Dakota; in fact, their nearest post office was at Haley, North Dakota.

From there to Bel Fourche was roughly a hundred miles on horseback but farther by wagon, for a wagoner must snake to the left or to the right so as to be accommodated by wagon crossings. At that time, the western half of the state had not been homesteaded and bridges were a rarity. Even though Jim drove a seasoned team, the trip required nearly four days.

At night the travelers camped by the trail where they staked the horses out on the prairie and fed them hay and oats which they carried along. Jim and his wife, Mary, rolled out their bed on top of the remaining hay in the wagon. Joe spread his tarp under the vehicle as did Jim's young son.* Sleeping out on the Dakota prairie in November is not the coziest of experiences, but fortunately there were no storms.

During Joe's absence from Nebraska, he hadn't spent a homesick day until that moment when he suddenly decided to head back. Then each day his excitement mounted. His train

---

* This boy, also named Joe, was Jim's eldest child. He died as a young man during the 1918 Flu Epidemic.

arrived in Atkinson late one Saturday, and he spent the night in the Stockman Hotel.

The next day the two Ziska girls, Annie and Ella at ages twelve and eight, were delighted when, after church, Joe asked their parents for a ride south. On the way, Joe took something from his pocket.

"Do you know what this is?" he asked.

"A pear!" exclaimed Ella. "I've seen pictures of them."

"Where did you get it?" asked Annie.

"Oh, a fellow was hawking them at one of the depots back yonder," he answered.

Joe cut the fruit in two, and gave each girl a portion. It was the first time either of them had tasted a pear.

Joe stayed all night with the Ziskas, and in the morning, after helping with the milking, ate pancakes made by the industrious Annie who, in spite of her young age, seemed to be as handy in the kitchen as was her mother.

Joe intended to walk the remaining ten miles home, but John insisted that he borrow their horse, Daisy.

It was a gray day, and when Joe stepped into his parent's house, Antonija squinted in the dim light. Who was this young fellow who had so boldly entered their home?

"Joe!" shouted Fred, leaping to his feet.

"Oh, Pepicek," exclaimed Antonija, tears moistening her eyes. Pepicek is a Moravian (Czech) name, an affectionate term which could be translated into "Joey" or "my dear Joe."

Joe was truly home.

Pilfered Beer
1905

The wagon load of beer pulled by four head of horses was pointed toward the Vaclav Krysl ranch when it bogged down in the mud. Christina, the oldest Krysl girl, was to be married, and a three-day celebration was under preparation. The beer, along with a barrel of wine which had been ordered from California, was a part of the provisions.

The driver of this heavy load recognized that his tired horses needed both rest and reinforcements. Unhitching them, he tied them to the side of the wagon while he, himself, walked to a nearby farm. During his absence, a couple of young fellows came upon the stalled wagon.

"It looks like that wagon is overloaded," said one to his

companion. "We could lighten it up by taking away a couple kegs of that beer."

"Yeah," said the other. "That would be a right neighborly thing to do. Never let it be said that we passed by a fellow traveler-in-need without lending a hand."

The youths wrestled two of the kegs off the loaded wagon and rolled them away. They secluded them behind a hay pile, and in the days to come, their own private party exceeded the three-day wedding celebration both in hilarity and in length.

Joe at Christina's Wedding
1905

Upon returning from South Dakota, Joe Dobrovolny found that the family was invited to the Vaclav Krysl place where they were celebrating the marriage of their daughter, Christina, to John Krobot. Joe and his brother Fred rode across the prairie to attend the festivities, and on the way, they crossed the land which would, in about forty-five years, belong to Joe's son-in-law, Don Krysl.

"The water level was high that fall," Joe remembered later. "When we went over that land, there were places where it stood belly deep on our horses."

Upon reaching the Vaclav Krysl place (where the Neale Hamiltons now live) they discovered that a platform called a "bowery" had been constructed for dancing, and day and night, music furnished by various fiddlers caught everyone up into a festive mood and set toes to tapping. Day and night, too, three course meals were served in the house. Coffee dipped from a boiler (usually used to heat water for laundering) was served in both the house and yard. Ladies were everywhere with huge pans of kolachy (*kolace*).

(At the time of Christina's wedding, she was one of eight children; her sister Mary, who grew up to marry Albert Ziska, was two years old. Christina's mother later give birth to two more children, John and Agnes, bringing the total to ten.)

Since Joe had been working in other states for three and a half years, he now enjoyed greeting old acquaintances. Approaching Vaclav, he held out his hand.

"Who are you?" asked Vaclav in Czech.

"I'm Joe, one of Tom Dobrovolny's boys," said Joe.

Vaclav looked him over, head to toe. Joe was fine-boned, and carried not a single pound of extra weight.

"I don't believe that! Tom's boys are all big fellows. Really, now. Who are you?"

Since Vaclav couldn't be persuaded, he finally called Tom over. "This bony kid, here, says he's your son. I told him that your boys are all well-fed, stout fellows."

"Well," said Tom. "He's mine. But I agree that he could use a few more biscuits under his belt."

"Biscuits!" said Joe. "About all I've been eating the last few years are biscuits."

"Well," suggested Vaclav, "then maybe you'd better spread a little lard on them."

It was the first wedding that Joe had attended, and he, still exhilarated from his homecoming, had a memorable time. He danced repeatedly with one of the Kosicek girls.

The Bachelor's Cats
about 1906

Joe and another young fellow, Stub, worked near Newcastle, Wyoming, for an old bachelor whom we will call Charlie. They were excavating a pit which, when completed, would be used to water sheep. The two hired hands bunked with Charlie in a small shack which was overpopulated with about two dozen cats. Charlie had made a small swinging door that the animals could push open themselves, thus allowing them to go in and out at will.

Joe and Stub weren't exactly overjoyed with the housing arrangements: cats walked boldly on the table, sniffed in the cupboards, slept in piles on the bunks, and all but snatched food off people's forks.

One day Charlie went to Newcastle for supplies and didn't arrive home until long after dark. When Joe and Stub went inside for supper, they decided they were going to enjoy this one meal without having to guard every bite lest it be intercepted by the reaching claws of the ill-mannered pets.

"Let's give them a good scare so they'll stay outside for awhile," said Stub.

Upsetting a bench, they placed the seat of it firmly over the low swinging door, thus confining the roomful of animals. Then emitting a few war whoops, they proceeded to slam their boots under the table and across the room. Immediately, yowling cats were everywhere, leaping on the furniture, springing in the air, and climbing the walls.

After some wild, noisy moments, Joe slid the bench away from the swinging door, and the scrambling mass of fur quickly rippled out through the opening. Sitting down, the men ate supper without having to fight off the troublesome felines.

The next day Charlie wondered why his pets were unusually alert and wary.

The Beating
early 1900's

On arriving at a new job site in Wyoming, Joe was directed to a barn that served as sleeping quarters for the work force. However, he couldn't sleep because the building was full of fleas.

While he was tossing and scratching, he suddenly heard angry voices outside the barn. He lay there listening, but he couldn't understand the words well enough to ascertain what the dissension was about.

Next, mixed with more strong language came the sounds of blows. It didn't sound like a fistfight—rather more like someone was being whipped.

Thud! Snap! Whop!

Joe lay there—intimidated—listening and wondering. From the mixture of furious tones, he decided there must be quite a group, and that the most sensible thing for him to do was to stay where he lay, hidden in the heavy darkness.

Sounds of beating, accentuated by angry expletives, went on and on.

The weary, red-eyed Joe appeared at breakfast with about ten other yawning workers.

"The fleas almost ate me up last night," he muttered to the young fellow beside him.

"They chew on you every night," his companion growled. "A bunch of us got up last night and beat our bedding and our clothes against the corner of the barn. After we shook out as many of those man-eaters as we could, we bedded down outside. It helped a little."

So that was it! All that anger was aimed at the fleas.

The Bad Winter
1906 - 1907

Most Dakota winters are cold and beset with blizzards.

However, there are some especially severe ones, and in the years of the big cattle ranges, the Bad Winter of 1907 stands out as the worst of them all. The first deep snow came in November of 1906, and on top of it came blizzard after blizzard, week in and week out. There was no let-up until May.

As was usual at that time, the cattle were expected to fend for themselves over the winter. Pastures, on the whole, were not yet fenced, and after the fall roundup when animals that were ready for market were cut out of the herd and shipped, the others were turned loose to rustle for their own food until the time of the spring roundup when they were gathered and herded back to home range.

Even though the herds were virtually unattended during the winter, most of the big ranches retained a few cowboys who occupied scattered shacks referred to as "winter camps." Their main duty was to keep water holes open by chopping through the ice, but also they kept an eye on any cattle in the area and did what they could to help them survive.

During this particular winter, all local cattle had soon drifted southeastward with the repeated blizzards, and in their wake came wave after wave of tired, starving Montana cattle, their ice-caked heads bent low. By mid-winter, the prairie was sprinkled with the carcasses of dead livestock, which were soon covered with more snow, over which trudged a new wave of bawling, hungry cattle.

Spring, though late, finally did arrive. Joe Dobrovolny, who had stayed with his Uncle John's family in Fremont for a good part of the winter,* received a letter from Jim Mitchell asking him to come to Ludlow in the northwest corner of South Dakota to help with the spring roundup.

The entire West River Country (that part of the Dakotas

Joe
Mary   Anna   Frank Joe

* In the fall of '06 a horse fell and crushed Joe's leg. He recuperated at the home of his Uncle John in Fremont where he and cousins, Anna, Mary, and Frank, became fast friends.

west of the Missouri River) had been divided into roundup areas. The roundups were a cooperative effort, and each one was bossed by a nearby cattleman who was familiar with the local terrain. However, all other cattlemen in the region sent representatives (called reps) to each of the various roundups. Each was to take charge of any cattle belonging to the particular ranch for which he worked.

Usually, the small ranches participated in only the local roundups; but in 1907, the cattlemen in northwestern South Dakota, southwestern North Dakota, and eastern Montana gathered to discuss the situation. Among the group were Jim Mitchell and his friend, Eli Green. This group decided to send reps to each of the various roundups.

In addition to locating reliable men to send as reps, they must outfit each man with a string of horses. Long hours in the saddle and hard riding required that a man change mounts frequently, making it necessary for each cowboy to have eight or ten horses in his string. Also, outfits (chuck wagons, cooks, and cowboys) were needed to trail the cattle back to home range.

Joe had worked for Jim Mitchell during the summers from 1904 to 1906, and a feeling of mutual respect developed between the two. Jim suggested that Joe be one of the reps and vouched for his dependability.

At the Mitchell Ranch, Joe picked up the string of horses collected for him as well as the information about the brands of the ranches for which he was to rep, and rode southeastward toward the Moreau River. As he followed it into the Cheyenne River Indian Reservation, he found the prairie covered with rotting cattle carcasses, a sight which dismayed the budding cattleman. Also, the fetid odor of rotting flesh continually exploded in his face with such force that, even though he had his silk scarf (which was a part of a cowboy's regular garb) tied around his face, he sometimes had to hold his breath.

The area where Joe repped was on the Cheyenne Indian Reservation, but it is not known with which of the cattle outfits he worked. The Turkey Track, so named because their brand resembled the footprint of a turkey, headquartered thirty miles south of present-day Dupree;* the Sword & Dagger, also named

---

* In 1986 Thelma Frame of Dupree said that the grounds of the Turkey Track had been visible until the 1960's. Then the owner, Bob Samuelson, hired Jim Frame to level the area and to fill in the cellar, thus obliterating all traces of that old cattle kingdom.

Above: Billy Green (Eli Green's son) looking out over the prairie where Jim Mitchell's buildings stood. Left: Dennis Mitchell, Jim's grandson. 1986. Below: This item from The Atkinson Graphic gives an idea of the severity of the flooding caused by the melted snow from the Winter of 1907.

August 2, 1907 — Some of the men in the northern part of the county are wondering whether they are in Holt county or not. Bridges have been out since the spring flood. No sheriff can reach them to pay taxes though.

for its brand, ran their herds in the southwestern part of the reservation; the Matador, whose brand was a cursive v (referred to as a drag v) occupied the area along the Moreau River. Joe's many references to the Moreau and to the Grand Rivers and to Murdo McKenzie and Con McMurry (who bossed the Matador) suggest that he repped on their range.

Just as in trail-riding, the roundup day began early. Beds were rolled, breakfast was over, and by sunrise the cowboys were mounted on one of their faster, long-winded horses. The wagon boss explained details about the area to be covered that forenoon, and, after dividing the riders into two groups, sent them in opposite directions to circle it.

Cowboys were "dropped off" at intervals around the arc of the circle, the ones with the sturdier horses galloping on to the farther side. Once positioned, the cowboys flushed the cattle out of draws and creek bottoms and drove them toward camp, arriving, if all went as planned, in time for dinner. The collected cattle were thrown into the "day herd".

In the afternoon the riders chose fresh mounts and rode a new circle. The cowboys took turns herding the cattle both day and night. When the herd became large enough, the critters belonging to the "big outfits" were sorted out and turned over to the wagon crews who trailed them home. Cattle wearing the brands of the smaller ranches remained in the day herd until the end of the roundup.

The reps joined the regular cowboys and were under the direction of the local wagon boss. When it came time to work the herd (sort the cattle) the reps checked the critters and took charge of all those which bore the brands for which they were responsible.

Unfortunately, Joe's family has very few details about his unique experience in the big roundup. They do know, however, that in spite of the droves of cattle collected, very few animals belonging to the smaller ranches were recovered. Years later, whenever Joe mentioned it, there was a note of apology in his voice, as if the fact that he was unable to retrieve the lost herds of the ranchers he represented was somehow his fault rather than that of the death-dealing winter.

He always ended his account with the words: "And when the last cow was sorted, there was nothing for me to do but cut out my string [of horses] and ride for home. That was the last big roundup. The cattlemen hadn't yet recovered from that winter when settlers swarmed in and took over the open range."

Throughout his life Joe told stories gleaned from his roundup experiences. Some were of incidents he had witnessed, while others were narratives that he had "heard tell" around the campfires. One that he particularly enjoyed relating was about Cap Mossman (pronounced Moze-man) and his famous, oft-repeated parlor trick. Even those Dakotans who hadn't witnessed it had certainly heard about it. Joe's story follows:

"Once when I was in a hotel restaurant, I saw a fellow light a cigar with a hundred dollar bill. It was Cap Mossman, the boss of the big Turkey Track spread. He took the bill out of his vest pocket, walked over to the cigar lighter, caught it afire, and then lit his cigar. People knew he was in the habit of performing this trick, and every eye in the restaurant was on him."

This story, related to Joe's wide-eyed children during the Great Depression, was mind boggling. Who could possibly be rich enough to waste a hundred dollar bill in such a manner? Joe's daughter supposed that after the cigar was lit, the remainder of the flaming bill was placed in an ash tray to burn itself out.

However, Ike Blasingame (in his book, Dakota Cowboy, page 110) described this same action in greater detail. First, said Ike, Cap folded the bill lengthwise several times, and after using it to ignite the tip of his cigar, he pinched out the fire on the end of it and returned it to his vest pocket. Thus the bill wasn't completely destroyed. However, this bit of drama captured everyone's attention, and it made a marvelous campfire tale.

Since Joe spent his entire life working with animals, often some surprising occurrence involving the unusual behavior of a creature would prompt a round of tales about an animal's uncanny instincts or peculiar conduct. At such times, Joe was apt to narrate his unusual story of the she-wolf.

"Various species of animals have strange habits," he would say. "For instance, as odd as this sounds, I've been told that a female wolf won't fight in her own den. She's a fierce and savage fighter otherwise, but doesn't fight back if she is attacked in her own nest. In fact, I met a little, wiry fellow in South Dakota during the roundup after the Big Winter who claimed that he crawled into a wolf den and tied a rope on a she-wolf so she could be pulled out. She didn't do a thing while she was in her den, but she sure came to life and tore things up when they pulled her out."

Was that wiry fellow Ike Blasingame? Ike tells, in

Dakota Cowboy, about performing this feat, and Ike and Joe both participated in the 1907 Spring Roundup. Ike's book is an authentic story of the big cattle ranges during that period of time. The incidents and the names of places and people are familiar to Joe's offspring.

The year of 1907 was a time when ranchers were concerned about the fact that homesteaders, armed with sickle and plow, were beginning to seep across the Mighty Mo to fence in the open range. The cattlemen referred to these settlers by the derogatory term of *honyokes*, pronounced hon-yocks, and scorned their way of life. Western Dakota, the stockman felt sure, was cattle country and would be ruined by attempts to farm it. However, there was not the organized resistance in Dakota that had developed in Wyoming when the homesteaders arrived there.

The year before, Joe, himself, had considered homesteading and had chosen ground along the Grand River near Lodgepole. When he mentioned it to Jim Mitchell, a man he respected, Jim said in fatherly tones:

"Now Joe,* you don't want to do that. The cattlemen around these parts think a lot of you. Crossing over to the other side of the range dispute will turn them against you. That's not a good way for you to begin your ranching career."

Although Joe gave up his plans for homesteading in South Dakota, his decision helped the cattlemen nary one bit. Asking one man not to homestead was like attempting to stop a flood by dipping out a cupful of water. Within a few years, there was a "honyoker" on every quarter section of land, and the days of the open range and the big cattle companies were gone forever.

The Sioux Indians

The Indians, after they were pushed north from Nebraska, roamed freely in Dakota for many more years. In the

---

* This instance was one of the few times when Jim Mitchell used Joe's given name instead of his nickname, "Smith." Because of Joe's hard-to-pronounce last name, Dobrovolny, Joe's friend, Charlie Miller, introduced him to the Mitchells as Joe Smith. The Mitchells had a son named Joe and, to forestall confusion, called their hired man by his supposed last name, Smith.

early 1900's, stories about them were still bouncing from campfire to campfire.

Decades earlier, Dakota was the scene of numerous battles between the Sioux and the Crow Indians who made war on each other, mainly for the purpose of stealing each others horses. Sitting Bull's father was killed by a Crow Indian when Sitting Bull was yet a boy; when Sitting Bull grew to manhood, he avenged his father's death by killing the Crow. Sitting Bull was born on the Grand River and lived in that area most of his life. He was the leader of the combined tribes of Indians who slew Custer and his soldiers in the Battle of the Little Bighorn (Custer's Last Stand).

The ceremonial dances of 1890 (about a dozen years before Joe arrived in South Dakota) also took place on the Grand River. Because the Indians wore white shirts meant to protect them from the white man's bullets, these rituals were called Ghost Dances by the settlers. Governmental representatives, uneasy because of the fervor of the dances, decided that it would be prudent to arrest and remove the leader, Sitting Bull, even though he did not participate in the dancing. During the arrest, fighting broke out and Sitting Bull was shot. A short time later (also in 1890) the final confrontation came in the form of the Massacre at Wounded Knee.

Joe told of the movement of the Sioux Indians back and forth from the Dakotas to Canada in search of food, this dire need having been brought on by the annihilation of the buffalo. Some of his stories give clues regarding the means by which the Indians survived after the buffalo were gone.

He said to cook a turtle, they built a fire in a large outdoor oven, and when the oven was sufficiently hot, they removed the coals and tossed the turtle in, shell and all. How they served it once it was baked he didn't know.

A rancher who had lost a dog, later saw a papoose wrapped in the dog's hide. When they inquired about the animal, the Indians indicated that they had eaten it. Probably these Indians would have chosen a buffalo roast in preference to baked turtle or dog stew, but they didn't have the option.

Painted Women

Joe rarely told about the "Ladies of the Night" who were a part of the South Dakota Gold Rush Days (which coincided with the time of the open range.) When he did mention them, it was with a quiet tone and a half-embarrassed smile which suggested that it was a subject that shouldn't be discussed. Once, however, when Gladys Parks (part-owner of the Wright Land) was visiting the Dobrovolny's, she suggested to Joe's two young daughters that they wear a bit of lipstick.*

"Oh, no!" said Joe. "At the turn of the century I saw enough painted women in the Dakota boom towns. My daughters don't paint themselves. They're not that kind of girls."

"Joe, I'm speaking of just a touch of color. Every well-dressed lady wears make-up these days. A modest amount is becoming."

"Not my girls !" said Joe. "I say it's not becomin'. I prefer the wholesome beauty of a girl's natural color."

Also, during the early 1900's, Joe saw in western Nebraska the "most ridiculous dress fashion" of his entire life! "Hobble skirts" were in style then—extremely narrow, ankle-length dresses.

"Why, a women couldn't even walk in them," he reported. "I saw a lady who needed to hurry to catch a train. She couldn't take a decent step because of her narrow skirt, and so she was hopping along like a kangaroo. When she got to the train steps, she couldn't get up them because she was completely hobbled! Since the train was already starting to move, the conductor grabbed her and drug her aboard. All the other passengers were grinning to themselves.

"Now tell me—what sense is there to a style like that?"

A Distraught Grandmother
about 1908

Joe had returned to Nebraska after completing the sheep-shearing season in northern Wyoming and Montana. When he

---

* The six quarters of Joe's "Wright Land" and also the place that is just west of it where Hank Dobrovolny now lives, were owned by George Wright. (Originally, as already has been stated, the land around Wright's Lake was Rosenberry land, but the Rosenberrys moved to Canada in the early 1900's.) When Wright died, the land rented by Joe was inherited by Wright's daughter, Laura Compton of Nebraska City. After her death, it passed to her children, Gladys Parks and Doris Staples, who eventually sold it to Joe.

stepped into the depot in Crawford, he could not fail to notice an overwrought woman who was tending a crying baby.

He approached the station agent who, after taking care of Joe's travel needs, asked, "Do you speak Czech?"

"Yes, I do," answered Joe. "I didn't speak anything else until I went to school."

"Then try it out on that woman over there. She's been here since early morning, and I can't find anyone who can understand a word she says. I think she might be Czech.

"Joe walked over to her. *"Dobry den! Mluvite Cesky?"* he asked. ("Good day. Do you speak Czech?")

The woman jumped up. *"Dekuju Ti Buh!* (Thank the Lord!)," she exclaimed tearfully. *"Prosim, muzes mi pomoci?"* ("Please, can you help me?")

During the course of the ensuing conversation, the woman told her story. Her daughter and son-in-law, impatient to make a quick fortune, had gone west to prospect for gold. While the son-in-law was pursuing the elusive yellow dust, his little wife gave birth, after which she died of child-bed fever (post-birth infection). The grandmother had come west to get the baby but was now having trouble making travel arrangements because she knew no English. Since she already had missed the train she should have taken, Joe helped her purchase a ticket for passage on the one leaving the next day. Then he assisted her in finding lodging for the night in a nearby rooming house.

The old lady thanked him repeatedly and complimented him on his ability to speak the Czech language as well as to translate it into English.

"Gosh, she was tickled," Joe commented many years later when he told the story.

(As a teenager, Joe had interpreted for his father. Whenever Tom had business in O'Neill, the county seat, he and one of the boys left by wagon in the middle of the night and drove to Atkinson. From there they took the morning train to O'Neill. While doing business at the court house, the boy interpreted for Tom, as Tom spoke very little English. They returned to Atkinson on the afternoon train.)

And Then What?
1912 and after

What happened to Jim Mitchell and other cattlemen after

the homesteaders moved in? Joe's accounts about South Dakota did not include that information. However, many years later, Billy Green (the son of Jim Mitchell's best friend, Eli Green) and Dennis Mitchell (Jim's grandson) told the story:

> The time eventually came when Jim and neighboring ranchers were hemmed in by the settlers who had taken up the land where formerly the cattlemen had grazed their herds. Winter was approaching, and Jim and Eli were concerned about where they could winter their cattle.
> Finally, Jim decided he would take his herd to the North Dakota Badlands, poor ground which no one cared to homestead. Perhaps the cattle could find enough grazing to survive the winter. Jim offered to take Eli's herd of four or five hundred cows along, and since Eli had no alternative except to sell them, he accepted.
> The next spring Eli received a letter from his friend:
>
> > Dear Eli,
> >   I lost all the cattle. Where shall I send the hides?
> >
> > Jim
>
> After a couple of years of confusion and indecision, Jim sold his remaining property and took his family to California where they lived for a year. Not liking it there, they returned to North Dakota and started over. Jim died in 1934 at age eighty-four.
> Eli Green decided that he would continue to operate on his drastically reduced acreage but would convert from cattle ranching to raising and training horses. The homesteaders, he reasoned, would need teams to pull those detested plows!
> Northwestern South Dakota was too dry for a family to make a living on a quarter or two of land. Slowly, many of the homesteaders starved out and left. Billy, Eli's son, tells of hard times and hard work, but eventually he was in a position to slowly buy back enough land to have a ranch where he raises both cattle and sheep.

A Country School in the Early 1900's

**Hundreds of these one-room schools
dotted the Nebraska prairies.
All grades, one through eight,
were taught by a single teacher.
A few of these schools continue
to be in operation yet today. However,
they have fewer pupils.**

V.J. and Christina Krysl
as Teenagers
They are the eldest of Vaclav's
ten children.

Chapter 8

Back in Nebraska

Impatient Pony
early 1900's

Since Anna Hytrek's father died when she was a girl, she often was required to stay at home from school to help with the farm work. One winter when Paul was sick with asthma, she and Mary missed the entire school term. John and Stencil were busy baling hay, and the girls picked the corn and hauled the hay for the cattle.

But other years, Anna went to school whenever she could—until she was seventeen years old.

She often rode a horse named Tricks to school. After school when she brought him out of the barn, he was so overjoyed to be going home that he wanted only to buck and run. One of Anna's schoolmates had to hold him until she was well-situated on his back, and as soon as the assistant let go of his bridle, he gave a leap and a buck and raced for home.

There were occasions when Anna lost her lunch bucket (a syrup pail) on the two-and-a-quarter-mile run, but she didn't get off to retrieve it. With no one to hold her impatient steed, she would not have been able to remount.

Skinning Rats
about 1908

Since game was plentiful during the early 1900's, much of the meat on the pioneer table came from wildlife. Stencil was the hunter in the Hytrek family, and often took Anna or Mary along to drive the horses so that he could have his gun ready.

Stencil also trapped animals for their furs. The sloughs were thick with muskrats, and each fur brought about ten cents. When he bagged more than he had time to skin, he gave his sisters five cents per animal to do it for him. While they skinned, he stretched the furs for drying.

Once Mary's knife slipped and slashed the fleshy part of her palm at the base of her thumb.

"Nowadays," said Anna later, "A cut like that would be sewed up, but in those days people doctored themselves as best they could. Mother washed it, and I remember her saying that salt would be good to kill the germs, but salt really stings in a wound. So she used sugar which is also good.

"She positioned Mary's hand just right to close the wound, bandaged it, and put it in a sling because she didn't want Mary to use it nor to move her fingers for fear the wound would break open again. It took a long time, but it finally healed."

Trip to Elyria

After the Benbens moved to a place south of Elyria, Paul Hytrek had a distance of about sixty-five miles to travel to see Victoria Benben, his girlfriend. Once he invited Anna to accompany him.

They thought they could save time by cutting across the prairie instead of going east to strike the usual trail. However, they got lost. They stopped at a soddy to inquire the way, and even though darkness descended, they continued on.

When suddenly the horses halted, Paul urged them on, but instead of proceeding, they stepped backward. Perplexed, he got out of the buggy to investigate.

The next sound Anna heard was the distant voice of her brother.

"*Annina!*" he called in Polish. "*Nyay yets tu yeh joora!*" [It is spelled phonetically and means: "Anna, don't drive here! There's a hole."]

Paul had fallen down an embankment into a deep ditch.

After he had clambered around in the dark and had managed to climb back up, he decided to unhitch the team and wait until morning. It was a long night of fighting mosquitoes and listening to the coyotes yodel back and forth across the hills.

The next morning, they completed their journey without further problems. However, when it was time to return home, they followed the trail rather than looking for a short-cut.

Hunting Weapons
early 1900's

As a boy, Stencil made bows and arrows. The arrows were fashioned of straight, slender sticks with wires in the ends. He also made sling shots, using for ammunition round stones or bits of brick which he filed into smooth, round balls. He was a good shot, and could bring down a bird at quite a distance.

When he was older, he made his own gun shells. However, gunpowder and shot both cost money, an article that was always scarce, and sometimes when he was low on ammunition, he reverted to hunting with his home-made bow or his sling shot.

Baked Squab

During the summer, the Hytreks sometimes had a special delicacy, baked squab, for Sunday dinner. The dish was prepared the day before, and was rewarmed for the Sabbath meal.

After Mary and Anna were old enough, they were sent on Saturday mornings to go through the many rows of pigeon houses that were located high on the barn and granary walls. They chose about a dozen of the young birds (called squabs) to butcher. One girl climbed to the nests, decided which of the squabs were large enough, and tossed them to the ground. The other collected them and with a detachment born of repetition, calmly pulled their heads off. The two girls then plucked and dressed them.

Johanna coated the birds with lard and spices and baked them. Halfway through the baking, she poured cream over them and let it bake down into a rich, golden gravy.

It was a dish that would have delighted a king!

A Ferocious Cat
about 1905

One fall day when John Hytrek (a year older than Mary) was digging a trench to plant rhubarb, he noticed a cat eating some parts of a pigeon that had been discarded by the girls who were dressing squabs. Thinking that the half-grown kittens in the barn would enjoy a few choice morsels and needing a break from shovel work, he procured a can of the pigeon scraps and carried them to the barn.

A big tomcat was interested in the contents of the can. John took out a string of the entrails and, wanting to tease the cat, swung it back and forth high above Old Tom's head. The animal made several leaps, but John managed to swing the prize away each time.

The cat's bright eyes were intent on the moving target, and those eyes were getting brighter by the second. The odor of the bird particles must have called forth some remnant of the wild that was stored in the tame cat's heart, for suddenly he leaped with the speed of lightening.

"Gr-r-r-r-owl!"

Digging his unsheathed claws savagely into the boy's hand, the angry cat claimed his prize and ran.

It took many days for the deep claw marks in John's hand to heal.

Train Accident
March 23, 1906

Dr. F. S. Hunt of Stuart (the husband of Jan Ziska's daughter, Barbara) was summoned to O'Neill as a witness in the Irwin murder trial, and he rode to O'Neill on the noon train. Learning that he would not be called to testify that day, he hurried back to the depot. It was his intention to return home on the early westbound passenger train. When he missed it, he decided to catch a ride on the freight train.

Since the train was already moving when he attempted to board, his foot slipped and he fell under the wheels.

He was killed.

The year before, Robert Cearns (an uncle to Vivian Cearns Krysl) and Myron Irwin gathered with a group of other men to fight a prairie fire. After the flames had been whipped out, the group dispersed, but Cearns and Irwin remained to continue an argument that had erupted some days earlier.

Finally, the two began to fight. Irwin pulled a knife and stabbed Cearns, killing him. Since Dr. Hunt had examined the body of the deceased and also the bruises of the accused man, he was asked to testify at the trial.

Irwin was convicted and sent to prison.

July Fourth Celebration
about 1909 or 1910
told by Henrietta Ries Dexter

"Mother got up at four o'clock and fried the chicken; she awakened everyone else at five to do the milking and other chores. Then we all piled into the car and headed for Stuart's Fourth of July Celebration.

"We kids were small, and we had been told that in Stuart we could have a carnival ride and an ice cream cone.

"The car that Dad was driving was a Jackson with no windshield, no top, and no doors. It had a two-cylinder engine and would hardly pull itself. With sandy, rutty roads like we had then, that car was just plain helpless.

"On this day, we got stuck in every rut and every sandy spot. Dad was the only one who knew how to drive, which meant that Mother had to do the pushing. We kids would get out to lighten the load, and Mother would brace herself against the back of the car and shove. It was hotter than the dickens, and since we had no protection from the sun, and since we were crowded in the little car, we were all as red as fire.

"By two o'clock we were still three miles from Stuart, and besides being hot, we were thirsty and tired and hungry. Dad found a little tree for shade, and we ate lunch.

"After lunch, Dad asked, 'Shall we turn around and go home?'

"'Yes!' we all shouted. Man, were we ever tickled to head for home! We were willing to forget all about the carnival ride and the ice cream cone!

"But we had the same fight with that old car all the way back. It was the most worthless machine!

"When we got home, we still had chores to do. Boy, were we worn out! None of us wanted to hear about Fourth of July for a long time to come."

Cow Pumpkins
early 1900's
told by Ralph Ries

"Our family, as well as other settlers at that time, grew pumpkins to feed to the milk cows. Each night we boys chopped a number of the big pumpkins into segments and tossed them into the cow yard. The cows went after them like a cat after a mouse.

"We had to stay nearby and watch the cows while they ate because sometimes in their hurry to get their share, they gobbled the chunks down too fast. A piece might get lodged in a cow's throat and choke her. Grabbing a piece of hose which we kept nearby, we would poke it down her throat to dislodge the piece of pumpkin."

(Pumpkins and turnips were stored under the hay pile in the feed rack to keep them from freezing. After the pumpkins were gone, the turnips were chopped and fed to the cows.)

A Moonlight Mistake
about 1910

The dance at Anton Tasler's place was attended by most of the people in the neighborhood and by the younger Ziska boys. Since it was a busy time of the year, however, John and Mary Ziska and the elder Blackburns decided to stay home, but

About 1914, Edd Ziska and Vince Freouf moved to Wyoming to homestead.

Top: Edd and Vincent eating lunch "on the job."

Lower: Edd's log chicken house. He was excited to find an area where wood was plentiful.

they permitted their young girls, Annie and Ella Ziska and Anna and Frances Blackburn, to go to the dance with Edd Ziska.

Five people were a crowd for the buggy which had been constructed for two, but a couple of the girls crowded into the seat with Edd, and the others sat on their laps.

The horses that Edd was driving were newly broken and were a lively pair. Edd often drove spirited horses, for he made extra cash by buying unbroken horses, training them, and reselling them at a profit.

It was the first time that thirteen-year-old Ella had attended a dance without her parents, and in the company of her tall, fun-loving uncle, her beautiful, slender sister, and her merry, laughing friends, she *almost* felt pretty herself.

Ella admired her sister Annie who was intelligent and attractive and tall and dignified. Ella was short, and because of her poor eyesight, had difficulty reading and was inclined to squint. Even though she was not unattractive, she, as is true of most girls in their early teens, did not feel pretty. She once said that she thought of Annie as "the pretty white swan" and of herself as "just a little brown mud hen."

But this night was a time of magic, with her popular uncle whirling her around the dance floor and advising her regarding with whom she might dance. He kept a close eye, and if a man whom he considered unworthy approached her, he winked at her. The wink meant that she was to say that she already had promised the dance, and her uncle would then come to claim her as his partner.

Even though some of the merry group would dance until dawn, as soon as midnight lunch had been served, Edd told his young passengers to prepare to depart, and he went out to hitch the horses to the buggy. Being anxious to get home, the lively team would not stand still long enough for the four girls to get into the vehicle.

Later, Ella said, "The fact that it was a top-buggy made it harder to get in, and there were five of us who needed some time to wiggle around and get settled."

However, Edd had a solution. "If this team doesn't want to stand still, then we'll let them go," he said. "Everyone stand back!"

He loosened the lines, shouted, and snapped his whip. The horses leaped forward. Edd drove them at a fast pace around and around the farmyard; after they had tired a little, he again stopped by the house. This time the horses stood still while the girls got into the buggy.

That night after Edd had put his team away, he slipped off his shoes and trousers and lay down on his usual summer bed, a corn husk mattress in the barn. He hadn't bothered to remove his white shirt.

When Edd's brothers, Fred and Anton, came home, one of them noticed, by a shaft of moonlight that fell across the bed, a gleaming white object there. He assumed it was their cat.

"I thought I had that sneaking cat trained to sleep somewhere else!" he exclaimed. He grabbed a buggy whip and flicked it smartly at the bright spot on the bed.

There was a rattle of husks and a startled howl as Edd, in his white shirt, leaped up.

Luella Olson's Sore Stomach
early 1900's

One day when Luella Olson (later, Mrs. Frank Brady) was a child, she was sent to the field to bring home the calves. She slipped up behind one, grabbed him by the tail, and as she did so, let out a loud whoop. He and all the other calves took off at a fast clip.

"Everything was fine for awhile," she said. "I was working my legs fast to keep up, and we were going home double-quick! Then suddenly the calf kicked me in the stomach and knocked me down.

"I rolled on the ground, groaning and crying, for a long time. Oh, but it did hurt! Finally, I was able to get up and go on home."

No one had seen the incident, and Luella knew that her parents would be cross with her if they learned about it, which prompted her to keep silent.

"I surely did have a sore stomach for some days to come, though," she said.

Valentine Joke
about 1910
told by Elsie Prussa Jungman

One Valentine's Day some of the older boys fixed a pretty box for their teacher, Olive Sturdevant. After opening it, she removed an object which was carefully wrapped in tissue paper and tied with a fancy, red bow. Inside, though, instead of finding a Valentine treat, she discovered a bristly pig's tail which one of the boys had collected on a recent butchering day. Olive laughed and enjoyed the prank along with the pupils.

Later, she became the wife of Dr. Neal McKee.

Two Bad Decisions
1923

It is unfortunate for a boy of ten years to lose his father in death; however, that misfortune is multiplied if he also loses the remainder of his childhood on the same day.

Even though Lark Moore was the eighth child born in the family of thirteen children*, he was the oldest boy at home when, in 1911, his father died. Edgar, at age twenty-two, had already married and had his own farm to tend; Clinton, who was fifth born, died of whooping cough at age three; and the only other brother, Earl, was a small tot and no help at all for some time to come. The other nine children were girls.

It is difficult for those who knew Lark as a friendly, caring adult to realize that, as a child, he had very little chance to develop social skills because he rarely went to school after his father died. Also, even though his descendants point to their trace of Indian ancestry with great pride, when he was young, he felt that it set him apart from other children in the neighborhood. His teen years must have been a lonely time for him, for he passed through them experiencing a succession of long, work-filled days.

When Lark was twenty-two and Earl sixteen, they decided one evening to get into the Model T Ford and visit a neighbor named Ray to collect a threshing debt.

"Oh, that was one debt I often wished afterwards that we'd have just ignored!" said Earl. "Ray was the kind of man who didn't pay a bill unless a fellow went in person to collect, but we'd have done much better to have stayed home that night."

Ray was inclined to be irresponsible and was more interested in banter and horseplay than he was in more serious endeavors. He began to entertain his two guest with accounts of his revelry—accounts which were almost beyond the

---

* The thirteen children of John and Mary Etta Moore were: Edgar Ray, Rosa Eldora, Veva Gertrude, Lilly Azora, Clinton Earl, Ethel Leeora, Zelma Furn, Lark Lester (1901), Eunice Lorene, Hattie Bell, Hazel Orcelia, Earl Elsworth, Edith Wilma.

comprehension of the two listeners who had grown up thinking only of the serious tasks at hand.

"We should have been alerted by his sudden friendliness," said Earl. "He had never bothered to pay us much heed before. But his conversation *was* entertaining. We couldn't imagine ourselves involved in the kinds of practical jokes and general clowning around that he was telling about."

Finally Ray said that he and some of his friends had a hankering to go on a watermelon hunt.

"There's a big patch of huge melons in Steve Carver's cornfield," said Ray. "We'd have good picking there. Trouble is, we don't have any way to get out there. Since you fellows have a car, how about joining the fun?"

"Why, we know Carver," said Lark. "He'd *give* us melons if we asked him. We wouldn't need to sneak into his patch to *steal* them."

"You're missin' the whole point. It's no fun if you just *ask*. Where's your sense of adventure?"

"Well, it just isn't right," said Earl.

"It's not that wrong, either," said Ray. "After all, Lark just said that he'd give them to us if we asked. It's all just for kicks. All we need from you is a ride to the field and back. You don't even have to get out of your car. Just leave the melon-hunting to us."

Finally, Lark made the first bad decision of the evening. He agreed to provide transportation, and off they rumbled in the little Model T to pick up Ray's friends.

Some time later, six jolly fellows, tightly packed into the tiny car, lumbered up to the cornfield which surrounded the melon patch. Lark stopped on the dead-end trail to unload his passengers. After four of them spilled out, Lark and the youngest of the group, fourteen-year-old Wilbur Jennings, drove to the edge of the field, turned around, and stopped.

Each person in the patch had chosen a bulging melon, had deposited it by the roadside, and had returned to select a second one.

"Hyah, there!" Carver's angry voice split the night air. "Get out of here!"

The melon swipers ran down the corn rows until they came to the car.

"Now what? We're trapped!" whispered one of them as they crowded into the little Ford.

"Since there is no other way out of here, I guess we'll

have to go back and listen to one of Carver's wild cussings," said Lark, wishing secretly that he had chosen to go home to bed instead of coming here to experience one of Ray's less-wise adventures. He continued speaking, "That old fellow knows every cuss word invented, and we're probably going to hear them all more times than once tonight." He turned the car and headed back.

As they approached the man standing in the road, Lark slowed the vehicle, intending to stop. Then the dim lights of the Model T reflected on the barrel of a shotgun which Carver raised to point in their direction.

Startled, and forced into an instantaneous decision, Lark most probably made the wrong choice a second time that evening: he hit the throttle lever, and the car bucked a little and lurched foreword. He passed the man in the trail road and picked up speed—but do remember, the speed of a Model T was no more than a labored crawl.

The occupants of the back seat were able to scoot down, but the three in front were more crowded and they remained upright.

Ker Wham!

The earth-shaking blast sent forth a burst of buckshot that cut through the top of Earl's arm which lay across the back of the seat and struck the boy Wilbur at the base of the neck. The lad's body sagged. The second explosion of the gun blew Earl's arm off the top of the seat.

Wilbur, though unconscious from the moment he was hit, did not die until three o'clock the next day. By that time a crowd had gathered and was waiting to hear news of the boy's condition. Some of Carver's friends, fearful that the mob might attack him, picked him up and took him to the sheriff's office.

The deep ragged hole in Earl's arm was slow to heal, but after a couple of weeks in the hospital, he was allowed to go home. His days of inactivity were difficult for him because he had nothing to do except berate himself for getting involved in an embarrassing action which had gone further awry and had snuffed out the life of a neighboring boy. As bad as his wounds hurt, they were less painful than the pangs of guilt he suffered.

Lark, too, was overwhelmed with self-accusations. Being older than Earl, he felt he should have been more responsible than to have consented to a foolish and illegal prank. He knew that his brother's injuries and the death of another lad would haunt him for the the remainder of his life. His daughter

Marva reported that he rarely spoke of the incident, but that when he did, it was with deep remorse.

Now, in his old age, Earl still carries a rough scar over the hole chewed in his arm, and also he can locate a number of scattered buckshot which continue to reside in the flesh of his upper body.

The boys were called to testify during Carver's trial. The first two on the stand, Ray and a young man named Cox, both claimed not to have been on the melon hunt. However, Carver's lawyer was able to discredit their testimony.

Lark, Earl and John Kyle answered the questions about their involvement honestly. However, neither of the lawyers asked them about Ray and Cox, and they were spared the necessity of saying anything about them.

Because the youths had been molesting his property, Carver was deemed not guilty. Soon afterward, he sold his farm and moved away.

The Colt in the Tornado
about 1911
as told by Mae Sypherd

This story definitely has the flavor of a tall tale, but everyone knows tornadoes are unpredictable. It is related here by a person* who experienced the tornado and believed every word she spoke.

"While I was visitin' my cousin, Rosie Ziska, in Fairfax, South Dakota, she and I were walking to the post office to mail a letter to my folks in Atkinson. Shortly before we got to the post office, we came to a place where the Red Cross was having a sale of donated items. We were lookin' at the different things at the sale when the wind came up. It began to blow the merchandise, and papers and cloth articles were flying everywhere.

"We saw the cloud as we ran for the Post Office. It was big and black and shaped like a long pipe with the stem hangin' down—like a big bed spring with the narrow end at the bottom. The whole thing was rolling.

"Just before we got to the door of the post office, a clerk

---

* Matilda Mae (Ziska) Sypherd, daughter of Joe and Antonia Ziska, was about thirteen years old at the time of this incident.

grabbed us and hiked us into the back room where they sort mail. About the same time, there was a huge crash as the big glass windows and the door broke.

"The noise of the storm was terrible—louder than a freight train. Hailstones the size of apples were hittin' the roof just as if someone were beating it with baseball bats. We girls clung to each other in fright—cryin' and prayin' for safety.

"When the storm was over, the postal clerk walked us home, and we saw that a corner of Uncle Anton's house had been ripped off. A big steel tank had blown several miles, hit the house, and rolled on. The family was in the building, but no one was injured.

"Someone's piano was blown out of their house and was set down unhurt in the ball park.

"Mrs. Hagadorn was sittin' in her rocking chair in her home in Bonesteel, South Dakota. The tornado whisked the roof off and sucked her up into the air, chair and all. She hung onto the chair and had a smooth but scary ride. The thing that terrified her the most was the fact that there was a black colt whirlin' around just ahead of her. He was sittin' on his haunches and she thought that if he moved backward any more than he was, he might knock her down out of the sky. She couldn't see anything below her—it was like she was in fog or smoke; she had no idea how high she was.

"The storm set her down unhurt in a pasture near Fairfax. Later, her daughter married my cousin, Ed Ziska—Uncle Anton's boy.*

"Uncle Anton had a huge Grandpa cup—much larger than an ordinary cup. He tried to put one of the big hailstones into it, but it just sat on top—it was too large to go into that giant cup."

---

* Ed Ziska was a nephew of Edd Ziska, for Anton and Edd were brothers.

Side-hitch Hay Sweep

Chapter 9
Laughter and Tears

V.J's Homestead
about 1909

Vencil (V.J..) was the only one of the second generation of Krysls to use his homestead rights. The Kinkaid Law allowed a settler in the more arid parts of the country to have a section of land instead of a quarter section. When the law came into effect, Vaclav and his father Albert each "took out papers" on three additional quarters. By that time, Holt County land had been settled except for the Sandhill area, some of which bounded the Krysl land.

Albert was advanced in years and in poor health, but it was his plan to hold the land until his eldest grandson, V.J., would be "of age" and eligible to homestead. As soon as V.J. was twenty-one (Sept. 22, 1909) Albert relinquished the three quarters. He died the following March.

V.J. built a one-room cabin on the quarter that was west of Vaclav's place, and because occupancy was a requirement for "proving up" on his land, slept in it each night. The winter before he married, he built an upstairs over this room and also built on a lean-to kitchen.

After his marriage, he and Anna continued to live on the homestead until the required five years had passed. Then Frank Kaup (father to a large family, including Paul, Bernard, Aloys, and Bill) moved from his land (which later became the home site of the Karo Ranch) and arranged for V.J. to occupy it. V.J. cared for the Kaup cattle in return for a share of the calves.

After a couple more years, V.J. traded his two north Kinkaid quarters to his father in return for the more productive quarter which became the home site of the V.J. Krysl Ranch. They moved the house from the homestead onto their new land and began living there about 1915.

Now in 1992, Bill Krysl (V.J.'s youngest son) and wife Theresa occupy the ranch. The tall center part of their home is the original house from the homestead.

Henry Krobot's Bone Orchestra
May 9, 1911

Henry Krobot was usually a quiet man, but when he was in the midst of a large celebration, he was transformed into a lively, fun-loving fellow.

At the wedding celebration of V.J. Krysl and Anna Hytrek, he collected bones from the kitchen and announced to the men in the dining room that, in order to provide after-dinner music, he was organizing an orchestra. He passed a bone to each person, and as he did so, told what instrument the bone represented and assigned a sound for it (such as whang, whang; toot, toot; hum, hum; or beep, beep.) These sounds were to be vocalized in unison to imitate an orchestra.

Standing in front of the group, he announced the name of the song to be played, raised his director's stick (a hip bone from a large ham), and shouted, "Hup! Hup! Hup!" as a signal for the music to begin.

To the delight of the other guests, the orchestra entertained merrily for some time.

Frank Crane, Fiddler

Albert Krysl told (in the loud voice and Czech accent that was typical of that family) of his early interest in the violin. He was ten years old when he heard the able, old-time fiddler, Frank Crane, play at V.J. and Anna Krysl's wedding dance. As an old man, Albert said of Frank Crane:

"That old boy could really saw out a tune! His son Harry played the fiddle, too, and his girls played the organ.

"But, oh-h-h—that old devil! Ah-h-h—that Old Man

---

* John Krobot, who married V.J.'s sister Christina, was a son of Henry Krobot. John and Christina's children: Joe, Mary (Hytrek), Rosie (Wedige) (Humpal), Hattie, Frank, Johanna (Skrdla), and Albert.

Crane! I could watch him all night. I said to myself, 'Someday I'm going to do that, too.' He could fiddle in them flats, and oh—did that sound good! He'd fiddle and beller out a square dance at the same time. I tell you, he was sumthin'! After listenin' to him, I got the tunes in my mind, and I went to work. Annie [V.J.'s new wife] helped me over the rough spots. I bought my first fiddle from Old Westrom for seven dollars and fifty cents. I bar-reed the money from Kate [his sister-in-law Catherine]."

As a small child, Sister Theophane Hytrek also was impressed with Frank Crane's music. After she became a noted organist and composer, she once commented:

"I remember the first time I heard Mr. Crane play his violin. When I was a small tot, we were at John Miksch's where they were going to have a dance in their big front room. All of a sudden, Mr. Crane came in and started to fiddle. I was so excited by the sound that I could feel the thrill of it all over—even in my feet. I had never heard anything so wonderful—I can't even explain it. When people noticed how I responded to the music, they began watching me. After I became aware of their attention, I got self-conscious and restrained myself."

A Thief at the Wedding

A certain talkative fellow and his son came to the V.J. Krysl wedding celebration. While the man was in the house partaking of the wedding meal, he commanded the attention of the other guests with his unusual tales and comical jokes. In the meantime, his son slipped between the parked buggies and wagons and gathered a number of useful items, such as ropes, buggy whips, lanterns, tools, and lap robes. These he moved to his father's wagon.

Other youngsters (among them, V.J.'s younger brothers) were playing various games of "run, chase, laugh, and holler", and they discovered what the boy was doing. They confronted the culprit, and threatening him with a buggy whip, forced him to return the stolen articles to the correct vehicles. Fortunately, he was wearing a heavy coat with a sheepskin lining which provided him with some protection, for as you might imagine, the commands were accented with a few snaps of the whip.

When the young do-gooders were satisfied that all the pilfered items had been returned, they wrestled the frightened fellow to the ground. Upon unbuttoning his coat, they discovered that he was shirtless. They scooped sand onto his bare stomach and into the woolly lining of his coat.

At the time that V.J. and Anna were married, Bill Hoffman had recently arrived in the valley, and since he wasn't acquainted in the neighborhood, he didn't attend the celebration. The next morning the sun was shining and Bill was working in the field when the Conrad Vinzenz family rumbled by in their wagon—going home from the wedding dance. Bill thought it unusual that people in this part of the country danced all night.

A Determined Wedding Guest
as told by Josie Ziska Noziska

Anna and I had been friends since we were girls, and oh, how I wanted to go to her wedding! Since the folks weren't planning to go, Dad finally said that if I cared to ride our old bay horse Cherv (Cherv is short for *Cerveny*, which means *red* in the Czech language), I could go.

I packed my best clothes in folds of paper and put them in a box which I tied behind the saddle. Then starting long before dawn, I rode to Aunt Barbara Hunt's house in Stuart—I suppose it was about seven and a half miles—where I changed clothes. From there, I walked to church. The wedding was probably at eight o'clock in the morning, but I was there in plenty of time.

Anna's brother, Stencil Hytrek, married Mary Miksch on the same day, May 9, 1911, making it a double wedding.

After the wedding the Paul Hytreks invited me to ride with them to the reception. We tied Cherv on behind their buggy and drove to the Hytrek place which was about ten miles southwest of Stuart. It was noon when we got there.

And, oh, the food! I'd been up since about 2:30, and I hadn't taken time to eat much. The sight of all those goodies made my stomach churn. There were beef and pork roasts, home-cured ham, and big juicy meatballs. The upstairs bedrooms had temporary shelves made from planks and wooden blocks, and they were covered with pies, cakes, and *kolace* (fruit-filled rolls). (In Czech, the e added to *kolac* forms the plural.)

Meals were served all day, but in the evening the tables were taken down and the dancing began. Mr. Crane's fiddle kept our feet going all night. I didn't even mind that I got blisters on my heels!

The next morning I rode Cherv home. I was so tired I almost fell asleep on the horse. There was a lot of work waiting at home, but Mother let me go to bed for a few hours.

Anna's sister, Stella Dlugosh, lived near us and when Anna was about fourteen, she came to help Stella with a new baby. We got acquainted then, and have been friends all our lives.

A Second Celebration
May 14, 1911

"When V.J. saw the Frank Kaup family drive into the yard in what we called a motorized buggy, he was wild with excitement," said Anna Krysl, years later. "He asked Frank if he could try driving it, and when Frank said he could, V.J.. got in and started asking questions about the levers. There wasn't much to a car in those days. No top. No sides. It looked about like a buggy with no tongue.

"V.J. didn't see another thing all afternoon. When other guests arrived with their teams and buggies, it was my brothers who met them and helped them take care of their horses. V.J., being just *crazy* to drive that car, was too excited and too busy!"

The occasion was a post-wedding party on the Sunday following the Krysl-Hytrek nuptials. It was customary to have the wedding and the main celebration on a Tuesday, but on the following Sunday the newlyweds hosted a second gathering at their home. At this time, neighbors and friends came to feast on left-over food and drinks.

V.J., of course, hadn't had any experience with steering a wheeled vehicle, and his long arms were all elbows as he struggled to control the little car. So as not to frighten the horses of approaching guests, he rumbled around the pasture, his ever-faithful dog trotting behind. Later, when he returned to the yard, he ran into a gatepost, but luckily, no damage was done.

(The picture on page 7 of Stuart Centennial 1884-1984 was taken that Sunday at V.J.'s homestead.)

Feather Stripping

When V.J. and Anna visited the elder Krysls, the men played cards, slapping the table with their jacks and jokers and laughing uproariously. Anna loved to play cards, but she was never invited into the game. Rather, she was expected to sit at a small side-table with her mother-in-law and help with the usual

V. J., being just crazy to drive that ca

as too excited to play host to his guests.

Top: Hytrek home. Anna Hytrek/V.J. Krysl and Stencil Hytrek/Mary Miksch weddings.

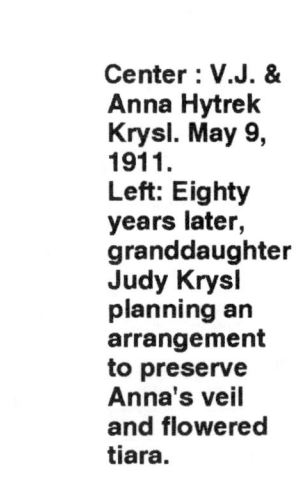

Center: V.J. & Anna Hytrek Krysl. May 9, 1911.
Left: Eighty years later, granddaughter Judy Krysl planning an arrangement to preserve Anna's veil and flowered tiara.

Above: Four generation picture. Anna Hytrek Krysl, her son Don, grandson Don Jr., great grandchildren Stephanie and Robert. 1982. The newness of the settlement of the Nebraska prairie is obvious by the fact that the only missing generation in the picture is that of Gregor and Johanna Hytrek.

Right: Don Sr.'s elder son Vincent with tiny daughter Adrienne. 1983. (This is a photo of a pastel drawing by Judy Krysl.)

after-supper task of stripping feathers. In Anna's estimation, this boring and endless activity did nothing to enhance the visit.

Anna was further incensed because the hilarity of the men's game made the stripping work even more tedious, for any slight air current would scatter the feathers. The fluff from the feathers was used for quilts and pillows. Most pioneers had large families, and it required a mountain of bedding to keep everyone warm on winter nights when the water bucket froze and snow sifted in on window sills, floor, and sleeping figures.

The downy feathers on the breast of a water fowl need not be stripped since they have soft spines. However, on other feathers, the fern-like sides must be pulled off the quill, making it possible to discard the coarse, sharp quills which would pierce the ticking as well as mar the softness of the pillow or quilt.

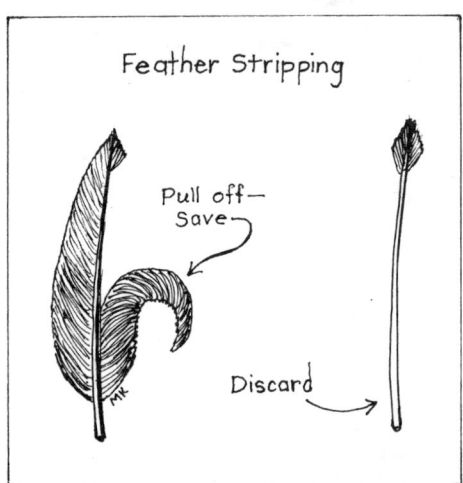

Feathers must be stripped from the tip down. When done correctly, the fluff pulls off as easily as the peeling from a banana. Stripping requires two motions per feather: one on either side. (Only waterfowl feathers were stripped because most feathers from land birds do not strip easily.)

A result of the pioneer's need for feathers was the cruel practice of plucking domestic ducks and geese twice. Soon after the young birds feathered out, they were caught and held down while the softer feathers on their undersides were plucked. After the feathers had grown again, the fowl were killed to provide food, and were, of course, plucked a second time.

When Ella Ziska's mother set the children at feather-stripping, she inverted a cup on the table in front of each child. The hard-to-confine bits of fluff pulled from the spines were slid underneath the cup. Ella said that no matter how hard they tried, never did they get the cups packed full to the point where no more feathers could be poked underneath.

Back to Cowchips
1911-12

Anna reported that the first years of their marriage were marked by poverty. One of their greatest shortages was fuel. At her parent's home, the family had graduated from the dismaying but necessary practice of burning cow chips (dried cow dung), for the groves they had planted now supplied firewood, and their fields yielded corn cobs. Anna's new Sandhill home, however, had neither grove nor cornfield which meant that she was again reduced to picking cow chips and making hay twists.

She walked about the pasture, selecting the chips that were dry enough and stacking them into piles. She used a stick to flip any half-moist chips so that they could sun-bake on the other side. Periodically, she drove a wagon pulled by a team of mules and picked up the piles of dry chips.

Sometimes V.J. brought slough grass from the low spots on his dad's land. Anna twisted the hay, folded it, and tied the ends with some of the longer strands. She then had a braid-like block of hay which was locally called "kran-soof-key." (The r was rolled.) Anna could not literally translate the word (or phrase) and did not know whether it originated from the language of the Poles, Germans, or Czechs. In English, the twisted blocks of dried grass were called hay twists. They burned much faster than wood, but not as fast as loose hay.

Lantern Light

When a man was working late so that he arrived home after dark, his wife usually came out with a lighted lantern to help him unhitch the horses.

The first year that Anna and V.J. were married, they had only ten cows to feed. V.J. baled the remainder of their hay and hauled it to town, using a four-horse team. Such a load pulled hard, and the going was slow. Even though he started before dawn, it was late in the night when he returned home.

Frequently, Anna went outside to listen, and when she heard the jingle of the harnesses, she lit the lantern.

Irene (Mayo) Teter
early 1900's in southwestern Nebraska

John Mayo lived on a farm near Medicine Creek. His daughter Irene (grandmother to Shirley Teter Krysl) loved horses. When she was small she was forbidden to go into the barn because her parents were afraid she might get kicked by one of the animals. However, she sometimes sneaked into the building to pet one of the tame riding horses that was stabled there. Occasionally, she climbed onto his back.

It was a happy day for the child when her parents decided she was old enough to ride, for thereafter she spent many delightful afternoons on the back of a horse.

Most of the Mayo children (there were two girls and five boys) terminated their education at the end of the eighth grade; however, Irene and her brother Harvey were exceptions. They and a neighbor girl, Eunice Johnson, "batched" in Cambridge in order to be able to attend high school.

After Harvey graduated in 1914, Irene worked for a family before and after school in return for the opportunity to live with them while she continued her high school education.

She graduated in 1916 and taught school in country districts for three years after which she married Earl Teter.

Washout
about 1913

One dark night, Freddie, Annie, and Ella Ziska rumbled along the trail road in a buggy on the way to a dance at Kubics. Water was high from spring rains, and this particular road was not familiar to them. As they trotted up to the bridge south of Slaymakers, the horses, Dick and Seal, suddenly leaped forward, and almost immediately the buggy lurched sharply.

When Freddie halted the team and got out to investigate, he found a foot-wide washout along the bridge. If the horses would have stepped into it, they surely would have broken their legs, but they had sensed its presence in time to leap it.

The other guests, aware of the washout, did not use the bridge. Instead, they drove down into the ditch and urged their horses across the sloughs and the fast-running stream.

You may be sure that on the return trip the Ziskas also abandoned the road and drove through the flooded stream rather than crossing the bridge.

(Forty-four years later, Ella's grandson, Donald Krysl Jr., was born in a speeding Ford as it crossed the bridge over that same stream.)

Rattlesnakes in Wyoming
1914

People tended to follow the rivers when laying out towns and choosing land on which to homestead. After occupying areas along the Missouri river, the settlers then spilled down the Platte, the Niobrara, and the Elkhorn.

By the early 1900's, most of the tillable ground in Nebraska had been homesteaded, and the sons of the pioneers were apt to move west to Wyoming or north to the Dakotas or even to Canada to find available land.

Among those who moved to the Glendo (Wyoming) area were the Paul Hytrek family (Anna's brother); the Bill Hytrek family (Anna's cousin); and Edd Ziska and his nephew, Vincent Freouf. Edd and Vincent left Nebraska about 1914.

George Hytrek, Paul's oldest son, reported that there were great numbers of rattlesnakes in Wyoming when he was a boy. They were especially thick through the 1920's and were still a constant nuisance in the '30's. However, the settlers waged a relentless war on them, and by the 1940's, their numbers had been greatly reduced.

"One of our neighbors had a steer who got snake-bit on the nose," said George. "His face and neck swelled up until he couldn't breathe, and he suffocated.

"Another neighbor killed so many snakes that he had a cigar box full of rattles."

The usual place for an animal to be bitten was on the legs, and if the bite didn't hit a vein, the critter most often survived.

"I think," said George, "that the severe swelling of the limb cut off the circulation to a point where the flow of poison to other parts of the body was slowed. Thus, the critter could fight it off."

The Hytrek dog, a beautiful collie, was struck four or five different times.

"He would swell up and get feverish," said George. "He'd lay in the cool mud by the water tank for a week or so, and recuperate.

"The day came, though, when he was struck one too many times. He was chasing a coyote, and leaped over a badger hole where a snake was hiding. The snake bit him on the underside. He came running home, wild with pain, and split the screen in the door as he dived through it.

"I immediately slashed the wound but couldn't get it to bleed. It was just as if the blood in that area was curdled. I could tell by the fang marks that it was a huge snake, and undoubtedly it had a lot of venom. That poor dog was just frantic with pain.

"He died after about twelve hours."

One day in 1985 when V.J.'s daughter-in-law was traveling in Wyoming, she happened to come to Glendo. She stopped at a service station. After the station attendant had serviced her car, she said:

"Almost seventy years ago my mother-in-law's cousin named Bill Hytrek moved here and I think the family still lives in the area. Do you know anyone named Hytrek?"

He looked at her a few moments, a bemused smile on his face. Finally, he answered, "I'm Cal Hytrek, my dad is Bill Hytrek, and my granddad was Old Bill." He put out his hand. "Hello," he said. "Who are you?"

(The wife of the elder Bill Hytrek was V.J. Krysl's sister, Annie.)

Moving a House
1915

"It was something to see: all those horses leaning into the harnesses and scratching the ground for footing and the men yelling and the dogs barking and the house a-shuttering and a-creaking. It about stopped your heart to watch." --Rose Hoffman

It took twenty-six head of horses, seven wagons, three days, and three kegs of beer to move V.J. Krysl's house from his Kinkaid Homestead to the site where he raised his family. The move was less than a mile, but the wagon wheels cut into the sand, and the horses could move the heavy load only a few yards at a time after which they needed to be rested. These frequent rest stops provided opportunity for any of the men who were so inclined to partake of the contents of the keg which, packed in wet gunny sacks, occupied the foremost wagon. This wagon, well out in front, was not attached to the house. In addition to carrying supplies and tools, it also, when there was a turn to be made or a knoll to ascend, became the director's stand.

Every half hour or so, V.J.'s youngest brother John was sent to the nearest water well to get a fresh bucket of water to pour over the gunny sacks that surrounded the beer. These treks kept the nine-year-old breathless even though he was a sturdy lad. Sometimes during brief periods of rest between trips to the well, he slipped unseen into the house and pretended to be a king whose castle was being transported by his loyal subjects.

Vaclav and all his sons had voices that rolled like thunder, but V.J. could out-shout them all. In his attempt to synchronize the efforts of the many men and teams, he stood in the back of the lead wagon and directed with long-armed gestures and booming voice. During times of movement, the intense hubbub of activity rolled over the usually quiet prairie, setting every heart pounding.

When the signal was given, men's voices exploded, the long leather lines cracked against horses' rumps, chains rattled, and leather creaked. Some drivers confined themselves to such phrases as "Giddap, there!" and "Hi-yah!" while others rolled out phrases in Bohemian, Polish, or German. Dogs barked, children shouted, women called warnings to the youngsters lest they venture too close, 104 firmly planted horse's hooves vibrated the earth, and the house groaned as the wagons labored over uneven ground. Above it all, V.J.'s explosive voice offered encouragement and instruction.

Standing unnoticed on the threshold of the shuddering house, the boy John pretended that *he* was the master of this great operation. His thinner voice could not be heard above the general discord, and he was free to shout his grand and lordly directions to the scores of horses and men involved in the operation.

After three days, the house was squatting like a mother hen over its new location, the beer kegs were empty, and the horde of willing helpers had evaporated—all of them, that is, except the boy, John. He, excited to have kinfolk living a mere half-mile away, returned daily to help V.J., Anna, and three-year-old Leo settle into the shell of a house—a house which to his wonder, was still propped up on stilts.

The plaster and lath had been removed from the interior of the building to lighten it for moving. The kitchen lean-to had been separated from the rest of the house and had been transported earlier. It now sat a short distance from the new home site and had become the chicken house. (Later, when V.J. had saved enough money to buy one of those wonderful, modern machines, a Model T Ford car, it became a garage.) Anna would now cook in a corner of the living area of the main house until the time when they could add on a new kitchen.

V.J., ever one to do a thorough job, decided that their home should have, for insulating purposes, two thicknesses of lath and plaster with dead air space between. The first layer would be installed *between* the rafters, and the second, which would form the inside wall, would be installed in the usual way. (This process of placing an extra layer of lath and plaster between the rafters was called "back plastering.")

Now while V.J. constructed new corrals, Anna spent every spare moment sawing lath and tacking it between the two-by-fours.

The Bull Snake
1915

"For a long time after that I couldn't stand to look a snake in the face—those stekly smart-mouthed, hissin' varmints!" — *John Krysl, many years later. Stekly, here spelled phonetically, is a foreign word meaning angry.*

One day soon after the move, Anna planned to go to the slough north of their place to make hay twists to use as fuel for heating and cooking. During the first two years of their marriage, Anna had reluctantly reverted to collecting and burning cow chips because their Kinkaid Homestead had no trees. The next two years they had lived on the Kaup Place where she enjoyed the luxury of having firewood to burn. Now, this new quarter was as yet barren of trees and since Anna did not want to *again* go back to burning cow chips, she worked relentlessly to harvest and twist the long, coarse grass from the nearby slough. Also, they now had some corncobs for fuel, as they had raised a small field of corn on the Kaup Place.

On this particular day, Anna had another problem. She

wished to mix and roll out some noodles so that they would be dry and ready for cutting when she and the children (Leo and John) returned from the slough. However, she was short of eggs because the hens, disturbed by the move to new quarters, had cut back on egg production.

She was aware that one wayward hen had made a nest under the house which was still propped up on beams. She herself could not wiggle into the narrow space, but when nine-year-old John arrived, she sent him in search of the hidden nest.

John crawled under the beams and lying flat on the ground, slithered toward the spot where Anna directed. Finally arriving, he lifted his hand.

"Yow!" The boy's scream was both loud and full of terror.

A huge bull snake, which was coiled possessively around the nest, had flung up its head and had hissed menacingly. John jerked back, whacking his head sharply on a beam. Hurriedly, he wiggled out of the narrow space.

That noon the Krysl family had dumplings instead of noodles while a short distance below, the bull snake dined sumptuously on a nestful of smooth, white eggs.

A Trick on Dad
about 1915

When Vaclav Krysl's first telephone was installed, he requested that it be placed high on the wall.

"There is no sense in having it down where the grandkids can reach the cord that dangles from the receiver," he said.

One day Vaclav, standing on tiptoe, was talking on the telephone. His son John took some bits of coal from the coal bucket and slid them under his father's raised heels. When Vaclav finished his conversation, he lowered his heels, and the coal crackled and popped.

"He didn't get mad," said John later, "But he didn't laugh, either. We could always tell when he was mad because his *caniri* stuck out!"

"*Caniri?*"

"Yeah. *Caniri* is *mustache* in Bohemian."

Anna Krysl with tots (Amelia & Josephine) and sisters-in-law (Agnes & Mary) on the horse-powered well rig.

Don Krysl's 1960 well machine.

Don and nephew Tom testing Don's new, self-designed well machine.

The Well Machine
1916

Shortly after the Krysls moved to their permanent home, V.J. and Vaclav bought a horse-powered well-drilling machine from Charlie Ammon, each of them paying sixty dollars. This implement was pulled to the well site by four head of horses. Upon arrival, the horses were hitched to the end of the rod that, when turned, furnished power to operate the water pumps. The horses walked single file in a circle, and each time one of them came to the spinning rod (the tumbling rod), he stepped over it.

After about a year, V.J. bought an engine for $125.00, and it supplied the power to operate the pumps. However, he continued to use horses to pull the machine from farm to farm until the time (probably 1928 or 1930) when he purchased a Regular Farmall tractor.

In 1937, V.J. rode to Sioux City, Iowa, with Herman Schneider, a trucker, and bought a 1934 V-8 truck for $170.00. After Ed and Joe Schneider brought it to Stuart for him, he mounted the well machine on it and christened it Old Herman.

Old Herman transported the well machine around the countryside until V.J. died in 1951. After that time, V.J.'s son Don took over the well business.

Quarrel in the Pig Shed

Eleven-year-old John Krysl was helping his older brother Ed clean the pig sheds when an argument erupted.

"Be careful with that pitchfork. You almost stabbed me," said Ed crossly.

"I did not! I didn't come within a foot of you."

"A foot? It was more like an inch. If I wouldn't have dodged back, you'd have got me right in the leg!"

The argument went on until the boys lost their tempers. When John picked up a handful of manure and drew back his arm, Ed ran. John pursued him which prompted Ed to race for the house. Just as he opened the door to bound inside, John hurled his handful of ammunition.

You guessed it! It missed Ed and sailed into the kitchen.

Ed was sent back to clean the pig shed, and John was set to work cleaning the house.

(In adulthood, Ed became the father of Kenneth and Melvin; and John the father of Ilene, Ray, and Larry.)

Breaking a Team of Horses
1915

> *"I can see Joe standing in the buggy and yelling yet. He had a hard time getting those horses quieted. Gosh! Don't write this down! If Joe reads it, he'll stomp all over me." -- Jim Ziska, fifty-two years later.*

Joe Dobrovolny was breaking a work horse named Chub, and had him teamed up with Old Bill, a well-trained horse. A few weeks before, Joe had broken another horse, Lucy, who by now was able to step along with Old Bill quite nicely.

It was Sunday, and Joe decided he would combine horse training with a visit to his girlfriend, Annie Ziska, who was in ill health. He hitched Old Bill and Chub to the buggy, and then, in order to also give Lucy some road practice, he tied her to the other side of Old Bill. The sight of this irregular, three-horse team was signal enough to other drivers of wagons or buggies along the way, and they all pulled their teams to the side in order to give the entire trail to Joe, this action being a common courtesy to a fellow traveler who was breaking a horse.

The distance from Joe's place, where he batched in a little cabin, to the Ziska place was about ten miles, but since he held the untrained team to a walk, it took a considerable amount of time to get there. His thoughts were on the tall, stately Annie to whom he was engaged to be married. His mind froze when he thought of her illness. She had tuberculosis of the lungs, and even though she had been treated by many different physicians, her condition was obviously worsening.

In the spring it was thought that she had been cured and a wedding date had been set. Then she had contracted the measles and was so weakened that the wedding had to be postponed. Joe wondered how she would be this day.

As he neared the Ziska grove, he centered his attention on the problem of turning the half-trained team into the driveway which was just beyond the orchard. Then suddenly, Annie's younger brother Jim, riding an old, tall bicycle that another brother, Freddie, had found in the junk pile of an abandoned homestead, came careening out of the driveway. When the boy saw Joe, he slowed the clumsy machine and swung into the orchard. However, it was too late.

In those days, a team was spooked by anything that moved without the assistance of horses. Lucy and Chub reared, breaking the buggy tongue. The portion of the tongue that was still attached to the buggy jammed into the ground, bringing the light vehicle to an abrupt halt. The two young horses were jerking sideways, trying to run. The traces were still hooked to the stalled buggy, and there was enough horsepower involved to really tear things up. Luckily, Old Bill did his best to hold steady while the other horses reared and plunged. Finally, Joe managed to quiet the team. Young Jim had the good sense to busy himself in the orchard for the next hour or two, giving Joe time to rise above his anger.

The Bereaved Bridegroom
1915

Everyone who was asked to comment about Annie was sure to mention that she was an especially kind young lady and was a diligent worker.

"She was like me in one way—she loved to dance," said Mary Balloon. "She was somewhat of a quiet person, but not shy. It was just that she had nice manners. And when she started going with Joe, everyone was pleased. Up to that time, she had never gone with anyone. One of the Dickaus wanted to go with her—and one of the Dierks boys. But I think as long as Joe stayed single, she was waiting for him."

Mary may have been right. When Joe, at age fifteen, first worked for the Ziskas, Annie was a child of about five and Ella was a baby. Ever after that, the girls were delighted to see Joe. On his trips home from Wyoming and South Dakota, he usually stopped at the Ziska farm. His tales of the open range most assuredly could be counted upon to impress the young girls.

"Annie always did like him," said Ella, "and we both thought he was the handsomest man in the south country."

May Sypherd said, "Annie was a lovely girl—so pleasant and happy. We all thought she and Joe were the perfect couple."

Ann Brooke said, "I saw them at a church dinner. Joe had such good manners. Almost all men lent their hand when a lady got into a buggy, but Joe handed Annie up with such grace! He was so courteous—so chivalrous. People remarked about it."

At first, Annie's pallor was overlooked—or if noticed, it was considered an aspect of delicate beauty. But when she became weary and faint in the middle of a task or when she preferred to watch the dancers instead of participate because it

both wearied her and quickened her persistent cough, her parents realized that something was seriously amiss. They called a doctor whose diagnosis was a shocking one: she had tuberculosis of the lungs or consumption.

Wedding plans were put on hold. Unwilling to accept the grim prognosis, Annie's parents and the determined Joe investigated advertised claims of cures, and Annie was sent on the train for treatment in several different medical establishments.

She seemed better when she came home (in the early spring of 1915) until the time when she got the measles. After that, she grew more and more wan.

Joe visited her often, and sent her letters and postcards between visits. He gave her one of those amazing, new machines, a phonograph, to help entertain her during her forced idleness. By late summer she was bedfast, and Joe knew that she would not survive the illness.

On November first, Mary left Annie in Ella's care while she went to the aid of a neighbor. Riding in a horse-drawn buggy driven by her son Freddie, she hurried to the Frank Dobrovolny home where she delivered Maggie's fifth child, a boy named Jay.

A couple of weeks later, Annie became violently ill. The doctor, summoned by telephone, drove out with a team and buggy.

After examining her, the doctor shook his head. "There's nothing more I can do," he said. "You'd better send for Joe."

They telephoned the Tom Dobrovolnys, and Fred carried the message by horseback to his brother Joe. Joe mounted Lucy, a horse broken to the saddle as well as to the harness, and rode the ten miles to the Ziska farm. He arrived minutes after Annie died.

"It was the saddest funeral I ever attended," said Mary (Dobias) Ratliff. "It was just unbelievable! Annie was dressed in white. Joe walked with the family and all of them were stricken with grief. Ella had cried until she had lost her voice, and she actually fainted in the cemetery.

"Everyone in the neighborhood had been pleased about the coming wedding—and now this."

Jim, the youngest member of the Ziska family, made these comments:

"Annie died in 'fifteen. Since I was born in 'oh-one, I was fourteen at the time. Some years later when I was in my early twenties, Doc McKee tried to send me to Arizona. He said my lungs weren't the best and I would get consumption, just like Annie did.

"'If you stay around here,' he told me, 'you'll be dead within the next ten years.'

"Shucks! In ten years I was far from dead. In fact, I could have gone into his office and could have tossed him out the window—probably with one hand."

Joe and Ella
1917

During the months following Annie's death, Joe continued to stop at Ziskas. Since he, as yet, had only a few cattle, he, using a four-horse team and a wagon, hauled load after load of baled hay from his ranch to Atkinson. The distance was too great for him to make the round trip in one day, and the Ziska farm was a handy place to stop overnight.

After the year of formal mourning, Joe and Ella put aside their qualms about the fourteen-year difference in their ages, and began "keeping company." It was not a long engagement, and again the Ziskas began planning a wedding. It was best to have a celebration during cool weather as there was, of course, no refrigeration. The date was set for the eighteenth of April.

From National Bellas Hess, a mail order house, Ella sent for a pale blue wedding dress with a white lace overskirt and a veil. This wedding ensemble cost ten dollars. Freddie, being the one with the neatest handwriting, wrote stacks of formal invitations. Days in advance, thinly rolled noodles could be seen drying on a line that was hung above the stove.

They butchered two pigs and a beef. The pork hams were placed in stone jars full of salt brine in preparation for smoking while the beef was cut mainly into roasts. At wedding dinners, it was customary to serve noodle soup as a first course. To make the soup stock, fifteen chickens and ten geese were cooked in a boiler ordinarily used to heat water for laundering.

Ella's aunt, Josephine "Jose" Regal Johnson, came several days in advance of the celebration in order to help with the cooking and cleaning. They scrubbed the floor with a lye solution that bleached the boards to a whitish tan, after which they scattered newspapers that would be picked up before the wedding party arrived.

Jose baked the tall, white wedding cake and decorated it with pink frosting. (When the newlyweds returned from the church service, the brides small, round bouquet was placed atop the cake.)

Joe's mother Antonija baked hundreds of kolachy; her small oven was on duty from early morning until late night for several days.

["Oh, but her kolachy were good!" said Antonija's daughter-in-law, Mag. "They were so tender and light that they just melted in your mouth!"]

The night before the wedding, Ella hung white crepe paper streamers near the ceiling and placed a large, white bell above the table. While doing so, she snipped one of her fingers with the scissors. Since she didn't want to wear a bandage on her wedding day and since the slashed finger was inclined to break open and seep, she had to be careful lest she get a stain on her wedding dress.

The men prepared parking space and hitching rails for the many buggies and wagons that were expected. They cleaned the barn and constructed a platform in a corner of the loft for the musicians and the square dance caller. Seating made from planks was installed along the walls.

John and Mary did not attend the wedding ceremony, as they needed to be at home to oversee preparations. However, they gave the bride and groom a blessing, called the Blessing

> Mr. & Mrs John Ziska
> request the honor of your
> presence at the marriage
> of their daughter
>   Ella May
>   To
> Jos. Dobrovolny at the
> St. Joseph's Church
> Wed. April 18th, 17
> at 8 O'clock A.M.
>
> Reception at the home
> of the bride's parents.
>   at 12 O'clock.

Joe and Ella's cabin: 1917-1925. The entryway was a later addition—as was the volunteer tree. 1972 photo.

Joe and Ella Ziska Dobrovolny, April 18, 1917.

of the Sheets, before the wedding party set off for the service. The blessing was a custom brought from Europe.

About two-thirty in the early morning, Joe, Ella, and the two attendants (Ella's brother Freddie and cousin, Josie Ziska), departed. Freddie drove the well-groomed horses that pulled the two-seated carriage that was loaned to them by the Blackburns. The harnesses were freshly oiled and decorated with tassels and bells. Two suitcases contained the wedding clothes, for they would dress at the rectory.

The Rebellious Fiddler
April 18, 1917

John Regal had been asked to play his violin at the wedding dance of his niece, Ella Ziska, but he didn't arrive. His brother Jim did most of the fiddling. In later years whenever Joe's daughter asked her father why John didn't fiddle at the wedding, Joe would smile, amused.

"He was mad at me," he would say.

"Why was he mad?"

"Oh, over a bunch of foolishness. He pulled some tricks on me, and when I got him back, he got mad. John never could take a joke, you know."

The inquirer decided there was more than one way to collect that information, and found opportunity to discuss it with John.

"You sure can make that fiddle talk, Uncle John."

"Well, I play by note, you know. In those fast pieces many fiddlers leave out some of the quick notes because they play by ear and don't know they're there. I play by note, and I get them all."

"Did you play at Mom and Dad's wedding?"

"No! Wasn't even there."

"Why, how come? I thought everyone in the whole county was there! Were you sick at the time?"

"No. Didn't go. I didn't get along with Joe very well."

"You didn't? Why not?"

"Oh, he always was pulling something. And Joe never could take a joke himself, you know."

It seemed plausible that someone else would know about the little feud. More inquiry produced a few stories, including this one which was told by a neighbor:

While the threshing crew had gone to the house for the noonday meal, Joe Dobrovolny and John Regal had remained in the field to maintain the fire in the fire box so as to keep the steam up. (By this time, John Ziska had a steam-powered thresher.) After the other members of the crew had returned to the field, Joe and John went to the house for a belated dinner. John finished the main part of the meal first and began to eat one of the two pieces of pie.

After the initial mouthful, John launched into his act. He grimaced and began to complain.

"What sour pie! This is awful. Someone must have left out the sugar. I don't know if I can eat it. It's terrible!"

He kept up a convincing barrage of grievances all the while he was eating the pie.

Joe finished his meal and shoved back his chair.

"Well, Joe," said John. "don't you want your pie?"

"No," answered Joe. "I'll not spoil a good meal with a bad piece of pie."

"In that case," grinned John, "I'll eat it for you." He proceeded to devour the pie, relishing every delicious morsel.

Another neighbor recalled that Joe came to work on the thresher one day when his eyes were puffy and he was obviously tired. He had been to a dance the night before. At noon, John Regal enjoyed razzing him: "Ha! Look at Joe. Humped down over his plate. Eyes all puffed up and blinkin' like an owl."

After several such remarks, Joe chuckled dryly and said, "You'd better watch out or your eyes will be puffed up, and it won't be because you danced all night!"

When Anna Hytrek Krysl was asked, she chuckled. "I don't know whether or not Joe could take a joke, but I know that John Regal couldn't." She then told this story:

"When we were kids at home, there was a group of young people, including John, at our place one Sunday afternoon. We were having a water fight, boys against the girls.

"The boys were filling their buckets at the pump by the barn and the girls were filling from a couple of barrels by the garden. My sister Mary ran around the corner of the house and came face-to-face with John. She swung her bucket, which was half full of water, and drenched him. He just stood there with water dripping off every side.

"One of the boys came running up and said, 'Ha, ha! John got wet!'

"'Yes,' said John, angrily, 'And John's goin' home, too!'

"He got his horse out of the barn and rode away."

The reason why John was too mad to fiddle at Joe's

wedding did not surface. If any of the neighbors knew, they didn't tell. For the rest of their lives, whenever the subject was mentioned in the presence of either John or Joe, John would bristle and Joe would chuckle.

Ed Bouska's First Dance

When Ed Bouska was fifteen, he had a job—a real, money-paying job! He was the oldest boy in school and earned one dollar a month doing janitorial tasks. He came to school early, emptied the ashes, started the fire, and scooped snow, including paths to the toilets. He swept the room and cleaned the blackboard.

Ed was proud when the end of the month came and he received his pay. A whole dollar! Think of it! However, pleased as he was to get the money, he would have been excited to do the work anyway because he was in love with the teacher, Rose Hayes.

She was wonderfully kind and equally beautiful. Ed hoped to marry her when he got a little older.

The Bouskas, of course, went to Joe and Ella's wedding celebration; and wonder of wonders, the teacher was there, also.

Ed watched the dancers swirl through waltzes and polkas and two-steps. He imagined himself dancing around the huge barn loft with the beautiful Miss Hayes on his arm. He never would have had the courage to ask her, but in those days neighbors, aunts, uncles, and—would you believe it—teachers took it upon themselves to encourage the youngsters to dance.

"Aren't you dancing?" the lovely Miss Hayes asked.
"I don't know how very well," mumbled Ed.
"Come on. It's easy! Let me show you."
The two shuffled across the floor.

"Oh," said Ed years later, "I was glad to go to school early to fire up the stove. But what I really was fired up about was that teacher!"

Freouf's Hotbed

The Joe Freoufs had a large, home-made hotbed in which they planted early radishes and lettuce as well as plants to be transplanted into the garden. These early vegetables were an immeasurable help in feeding a family in those days when money was scarce and trips to the grocer were infrequent.

The morning of the wedding was chilly and rainy, but the temperature was above freezing. The Freoufs decided to leave the hotbed open. However, during the day, the rain changed to sleet and later, to snow. That night while the dancers swirled inside the haymow, snow and wind swirled outside.

"We better go," Frances Freouf repeatedly told her husband Joe. "The hotbed needs to be closed." However, Joe was enjoying the party, and her gentle comments were unheeded.

"It was four o'clock a.m. when the Freouf wagon reached home. Joe left the team standing at the barn door while he lit a lantern, pumped the sprinkling can full of water, thoroughly soaked the plants, and closed the hotbed. Then he returned to put the horses in the barn and unharness them.

The next day they found that the hotbed plants were all frozen.

(Frances Freouf, being a sister to John Ziska, was Ella's aunt.)

Even with glass doors to cover the hotbed, how could people plant seeds in March or April and hope to protect them from freezing? The pioneers had a way to generate the necessary heat.

They dug a hole the size of the hotbed frame to a depth of four or five feet. They filled the hole with about three feet of fresh horse manure. Above the manure, they placed the dirt in which the seeds were planted. As the manure rotted, it generated enough heat to warm the soil above it. A wooden frame was placed around the seed bed and during cold weather, all was covered with hinged doors—and perhaps straw or a blanket.

Others Remember the Wedding

Ella Dobias was thirteen at the time of the wedding, and was a pupil in School District 213. When Bouskas, driving a matched bay team on a buggy, were enroute to the wedding reception, they passed the school. Ella Dobias was sitting near the window and waved to them. The teacher scolded her and gave her a small tap on the cheek to let her know that she had behaved in an unacceptable manner.

Charlie Mlinar, who was about eighteen, said that he enjoyed the hay loft dance immensely. He danced with everyone, including the bride who was a wonderful dancer.

Ella and her brother Freddie danced a jig.

"I had never seen anyone dance like that!" said Charlie. "Their feet just flew. Everyone stood and looked, then clapped them back for more. It was great. We danced all night, went home for chores, and in spite of the storm, came back the next day to continue the celebration. The dance continued on the second night, also."

Frank and Mag Dobrovolny lived a couple miles south of the Ziskas. They had five young children, the smallest, Jay, being about a year and a half old.

"What I remember most about the day was the cold, raw weather," said Mag. "My dress clothes weren't very warm, and I was shivering all day. It was hard keeping track of all the kids with the older ones going to the barn to watch the dancing. When night came, it was even colder. I was glad when toward morning, we put the kids in the wagon, covered them with quilts, and went home.

"The next day after Frank had finished feeding the cattle, he and the older kids went back to Ziskas, but not me. I was glad to stay home with the smaller children."

At the time of the wedding, Agnes Krysl was about eight years old. Because she had outgrown her "Sunday" shoes, she had to wear a pair that had belonged to an older sister. One of the boys noticed that her shoes were too big and began teasing her.

"Hey fellas!" he yelled to the other boys. "Do you wanna be ready to go fishin' when the weather clears? If you do, Agnes has two boats you can borrow. She's wearing them for shoes, but really they are boats."

"I was about eleven years old at the time," said Barbara Mlinar. "What I remember best is how pretty my mother looked that day. She wore a white, embroidered blouse with a stiff collar that stood up on the sides and back. Her wavy brown hair was done in a fancier bun than was usual and was decorated with an ornamental comb. She wore several petticoats edged in lace ruffles underneath her black skirt.

"I thought she was beautiful."

(Barbara's mother Mary was John Ziska's sister; thus Barbara and Ella were cousins.)

After the Wedding

The day after the wedding, Thursday, the force of the spring storm increased, there being howling winds along with more snow. Even though the party continued, Ella helped with the morning milking, and Joe offered to assist Freddie who was going to the meadow to get feed for the cattle. At first, the wind was in command, for it unceremoniously hurled each forkful of hay off the rack as soon as they pitched it on.

Finally, they backed the rack up to the stack so that the wind hit the end rather than a side. (The sides of a rack are more open than the ends.) They finally managed to get home with some hay.

By Friday, the celebration was winding down and Joe slipped away to ride to his little cabin to check on his own livestock which he had left in the care of his brother, Fred. After he returned to the Ziska place, he and Ella went to O'Neill, probably on Monday, to get their wedding pictures taken. They packed their fine clothes in layers of tissue paper and put them in suitcases. After driving a team and buggy to Atkinson, they took the morning train to O'Neill.

Unlike the settlers who used sun time, the railroad functioned on Standard Time which in their particular area was forty-five minutes earlier than sun time.* Since about three and a half hours were required to drive to town, it was necessary for Joe and his bride to depart in the middle of the night in order to catch the morning train.

After their visit to the photographer, the newlyweds stopped at St. Mary's Academy where Ella's friend and neighbor, Margaret Blackburn, was boarding while she attended high school. Margaret was expecting them, and when they knocked, she and her fellow boarders exploded out the door and showered them with rice.

Visiting the academy was an exciting event for Ella. She had never before been in any school except the neighborhood, one-room, country schools.

---

* Any person who wished to set his watch or clock by sun time must first choose a clear day, after which he consulted the almanac to see what time the sun would set on that particular day. Next he viewed the setting sun, and when the final edge of the blazing orb disappeared behind the horizon, he set his timepiece.

Joe and Ella in a buggy pulled by Old Bill.

The couple returned to Atkinson on the evening train and stayed in a hotel overnight. The following day they drove the buggy back to Ziskas, loaded Ella's possessions in Joe's wagon, and by nightfall were in their own two-room cabin on Joe's budding ranch twenty-two miles southwest of Atkinson.

The Fennison Quarter
1917

Vaclav Krysl rented a quarter (located north of Schoolhouse 205) from Mrs. Fennison, a lady who lived in Illinois. One day he received a letter from her, and since he couldn't read English, he asked his son Frank to translate it.

Frank thought it was an ordinary friendly letter. Mrs. Fennison told about some recent events in her life and mentioned that taxes were so high that she intended to sell some property that she owned. Frank assumed she was referring to Illinois property, and completely missed the point of the letter, which was to notify Vaclav that she wished to sell the quarter he was renting.

Since she got no reply from Vaclav, she wrote to Harry Kopp who bought the quarter for eighteen dollars per acre.

When Vaclav learned of the transaction, he confronted Harry.

"How is it," he asked, "That you bought that quarter out from under me? I didn't even have a chance to bid on it."

"Why, Mrs. Fennison said that she had written to you, but received no answer. She assumed you weren't interested."

Three young fellows and a Harley Davidson motorcycle. V.J. Krysl is at the far right.

About a year later, V.J. bought the quarter for thirty-seven dollars and fifty cents an acre. Kopp more than doubled his money. The quarter is still owned by V.J.'s son, Bill, and is referred to as the Fennison Quarter.

Saved String
1913-1918

One day Ora Whipple, a teenager, was in the country store and post office at Tonawanda (perhaps twenty-five miles southwest of Atkinson),* and while she was looking at a magazine, she came upon a picture of a crocheted bedspread.

"I was just delighted with it!" she reported later. "I

---

* When Joe Dobrovolny began living in his cabin south of Holt Creek (where his son LeRoy lives now in 1993), his address was Tonawanda, Nebraska. However, the place which was the location of the community building and of the Jonas ranch house (that served also as a postoffice) is now pastureland.

thought I'd never seen anything so beautiful and I decided to make it. I didn't have money to buy the magazine, but I asked to copy the directions. However, Mrs. Jonas gave the magazine to me. She told me later, though, that she never expected to see that bedspread. What Sandhill child who couldn't afford to buy a ten-cent magazine could afford enough thread for a bedspread?

"But I was determined! In those days, everyone "ripped out" flour sacks to reuse the material for dish towels, night gowns, underwear, quilt blocks, and the like, and they also saved the string that the sacks had been sewn with. I got my mothers crochet hook and our ball of flour sack string and went to work.

"Also, everything you bought at a store was wrapped in paper and tied with "store string". If the articles were put in a paper bag, the top of the bag was probably rolled down and the whole package securely tied. Even the bristles on a broom were wrapped and tied, as was a box of shoes. Otherwise, groceries and new clothes might get dusty or muddy in the open buggies and wagons.

"Store string was heavier than flour sack string, but I discovered that if I unraveled it and took out one strand, it was the right thickness. So my mother's ball of store string was the next thing to disappear! But when it was used up, my creation

Ora's Bedspread Made from Saved String

was only about a foot and a half square.

" However, when Mrs. Jonas discovered that I *really was* determined to make that bedspread, she told the other neighbors who lived out there in the hills, and they gave me their extra string. Also, my cousin, Ruby Newton, lived in Ewing where a group of ladies used flour sacks from the bakery to make clothes for the poor. She saved the string for me.

"I had to tie the pieces of string together which meant that there were a succession of knots to deal with. I worked them so that the knots and the loose ends were always on the back side. The bedspread had a rose design crocheted in it with a puffy stitch that resembled the popcorn stitch.

"Eventually, people far and near were collecting string for me, and after about five years, the spread was completed."

"Do I still have it? Well, until a few years ago, I did. Then my niece [Doris Slaymaker Vogel] admired it so much that I gave it to her."

Ora Whipple lived for more than eighty years in her parent's two-room homestead cabin located in the hills near Whipple's Lake, a place far beyond the "end of the road". Her days, spent in virtual isolation, were filled with tending her garden and with preserving food. On into modern times, she continued to cook on a wood stove, to carry water from an outside well, to wash clothes on an old-time wash board, and to do battle with the coyotes who teased her dog and attacked her cats. During the 1980's, she moved to Parkside Manor in Stuart.

Originally, there had been only one room in the Whipple cabin, and it had been built on the line between Ora's parents' land and her uncle's land. Such an arrangement allowed each landowner to meet the requirement of "occupation" by placing his bed in that portion of the room which was on his land. Eventually, they added a second room.

One day after Ora was advanced in years, her nephew chided her for her shaky handwriting, telling her that she should write a little more carefully whenever she signed a check, or the bank wouldn't be able to read her handwriting.

"Well, then we'll be even!" snapped Ora. "I never could read theirs!"

The binder cut the grain and tied it into bundles, thus making the scythe virtually obsolete!

Balloon's Home-Made Bean Thresher

That wonderful invention,
the automobile,
was beginning to appear in Green Valley.
Also, notice the appearance of
a grove of trees on the
once-barren prairie.

Chapter 10

World War II and Beyond

The Great Flu Epidemic
1917-1918

During the First World War, there was a widespread epidemic of influenza. Thousands died in Europe, the United States, Asia, and Australia.

Conrad Vinzenz,* since he lived only three miles from Dora Lake, decided that while his wife and four children were visiting the Frank Goldfuss family (Mrs. Vinzenz' parents), he would go fishing. It was a raw day and he came down with a chill. However, since he had told his wife that he would come for the family the next day, he ignored his illness, got in his car, and drove north.

The car was a Model T Ford, and like the cars of that time, had no heater and nothing except curtains to cover the windows. It afforded quite a cold, breezy ride.

The Goldfusses lived about thirty miles away, and the country roads were rough and rutty. Since Conrad was not yet adept at driving a car, it was a long, slow trip.

The next day he was so ill that his wife called a young Atkinson physician, Dr. William Douglas, who came by horse and buggy to treat him. The family was not surprised when

---

* Conrad's parents lived on the Gruenberg place south of Bill Krysl's hills. Conrad lived a half mile south of his parents. When he died, his oldest son, George, was seven years old. The other children were Louis and twins, Catherine and Josephine.

the doctor reported that Conrad was suffering from the perilous flu which was sweeping the country.

On May first, his thirty-second birthday, Conrad died.

At the same time, V. J. Krysl's wife and three small children had the flu.

"How do *you* feel?" the doctor asked V.J.

"I'm perfectly healthy!" shouted V.J., jovially. "I'm far too tough to be invaded by flu germs."

However, after a few days V.J. also became ill.

To treat the victims, the doctor traveled south on alternate days, following a route which included the homes of those people who were infected; on other days he traversed a similar route that lay north of Stuart.

All of V.J.'s family survived.

Mary Disterhaupt loved to dance. Her mother once said to her, "Mary, I think you'd rather dance than eat!"

Mary answered, "You bet! I'd rather dance than do anything else!"

The Disterhaups went to a Red Cross Benefit Dance in Atkinson. Nationwide, people had these dances in every town and also in homes in the country.

At the dance Mary, then a young woman, must have picked up the flu germs, for she came down with the disease.

Even though Dr. Douglas came regularly, Mary wasn't getting better. It was thought she surely would die. Finally, she was able to get some food past her swollen throat and slowly began to improve. Her recovery stretched out to eight or ten weeks.

One day Mary overheard her mother talking to a niece.

"Mary is slowly improving," she said. "But she had such a high fever for so long that I'm afraid she's permanently weakened. Most likely, she will always sicken easily and will die young."

These words distressed Mary and gave her cause for concern for many years.

"And do you know," she remarked at age eighty, *"I've outlived Mother twenty-one years! She died when she was fifty-nine!"*

Luella "Ole" Olson Brady had the flu when she was fifteen and lived in Iowa. Initially, everyone was sick except her father. He drove thirty miles to Ceresco, Iowa, to get a nurse. Shortly thereafter, he also took the flu.

Because he was extremely ill, the nurse called the doctor, but the doctor was so busy with the widespread epidemic that he couldn't come.

The nurse arranged the sick on cots and make-shift beds in the dining room. Luella's dad, a man of six foot four, usually had a hearty appetite, but while he was ill, he didn't eat. The only nourishment he took was an occasional pickle which, he felt, momentarily helped clear the congestion in his throat.

Even though a number of people in the area died, everyone in the Olson family survived the epidemic.

Donat and Emma Kunz had ten children. The entire family except Marcella (who was nine years old) had the flu. An aunt came to take care of them until she, too, became ill, leaving little Marcella to nurse them all.

The neighbors brought kettles of soup and set them on the porch. So as not to expose their benefactors to the deadly influenza germs, the girl waited for them to depart before going out to get the food they had brought.

The chore that Marcella most dreaded was emptying the chamber pots. She carried them to the outdoor privy and dumped the contents there. Then, worse yet, she also had to rinse them.

The aunt was sick for three or four months, but all of them survived.

Ed Jones, uncle to Keith and Kenneth Jones, was in the army when the flu struck him. While he was sick, he completely lost his voice, and it was slow in returning. His buddies nicknamed him "Whisperin' Jones."

One of the Waters boys, a brother to Della Waters Dickau, died of the flu while he was serving in the army.

Carrie Ottele Kramer's sister Polly, a young woman married to Hank Baum of Stuart, died in October, 1918, of the influenza.

Broken Hay Baler

During the time that the United States was involved in

World War I, the Krysl brothers (V.J., Frank, Joe, Ed, and Albert) baled 3000 tons of hay, using a horse-powered baler. During a moment of foolishness, they broke the baler.

While Joe and Ed were pitching hay down from the stack, they came upon a cow bone.

"Hey, V.J.!" Ed shouted playfully, "Do you want to sharpen your teeth on this?" He tossed it down onto the hay table.

"Whatever you pitch down, I bale," bellowed V.J. who was feeding hay into the machine. He picked up the bone and tossed it into the baler, thinking that it would be pushed into the middle of a bale of hay.

However, the bone caught in the mechanism, the entire machine shuddered, and the ribs of the baler rose up and broke.

A Bolt of Lightning
about 1918

When the violent thunder storm descended, the Jim Gaughenbaugh family was in a spring wagon on the way home from O'Neill. The two small girls, Nelle* and Margaret, were crying in fright as they clung to their mother, Mary.

"This lightning is terrible!" exclaimed Mary, "So close! Isn't there a place where we can stop?"

"The Ditch Camp is just ahead," Jim said, shouting above the noise of the storm. "We'll pull in there."

By the time they reached the sought-after driveway, they—along with the groceries—were completely drenched. The girls continued to wail but probably couldn't be heard above the roar of the storm.

The farm known as the Ditch Camp was occupied by Everett Brown. It had two driveways, one leading to the house and the other to the barn. Just as Jim turned into one of them, a team, which was coming from the opposite direction and was pulling a manure spreader, turned into the other.

Suddenly there was a sharp crack, a startling flash of blinding light, and an earth-jarring boom. It was followed by an incredibly loud rumble. The horses that were pulling the manure spreader dropped to the ground, killed instantly by the lightning bolt.

---

* Nelle Gaughenbaugh, as a young woman, taught the Joe Dobrovolny children. Later, she married Clarence Gilg.

The Gaughenbaugh team plunged in fright, but Jim kept them under control and was able to deliver his terrified wife and children to the door of the house. After tying his horses to the hitching rail, Jim ran to offer assistance to the man who had been knocked off the seat of the spreader. Miraculously, he had not been seriously injured.

Mrs. Brown supplied her dripping guests with dry clothing and helped them repack their rain soaked groceries.

A Letter from the President

When Clarence Tasler was in France during World War I, a soldier's pay was thirty-two dollars a month. However, a sum of seven dollars was withheld as a premium on life insurance, and another amount of seven dollars and fifty cents was deducted for United States Liberty Bonds, leaving each soldier with a monthly check of seventeen dollars and fifty cents.

"We figured it was a ruse," said Clarence, "to cut our pay without actually saying so. We could do nothing but shrug our shoulders and take what they gave us. We figured the bond money would never be seen again."

Fifteen years later, the Great Depression of the Thirties seemed to have devoured every dollar in the entire country. Most people, including the Taslers who lived about thirteen miles southwest of Atkinson, had long ago used all their funds, had bills all over town, and had borrowed from the bank until their credit was exhausted.

Then one day Clarence received a letter from President Franklin Roosevelt. In it, the president said that the money Clarence had saved in bonds in 1918 was being returned to him. It would be sent to the post office where he could receive it on a designated day.

"Possibly you can use these funds better now than at any other time in your life," the president wrote.

Clarence and his wife Nettie went to the post office as directed and received a large, white envelope. They took it, unopened, to Fred Swengley at the bank. They had no idea how much money was inside, but even a few dollars would be a godsend.

When Swengley opened the envelope, a check for one thousand three hundred three dollars fell out. For a moment, Clarence and Nettie stood frozen, shocked into immobility.

"Why, it was a *jackpot*!" exclaimed Clarence in telling the story. "In those depressed times, it was a *gold mine*!"

Swengley held out two check books and said, "Go pay your bills."

The pair recovered their senses.

"Away we went!" said Clarence, "Nettie one direction and me the other. A couple of times we met at a corner to compare notes. When we finished, we went back to the bank."

"How much do you have left?" asked Swengley.

"About three dollars," answered Clarence.

"Eat it up!" said the banker, "and from now on, buy what you need. Your credit is good again."

They bought groceries for a celebration supper. In those days, three dollars would buy many times more than it does today.

Later Clarence said, "That was the turning point for us. That morning, we had been destitute—not a penny to our names. By afternoon, thanks to those bonds, we were back on our feet."

Broken Noses
around 1918

Lark Moore, driving a team, came home from the field and saw his younger brother Earl playing with an old tire inner tube. Earl had anchored one end of it to the wheel of a mower that was parked on a hill. Grasping the other end of the tube, he struggled down the hill to see how far he could stretch the rubber.

"I can beat that," said Lark. He grabbed the rubber tube and walked backward, digging his heels into the hillside. Suddenly, the other end of the tube came loose from the mower wheel and blasted him in the face, breaking his nose.

Lark received no medical attention, and as time went by, the crushed bone healed—but his nostrils grew closed. Years later, this excess bone had to be removed, a procedure which changed the shape of his nose, making it flat on the end.

One day Lark told Earl to bring the horses in from the pasture when he came home from school, thinking that the boy could cut cane in the late afternoon. As Earl drove the horses, an old mare got in the way.

When he attempted to drive her to the side in order to let the other horses by, she kicked and hit him in the face.

"I remember seeing that big hoof in front of my eyes, and immediately I was on the ground, my nose smashed," said Earl. "I didn't cut any cane that day!"

His sister Edith took him to the doctor who stuffed his nose with gauze saturated with vaseline.

"It had quit bleeding by the next day and I went to school," reported Earl. "I looked at that big nose for quite awhile. No way was I tempted to get into tussles or jostling matches for some months to come."

Assaulted Game Warden
early 1900's

In the Early Days (except for the time after the fires and the drought years in the 1890's) there was a profusion of wildlife, the vast numbers of which would astound a present-day hunter. In addition to the grasslands and the sloughs filled with rushes, numerous grain fields planted by the homesteaders provided an abundance of food and cover for the furred and feathered creatures of the plains.

Some of the settlers met all their summer meat needs by hunting game. Also, there were those who hunted to supply eastern markets. In those days it was difficult to obtain cash, and prairie chickens and ducks could be sold for perhaps thirty or thirty-five cents each.

To ship meat to Chicago or New York, Holt County hunters "salted it down" in barrels.

When it became obvious that the killing of wildlife needed to be regulated, game wardens came into existence. Initially, however, these wardens were not well-received by most landowners.

"The wildlife feeds on the grain in our fields," the farmers were apt to say. "The state has no right to come onto our land and tell us when we—or anyone else—can or can't shoot the game that consumes a sizable share of our crops!"

Two hunters from central Green Valley were spending long hours traversing the prairie in an effort to fill their shipping barrel with meat. Their wagon box floor was covered with dead prairie chickens when they were intercepted by a game warden.

However, it was the warden who was in trouble that day. The two men grabbed him, pinned him down, and tied him hand and foot. After setting him on the seat of his wagon, they proceeded to lecture, in terms they were sure he could understand, on just why they insisted that neither he nor any other employee of the state had a right to scrutinize another citizen's hunting activities.

After exhausting their collection of abusive and threatening terms, they turned the horses to face the direction of the warden's home, tied the lines loosely to the front of the wagon, and started them down the trail. The horses went home without a driver's guidance, and the two men saw no more of the warden.

It was necessary for wildlife to become more scarce before many of the settlers accepted the regulation of hunting rights.

(For those wishing to gain an idea of the abundance of wildlife in Nebraska during pioneer days, you may look in the July, 1979 issue of Nebraskaland Magazine: Sportsman's Scrapbook. On pages 12-13, is a picture of five hunters with their two-day "bag" of 132 ducks and geese.)

Krysl Hunting Stories
early 1900's

Tom Mains found himself in trouble one day when he was hunting. He had waded into a pond to get a duck and had mired down into the mud. Since he feared that he might continue to sink, he used his gun to help hold himself up.

"Just wait," shouted a friend. "Stop struggling. There's an old post here in the edge of the pond. I'll pull it out and use it to come in and get you."

After Tom was rescued, he discovered he had left his gun in the pond.

Again using the post as a support, his friend went back to retrieve the weapon. Sometime later, Tom decided to sell the gun and demonstrated it for Ed Krysl, who then bought it.

One day Ed shouldered the gun and went hunting. When he shot at some prairie chickens, he killed the chickens, but the gun exploded.

No one could explain why the gun functioned properly during the demonstration; then later blew up. Perhaps there was no connection between the mud bath and the explosion. One theory was that a part of a defective shell might have remained in the gun; another was that, since Ed had stored it on an open porch, wasps might have built nests in the barrel.

Ed Krysl had a hunting dog named Puppy which was his loyal companion, especially if he had a gun along. Ed often bragged about the dog, saying that it didn't much matter where a downed bird fell because Puppy would find it and bring it in.

One cold day Ed shot a duck which landed in an open spot in the pond. The dog bounded over the ice, leaped into the freezing water, and got the duck; but when he tried to climb out, the thin ice that surrounded the water hole repeatedly broke under his weight, thus plunging him back into the frigid pond.

Ed shouted encouragement: "Come on, Puppy! We don't need that duck! Just drop it! Come here, boy. Keep trying!! You can do it!"

But the faithful animal hung onto the bird as he struggled, and his efforts grew obviously weaker. With no way to help the floundering dog, Ed could only stand and watch.

"I tell you," he said later. "That was a terrible thing to see. My own dog. My good friend. And I couldn't help him—just watched while he struggled in that icy water till he played himself out. When he finally went down, the bird floated to the surface. A hard thing to see. A mighty hard thing to see."

John Krysl and his nephew Joe Krobot went hunting at Goose Lake one beautiful, fall day. They sneaked up behind a knoll, and cautious peeks through the rushes informed them that there were numerous ducks on the lake. What they didn't know was that off to one side was a pool full of geese.

When they got close enough to the ducks, they stood up and fired. At the first shot, the geese raised up.

"Geese!" John yelled, and both of them turned to aim at the geese.

They got eight geese.

John ended his story: "We didn't get many ducks that day—ten or twelve, maybe."

Joe and Ed Krysl took one look at a brighter-than-usual winter morning and decided to go hunting. They took their guns and walked to Johnson Lake. After they had trudged around it, they went to Otter Lake where they shot some ducks. Next they hiked to Wolf Lake, and shot a few more ducks as well as a goose.

"I guess we have about all we can carry," said Joe. "We had better head for home."

"Those mallards that flew off the other side of Otter

Lake seemed to be headed for Goose Lake," answered Ed. "I'm curious to see what is over there."

"Why don't we hide these birds under the snow by that hay pile yonder? We can check out Goose Lake, and then pick them up on the way home."

At Goose Lake, the two hunters got a couple of geese and more ducks. Carrying their guns and all their game across the hills was no small task, but another job yet awaited their attention when they finally arrived home: they had to pluck and dress their game.

"That still wasn't the end of it," said Ed. "We saved the feathers for the women to make bedding, and every night after supper Ma pestered us to strip them—that is, pull the fluff off the spines of the feathers. She would put a pile of them in the middle of the table, and we'd take a few at a time to work on. Couldn't laugh or cough or sneeze or the feathers would all roll off the table. Almost didn't dare breathe."

Hunting stories, like fishing tales, sometimes get inflated, but Ed Krysl told this tale with a genuinely serious expression:

"In the days when game was thick, Old Man Johnson went huntin' and sneaked up on a big flock of ducks. The lake was just black with ducks! Before he was quite ready to shoot, the whole bunch raised up into the air, coverin' the sky like a huge, black cloud.

"He quick shot but aimed too low. All he got was a half bushel of duck feet."

"Really?" asked his wide-eyed guest. "Can that be true?"

"So they say!" said Ed in his slow, gravelly, Krysl drawl. "So they say."

Handling a Model T Ford
about 1920 in Wyoming

George Hytrek (nephew to Anna Hytrek Krysl) remembers the winter nights when he and his friends came out of a dance hall at about three o'clock in the morning and were faced with the problem of getting the Model T started.

"We'd jack up one of the hind wheels, and one guy would spin it while another got on the crank. Just jacking a rear tire off the ground would make it crank easier because there was less friction, but spinning a wheel helped more yet.

"Another problem we had was going up a hill. It was rough country there, it being near the mountains. A small hill was no problem, but a steeper one would burn up all the gas in the carburetor, and the motor would die. Then a person had to let the car roll down the hill and get it turned around backwards. You had to *back* up the hill. The gas tank was under the front cushion. If you went up backwards, the gas could continue to flow to the carburetor."

The Sensible Horse
1920's

When Ora Whipple was teaching at the Jonas School, she drove a rickety buggy pulled by a horse named Molly. There were several pasture gates to open, pass through, and close. The trusty Molly always waited patiently while the gate was being closed. Ora, being in a hurry to get to school, would crack her whip as soon as she was back in the buggy, and the horse would leap forward.

On this particular morning after Ora closed a gate, she hurried back to the buggy, and because the step was unsound, she grabbed the seat with her right hand and the front wheel with her left in order to steady herself as she climbed aboard. At that moment, Molly apparently decided Ora was in the buggy, and anticipating the crack of the whip, she bounded off at a gallop.

The sudden motion threw Ora backwards, causing one foot to lodge between the seat and the side of the buggy. The other foot bumped along on the ground. Luckily, she was able to retain her grip on the light wheel with one hand and was strong enough to hold it from turning. With the other hand, she clung desperately to the seat.

Ora feared that Molly would make a sharp turn to cross a bridge that lay ahead, an action which would probably upset the buggy on top of her. However, the horse sensed that all was not right and stopped.

Ora had some difficulty loosening her lodged foot, but once the task was accomplished, she climbed into the buggy and went to school.

Thanks to the wise horse, she was not seriously injured; but for a few weeks, the stiff and painful muscles in her legs prevented her from joining the children in recess games.

Mower Accident
early 1920's

It was mid afternoon when five-year-old Earl left the house to carry a drink of water to his father, Henry Dickau, who was mowing in a nearby field. When Earl reached the "land" (that portion of meadow chosen to be a unit for mowing, raking and stacking) he found that his father had recently passed, making it necessary for the boy to wait until the mower had made another journey around the outer boundary of the "land."

Earl was tired. Every morning he, using a gallon lard bucket in each hand, trudged behind his dad, back and forth, back and forth, carrying water to the pigs. Then on this particular day, the father had said at noon:

"Earl, it's a hot day today. Those pigs could use extra water. As soon as we're finished eating, we're going to have to carry them some."

Now, as Earl waited, he sat down in the tall grass. For awhile, he watched the creatures around him—the meadowlarks, the dragon flies, the honeybees, and the inchworms. He caught a grasshopper and watched it spit "tobacco juice." As he sat, the warm sun on his back accentuated his drowsiness; he lay over on the ground and was soon sound asleep.

Neither the noise of the plodding horses nor the staccato clicking of the approaching sickles were enough to arouse the child. Rather, just as the mower bar was passing, Earl jerked awake.

Startled, the boy lifted his arm at a precise moment for the sickle blades to catch it.

Henry, whose eyes had been on the sickle, saw the hand as it popped up in the grass. He stopped his team and rushed to the child. The little wrist had been severed, bone included, except for the cords on the underside.

Henry grabbed the limb above the wound, snatched up the child, and ran home. Upon reaching the yard, he plunged the boys arm into the cold water in the horse tank.

"Della! Della!" he shouted frantically.

Della, having heard the screams of the child, was already coming.

"Call the doctor!" said Henry. "I mowed Earl's arm almost off!"

It was an hour's drive for the doctor in his Model T Ford. In the meantime, Della and Henry tied a cloth tightly around the wound and kept dousing this bandage with cold water. They assumed that the doctor would find it necessary to finish amputating the hand.

Finally, when the doctor did arrive, he decided to attempt to save the limb. Laying Earl on the kitchen table, he gave an anesthesia and sewed his hand back in place.

The doctor then took Earl to town with him, and placed him in the care of the boy's grandmother, Mary Dickau.

The arm was saved, though Earl had a stiff hand from that time on. In spite of this inconvenience, he has always been an energetic and efficient worker.

Stencil's Toothache
1915 or 1920??

Stencil Hytrek had a toothache. It had bothered him at brief intervals for some months, but finally had reached a point where the pain was constant and excruciating.

He tried a number of suggestions aimed at bringing relief: with the aid of a toothpick, he put a bit of cotton soaked in peppermint extract into the cavity; he put sulfur in it; he rinsed his mouth in a strong tea made of dill seed; and he dipped a piece of cotton in whiskey, and placed it between his teeth.

His tooth continued to throb. His entire jaw was as sore as a six inch boil! There were shooting pains in his ear and more of the same down his neck.

Finally, an acquaintance said to him: "I can tell you how to get relief—sure and lasting."

"I'll bet!" said Stencil. "I suppose you're going to say for me to drop dead."

"Not quite that drastic. The way to do it is to kill the nerve in the tooth. To do that, you use a piece of baling wire and bend it so that you can insert one end into the cavity without touching your mouth or tongue. Then you heat it in the hot coals in the stove, and when the tip gets hot, insert it in the cavity. That kills the nerve, and the pain is gone."

At first, Stencil didn't regard this suggestion as a practical one, but finally when he was worn down by the day-and-night agony of the toothache, he decided that as torturous as the cure sounded, it would would at least end the constant pain. He got a piece of baling wire and took out his pliers.

He followed the directions carefully.

His toothache disappeared.

Teter Ball Team
1921 in southwestern Nebraska

In the days when neighborhood baseball games were a popular form of Sunday afternoon entertainment, the Bartley community had a team. Because the Teter boys, Jack, Bill, Earl (Tobe), Ora, and Boyd and their brother-in-law, Frank Smith, were the backbone of the team, it was called the Teter Team. Also, the boys' father, Frank Teter, was a sports enthusiast. He encouraged his sons, coached them, and often umpired.

On the Fourth of July that year, Will Teter broke his knee while sliding into second base and thereafter couldn't play.

Later that summer Cambridge wished to feature a game on the Legion Baseball Field. A local group, called the Minnick Team, challenged the Teters. Excitement was especially high because the winners would receive genuine baseball uniforms.

Being short a player because of Bill's injury, the Teters looked over the neighboring areas for a replacement. They decided on a young fellow, Bill Reiner, from Indianola, a small town about six miles west of Bartley. Boyd Teter, who usually occupied the mound, happily decided that Reiner should pitch. They arrived in Cambridge in high spirits only to find that the Minnick Team had hired a league pitcher from Ogallala.

The Teters held a meeting. These were neighborhood teams, and pulling in talent from afar wasn't legal. They considered protesting—but the fans were waiting! Finally, they decided to proceed with the game.

If the hired player was a great pitcher in Ogallala—and in Witchita, Kansas, where it was said he had also played—his expertise didn't blossom in Cambridge. The fans were about ninety-five percent in favor of the Teters. They teased and taunted the hired pitcher until he lost heart. With a score of two to nothing, the Teters won the uniforms.

Bill's leg didn't heal properly. He finally had surgery which helped, but he had to wear a brace the rest of his life. All the other Teter boys farmed, but Bill operated a drug store.

Home-Made Bread

Irene Teter made wonderful home-made bread, but unlike most other people, she did not slice it before she placed it on the table. Rather, she put a loaf and a sharp knife beside Earl's plate, and he sliced the bread as it was needed.

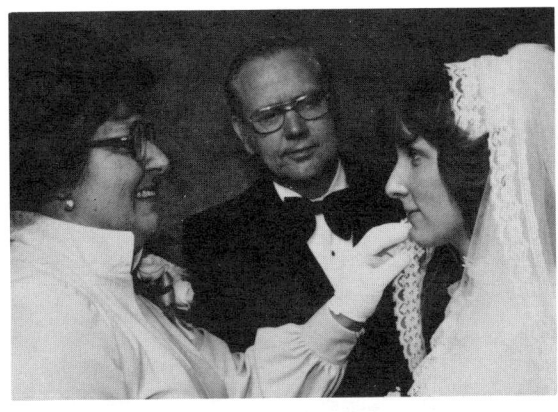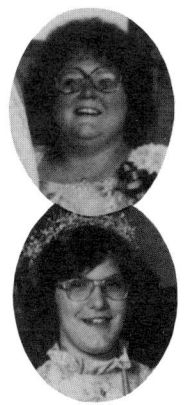

John Teter and Marva Moore Teter with their daughter, Shirley Jo Teter Krysl. At right, Shirley's sisters, LeAnn (top) and Ivy.

Left:
John's parents, Otis Earl (Tobe) Teter, 1897-1953; and Irene Mayo Teter, 1897-1986. Married: 1917.

Right:
Irene Mayo Teter with her second husband, Clyde Wyeneth.

Marva's parents: Lark Lester Moore, 1901-1983; Nellie Marie Premer Moore, (1906-1980). Married: 1928

Marva's Grandparents: Frank Albert Premer, 1882-1929; Ellen (Nellie) Daniels Premer, 1881-____. Married: 1904.

Marva's Grandparents: John Franklin Moore, 1860-1911; Mary Etta Miner Moore 1869-1953. Married: 1888

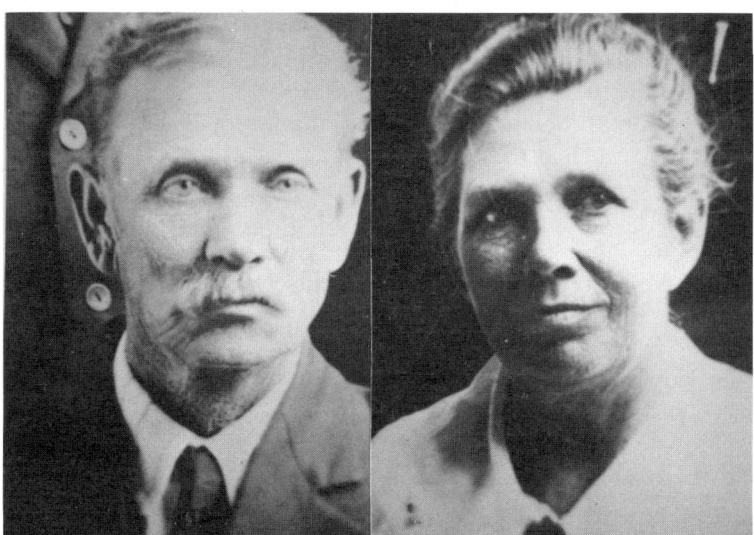

John's Grandparents. Top: Frank L. Teter (1867-1939) and Mattie May Phifer Teter (1876-1929). Married 1892.

Bottom: John William Mayo (1854-1931) and Sarah Emily Bossort Mayo (1862-1930). Married: 1881.

Sometimes when Boyd and his family were going home from town, they stopped at Earl's place and Irene invited them to stay for supper. The menu was always the same: a generous pan of gravy which was eaten over bread.

When Earl cut bread for Boyd, he tossed it across the table to the brother who had been a fellow ball-player, and Boyd deftly caught it.

Kitchen Table Surgery
probably 1920's

Lark Moore's mother, Mary Etta, had an ear and sinus infection which was getting worse rather than better. It was long before the discovery of antibiotics, and by the time her condition was extreme enough so that Dr. Arbagest was called, she was deathly ill.

Immediate surgery was necessary, but the small town doctor did not have the necessary instruments, and there was no time in which to obtain them. After consideration, he went to the general store and bought a chisel and a wooden mallet. (The latter object was actually a potato masher.)

Jack Crawmer, the storekeeper, asked, "What in the world are you going to do with those?"

"I'm going to Frank Moore's place to operate on Mrs. Moore. She has a bad mastoid infection."

"Great Scott! Don't you think you'll kill her with instruments such as these?'

"Well, if I don't operate, she is going to die for sure."

The doctor returned to the Moore farm. After stretching Mary Etta out on the kitchen table, he gave her an anesthetic. He made an incision behind her ear and chiseled through the bone in order to drain the infection.

Mary Etta did not die from the unorthodox operation. Her daughters nursed her back to health, and she lived for many more years.

Shut the Door!

George Hytrek (the eldest of Paul's seventeen children) said that once when he was a kid, he opened the door and stuck his head out to view a blizzard. The wind and fine snow suddenly blasted into his face with such force that he couldn't breathe.

"It was as if someone had put something tight over my face," he said. "No way could I get a breath of air. Not one bit."

For a moment, he stood there in a surprised stupor.

"Shut the door!" yelled another member of the family.

As soon as he pulled his head back into the room, he was able to breathe.

"That kind of experience is something you never forget," he said. "It was the only time it ever happened to me, but from then on, I respected the violence of a blizzard."

The Coyote on the Stairs
1920

Anna Krysl knew what it meant to be busy. In addition to the usual routine of cow milking, chicken feeding, garden weeding, housekeeping, and child watching, she had the added task of cooking for the carpenters who were remodeling their farmhouse. Two of the children required relatively small amounts of care: eight-year-old Leo tried to stay out of the way in order to avoid some of the never-ending jobs of carrying water, firewood, and corncobs; and Christine was a tiny baby and not yet capable of mischief. It was Josephine at age two and Amelia at age four who required the watching.

The carpenters had built a stairway that led off the kitchen, and they were now finishing an upstairs room. The little girls loved playing on the new steps and were often in the way of the men who carried tools and supplies up the stairs. Anna hadn't time to ride herd on the two children, but something must be done to keep them out of the way. She devised a plan.

Going out to the barn, she caught several of the more wild cats and put them in a gunny sack. She stowed the sack behind the house and went inside. After depositing some potato peelings in two small buckets, she called to the toddlers.

"Help me girls. Take these peelings outside and throw them in the chicken yard."

While they were gone, she brought the sack of cats into the house and placed them on the landing of the stairway.

When the two mischief-makers returned, Anna told them: "The men are tired of you girls being in the way. Today they brought some wild coyotes along, and they have them upstairs, tied in sacks. If you keep bothering them, they are going to turn those coyotes loose to chase you away."

The girls went to the stairway and gazed up suspiciously.

They had already learned that their mother was inclined to be tricky.

Anna came up behind them, broom in hand.

"One of the coyotes is right there in that gunny sack. Let me show you."

Using the straw end of the broom, she reached up to the landing and gingerly poked the sack. The startled cats leaped up inside the bag and conveniently emitted a few yowls.

The girls jumped back. There really were coyotes on the stairs! It was no joke! They found another place to play.

Anna's account did not make any references to the children's sleep habits after this episode. Did they lie awake all night and worry about coyotes in the house?

Dragging Dora Lake
1921

Water was deep that wet spring when Dr. Dale Stuart, Forest Shearer, John Kaup, and Charlie Anstine upset their newly-built rowboat in Dora Lake. It seems that it was a disagreeable day from the beginning, but the men were determined to try their four-man boat. It had especially high sides, a feature that would add to its safety, they thought, for a heavy load could settle it lower in the water without sinking it.

The boatmen were rowing along, quite satisfied with the way the craft was riding the waves. However, since John Kaup couldn't swim, he was tense about the rough water and was anxious to return to shore.

Suddenly, a yet stronger gust of wind caught the little vessel broadside.

"Look out!" yelled John Kaup, frightened by the rocking of the boat. For some unexplainable reason, he jumped overboard. Perhaps he thought the water was more shallow than it was, and that he would leap out and steady the craft. As he jumped, the boat tipped over, plunging everyone into the lake.

John yelled just once. "Help!"

By the time the other three had righted themselves and had struggled to gain a hold on the overturned boat, the waves had scooped John away, and had rolled him under.

He was gone!

The others, weighted with heavy boots and coats, managed to hang on for a time. However, before fellow fishermen were able to come through the rough, cold waters to their assistance, Shearer and Anstine lost their grips on the boat and sank. Dr. Stuart, Navy veteran of World War I and a strong swimmer, managed to stay afloat until he was rescued.

Two fishermen who had cars were sent to Stuart to report the accident and to bring back help for retrieving the bodies. Since it was known that V.J. Krysl owned a rowboat and was adept at handling it, one of the messengers stopped at his ranch to ask his assistance.

V.J. and several other men spent the cold, windy afternoon dragging Dora Lake. They used long strands of barbed wire from which they dangled a series of fishhooks. Positioning a boat on each end of the barbed wire, they rowed back and forth across the lake.

"I had never before been to the lake when it was so windy," said one onlooker. "The waves bounced those little boats around like a bunch of corks. I was almost afraid to watch, fearing we'd yet have more accidents. I kept counting the boats, and each time I was surprised when they were all still afloat."

When John Kaup's body was found, the searchers came to shore to compare notes and to develop a new strategy. An observer offered a suggestion.

"Perhaps we should tie guy wires to the boats to help steady them," he said. "And also we'd have a way to pull them to shore in the event any of them capsized."

"I don't want anything tied to *my* craft," said V.J. "Holding back a boat against these high winds could drag it under. I want it to be free to respond to my oars."

Before nightfall, a second body, that of Charlie Anstine, was recovered; Forest Shearer's body was found the next day.

(Forest Shearer was a brother to Mahlon Shearer and an uncle to Dick Shearer who survived the World War II Death March in Germany.)

Picking Corn
early 1920's

Each fall John and Christina Krysl Krobot's two oldest children, Joe and Mary, were taken out of school to help harvest the corn. The family operated two wagons: the boy Joe worked with his grandfather, Henry, while Mary aided her father, John.

"Oh, I hated that job!" said Mary in her old age. "Many a morning I bawled all the way to the field. I'd look the other way, trying to hide the fact that I was crying because I didn't want Dad to think I was lazy. Even though we had done chores—everyone helped with the milking chores—it was still dark when we went to the field. Thus, it wasn't too hard to hide my tears.

"When we arrived in the field, like as not we'd find there was frost on the corn. Our mittens would soon get wet and our hands stinging cold. Sometimes after the sun came up, it would be warmer. But, oh, those cold mornings! And we didn't really have warm clothes, although we wore winter underwear and bundled up as best we could.

"I usually picked the row beside the wagon, and Dad picked the next two rows. By noon we'd have the wagons loaded and we'd go home for dinner. Dad and Grandpa would shovel the corn into the crib and we'd go back to the field and get two more loads in the afternoon. We'd get back at four or five o'clock because, of course, we had to be home for chores.

"Oh, how I envied the other kids who sat in their desks in the warm schoolhouse all day and studied their lessons. School was a picnic in comparison to being out in the raw weather, with wrists and elbows aching from yanking off those corn ears. Sometimes at night my joints hurt so bad that, tired as I was, I couldn't sleep."

To pick corn by hand, a person used a team of horses on a double-boxed wagon (twice as high as a usual wagon) with the right side of the box built up higher yet. That high side, called a bang board, caught the ears tossed by the pickers and dropped them into the wagon.

Each picker used a steel hook which was firmly anchored to his right palm by a leather strap around his hand and another around his wrist. He grabbed the ear of corn with his left hand and slashed the husks with the hook that was on his right hand. With the same motion, he slid his right hand inside those husks to grasp the bare ear. He broke it off and tossed it against the bang board, after which it dropped into the wagon. The empty husks were most often left dangling on the cornstalks.

If one person were working, he walked between two rows of corn, picking first on one row and then on the other. If two people were working, they probably picked three rows: each person picked one row, and they alternated on the middle row.

After a day or two, a well-broken team could function without a driver. They moved down the rows, responding to the

"Giddap" and "Whoa" commands of the picker.

Andrew Miksch
1923

A work horse had pulled loose in the barn, and when fifteen-year-old Andrew Miksch walked in, the horse kicked him in the face. About a half hour later, Cecelia went to the barn, figuring that Andrew would, by then, have the milk cows inside. She found him sitting by the barn, bleeding from the hoof mark on his face.

The younger Dr. McDermott of Stuart came to the farm and sewed up the wound. He thought Andrew should be brought to town, and he called a nurse from Omaha to care for him. Andrew was taken to the Stencil Hytrek home in Stuart (Stencil had married the boy's sister, Mary Miksch).

A few days later he became delirious and seemed to think he was hunting crows. He kept asking his sisters to pick up the birds that he insisted he had shot.

"There they are. See them? Why don't you get them?" he'd say, pointing.

There was a ten-cent bounty on crows, and Andrew liked to hunt them.

By then, Dr. Ben McDermott, the older of the two brothers, was back in town, and he sent the boy to Omaha.

Because of the head injury, Andrew got spinal meningitis and soon died.

The Backward Mules
probably 1920's

Joe Mlinar Sr., father to Charlie Mlinar, was going to haul some pigs to town. He had a "triple box" wagon (an especially high wagon box) pulled by a team of young mules.

When the wagon began to move, the pigs were startled and gave a couple of loud snorts which frightened the mules. They began to run.

Joe braced himself in the bottom of the tall box, pulling on the lines. The mules ran toward a tree, and one went on the right side of it while the other went on the left. The wagon stopped with the crack of breaking wood and the snap of harnesses.

When Joe raised up to look out of the wagon, he found

himself face-to-face with the mules. The wagon tongue had hit the tree, had broken in three places, and had whirled the team inward.

Joe unhitched the mules and used an older, more experienced team to haul the pigs.

Incubator Light
1920's
as told by Orval Monson

When I was small we lived near Spicer, Minnesota on Green Lake which was about a hundred miles west of Minneapolis. Each spring my mother hatched chicks in two incubators which were located upstairs in our bedroom. They held about a hundred eggs and were warmed by kerosene lamps.

One of the incubators had a small glass window in front through which some of the yellow rays of the lamps escaped. Whenever I awoke in the night, I liked to gaze at the light. If I squinted my eyes, I found the rays would form patterns which would fluctuate according to the changes in the positions of my eyelids.

Also, the incubators needed to be closely guarded because of the temperature, and Mother got up in the night to slip quietly upstairs to check them. Her coming and going and the friendly light and the smell of the burning lamps are among the most pleasant memories of my childhood.

Most mornings I awakened to the sounds of Mother turning the eggs and replenishing the kerosene in the lamps. But of course, there finally came a morning when the first sounds I heard were the peeping of the newly-hatched chicks.

Mother always made our nightshirts from flour sacks and all of them were the same size. Since I was one of the smaller kids, the shirts fit loosely enough so that I could put a baby chick in my sleeve and it would walk around in there, tickling my arm with its downy feathers.

A less happy remembrance is of a time that my older cousin Cliff was staying with us. Cliff was a tease. He had a candy bar that he had stored on a high shelf in the closet.

Every night he would take a bite of the candy; then he'd hold the remainder out to the rest of us for each of us to have a smell of it, after which he'd wrap it up and put it back on the shelf.

Top, left: Patti Monson Krysl, her step-father, Orval Monson, and daughter, Eve Willadsen, 1979; top, right: Orval's parents, Molly & Ephriam Monson; bottom, Eph's children: Sanford, Herman, Thelma, Ruby, Alvah, Orval, & Archie. (Elmer & Myrtle were not born yet.) About 1924.

Above: Sanford Monson on a triple-box wagon with two side-boards on top! The size of the load displayed here is impressive. Notice how each of the top two wagon boxes is fastened to the one below it by the use of cleats. As is usual, at the middle and at both ends, the second wagon box has strengtheners (steel rods going across the width of the box). The black dot in the center of the box is the end of a strengthener. The bang board, nearly hidden by the load, can be seen peeking above the corn. One old-timer who saw this picture said, "It took mighty good corn, a mighty good man, and more than a half-day to pick such a load as that!"

Opposite page, top left: Gladys (maiden name unknown) Crepps Schriner, about 1900-1985, maternal grandmother to Patti Monson Krysl. Very little is known about Gladys' first husband, Glen Crepps (not shown). It is said that he had red hair, spoke both German and English, and was a pilot in the U.S. Armed Forces. Top, right: Phyllis Crepps Monson and her second husband, Orval Monson. Center: Phyllis and Cliff Monson (first husband) with their baby Patti, 1950.

Bottom: Eve Willadsen, daughter of Patti Monson Willadsen Krysl and Vince Krysl. Eve's birth father is Carl Willadsen.

Top: Monson corn, all of it picked by hand, piled beside the chicken house.

Bottom: Bundle wagons heaped unusually high, heading toward the thresher. (The half-grown horses loitering behind the wagon are probably the nursing colts of mares that are working in the field. Sometimes colts were permitted to tag along with their mothers.)

The candy bar lasted about a week. After that, he saved the paper and let us sniff it each night.

You know, I still feel irritated when I think about that ornery Cliff and his candy bar.

(Orval Monson ,1917-1990, was Patti Monson Krysl's step-father. Orval's father, Ephriam Monson, was a hard-working farmer.

Cliff Monson, Orval's cousin, was Patti's birth father. He was the son of Conrad, whose family members were great outdoorsmen and wildlife enthusiasts. Cliff died young of rheumatic fever.

When Patti was seven, her mother, Phyllis Krepps Monson, was struck and killed by a drunk driver. Orval, who was Phyllis' second husband, was walking with her at the time, and he was seriously injured in the same accident.

For a time after her mother's death, Patti lived with an aunt in California. When she was in junior high school, she went to Iowa to live on the Monson farm with Orval and Orval's mother. Orval became her parent and dearest relative. Later, he was the beloved grandfather of Eve, Vincent, Adrienne, and Renee.)

Minnesota Storm
1920's
as told by Orval Monson

My dad, Eph Monson, shipped cattle to St. Paul which was about a hundred miles away. One warm, misty, fall day, he drove his cattle to town and loaded them on a train.

Dad knew about Minnesota weather, including how fast it could change. As a precaution, he put straw in the bottom of the boxcar and covered the north side of it with tar paper. Shortly after the train left, a howling blizzard blew in.

When the train got about halfway to St. Paul, it was ordered to stop out on the open prairie.

There were several other cars loaded with cattle, and a great percentage of them perished in the severe weather, but since Eph had taken some precautions, his animals survived.

The railroad did not compensate the farmers for their dead cattle because the storm was considered to be "an act of God."

Remembering Cliff Monson
as told by his sister, Pat Wigtil

Since our mother died when I was twelve, Cliff went to Chicago to live with our oldest brother, Sydney. Thus there were many years when I rarely saw him. Besides, Connie and Cliff were older than me, and I was merely the pesky little sister.

First, I recall that Cliff once took a punishment in my place. Mother was upset with me and was going to spank me.

"Oh," said Cliff, sympathetically, "Paddle me instead."

I suppose Mother thought it would hurt me worse to have my brother spanked for my misdemeanor, for she *did* spank him. I fled the scene, and worst of all, I can't remember if I ever thanked him.

Cliff loved animals and always had several pets. When I was about five, one of his squirrels got out of the cage and came darting toward the door where I was standing. I was frightened and began screaming and jumping up and down in an attempt to scare him away. But he ran right under my feet, and I stomped on him! Cliff nursed the little thing tenderly, but it died.

Another time, I decided to be especially good to one of his rabbits and fed it cream instead of milk. It died, too.

When Cliff was older, he was an avid hunter, but I wasn't around him then and don't know any of the details.

My dad, Conrad Monson, liked to buy broncos and break them to ride. A certain one that was tied in the barn was especially beautiful, and once when the folks weren't home, Cliff decided to ride it. I was instructed to let him out of the barn when he was ready. I stood outside by the door, waiting.

Finally he yelled, "Open up!"

I swung open the door, and the horse—he was named Arthur—thundered out like a cyclone. Instead of going toward the open corral gate, he veered to the right, jumped a closed gate, and galloped away. Cliff was hunched over and was bouncing like a salt shaker, but he was hanging on! They disappeared over a rise, and in a little while, I couldn't even hear the beat of the horse's hooves.

I was worried and climbed on a fence for a better view. I couldn't see a thing of Cliff or Arthur anywhere. Would the horse keep going until they were in unfamiliar surroundings? If so, how would Cliff find the way back?

Finally, they reappeared, and Cliff was sitting tall in the saddle, grandly riding the panting Arthur. Boy! Was I relieved!

Rabbit Burgers

Frank Hulinsky of Burwell carried a gun along when he picked corn. So that it wouldn't get dusty, he kept it in a flour sack in a corner of the wagon. Rabbits were thick in those times, and occasionally he stopped to shoot some. There were days when he bagged only a few, but he remembers that on one particular day he got fourteen.

The horses soon learned that whenever Frank tightened the lines around the stick at the front of the wagon box and pulled his gun from the sack, they were to stand still and wait. When he returned, loosened the lines, and began tossing corn against the bang board, they started moving down the row again.

In the evening, Frank and his wife Emma skinned the rabbits, removed the meat from the bones, and stored it in a cold room. After several days, Emma ground it, adding some pork as she did so, and fried it into rabbit-burgers. She placed the burgers in a stone jar and covered them with hot lard.

Up to this point, Emma's story was familiar. In late winter when warming weather threatened to thaw the meat supply which probably hung in an outdoor building, most old-timers "fried down" meat—hamburgers, steaks, or sausages. The stone jars with the fried-down meat were set in a cool place. To use, one dug around in the solidified lard and removed the amount of meat needed for a meal. The remainder was saved for other days. If stored in a cool place, it kept for weeks.

However, Emma said that she sealed her stone jars of fried-down meat in a most unusual way, using brown wrapping paper. After smearing the paper on both sides with egg white, she placed it over the hot jar, folded the edges down over the outside of the rim, and tied it firmly with strong cord. The egg white dried and effectively sealed as it did so.

Once the jar was opened, the meat was used, day-by-day, in the usual way.

Four Lame Legs
1920's

When Charlie Mlinar was a teenager, his father sent him to haul some hay to town. He was using four mules, one of which was a colt named Jack. Since Jack was skittish, his halter rope was tied to one of the older mules. Upon arriving at a bridge, they found it frost-covered, and the mules, afraid of the strange, white boards, were reluctant to cross it.

"I finally got them onto the bridge, but they were shying to the side, and since Jack was on the outside, he got pushed over the railing," said Charlie.

When Charlie looked over the side of the bridge, he saw the young mule suspended by the head, his feet kicking the air frantically.

Taking out his knife, Charlie cut the halter rope, and Jack dropped into the slough. He scrambled to his feet and limped out of the water.

"He didn't know which one of his legs to favor," said Charlie. "I guess all four of them hurt."

Flapper Days
mid 1920's

The "Flapper Days" of the 1920's were in rebellion of the tightly laced corsets, the form-fitting bodices, and the narrow, pointed shoes of the 1800's and the early 1900's. The shapeless dresses of the twenties looked untidy in comparison, especially to the older generation.

Vaclav Krysl was once heard objecting to the dresses worn by his younger daughters. He threatened to throw "all those rags" out of the house.

It is true that the nipped waistlines had been carried to extremes. In order to keep their waists small, some women wore their corsets to bed.

It was said that the reason Grace Regal died young was because she "laced herself to death." After putting on her corset, she put the ends of the laces around the bedpost, after which she reared back to tighten them.

When young people finally rebelled, they went to extremes in the opposite direction, and the dress styles were shapeless. The term "Flapper Days" came from the loose, floppy, unbuckled galoshes that the girls began to wear instead of the pointed, narrow shoes.

The Threat at the Wedding
May 6, 1925

A gala celebration was prepared at the home of Joe and Antonia Ziska in preparation for the wedding of their daughter Mary to Albert Krysl. There were to be three-course dinners served throughout the day, and a "bowery" had been constructed for outdoor dancing in the evening. People from far and near had been invited, and the first of the guests were arriving.

Then a most disturbing rumor was reported to Joe: a

man named Walter Gregor (no relation to the Greger family of Stuart) who was enamored with Josephine Verzal had made a threat on her life because she was rejecting his attentions. Furthermore, he had stated that he might possibly commit the crime at the Ziska wedding dance.

Joe asked his brothers and his sons to help him guard against any trouble; otherwise, he attempted to confine news of the threat so as not to ruin the festivities.

The oldest Ziska son, Charlie, and his cousin Freddie guarded the road in order to intercept Walter should he come. Joe and his brothers Fred and John greeted the guests and helped them find parking for their cars or buggies.

After the Verzals appeared, the Ziska brothers spent a watchful evening on the outer fringes of the group where Josephine happened to be.

"That was a wedding dinner," said John Ziska, "that might as well have been made of chopped corn cobs. I was so intent on watching the crowd during my meal that, once I was finished, I had no idea what I had eaten."

Walter did not appear that night. However, four days later when Josephine, her mother, and her little brothers were walking home from the movie theater in Atkinson, Walter stepped out from behind some bushes and shot Josephine. She died about thirty minutes later.

In July, Walter was sentenced to life imprisonment. Also, on each anniversary of the girl's death, he was ordered to spend the day in solitary confinement.

The Third Bolt of Lightning
1927

Joe Freouf's first encounter with lightning came when, after a summer storm, he went to the pasture to check his cattle, and another rain shower developed. Just as he was crawling through the fence, lightning stuck and knocked him unconscious.

His dog Shep ran home and darted from one member of the family to another, barking incessantly. Joe's son Anton mounted a horse and followed the dog who led him to where the stricken man lay.

Joe was beginning to revive. He struggled to his feet and staggered about. After Anton managed to hoist him up onto the horse, he carefully walked the animal home.

A few years later when a couple of the milk cows got out

Joe and Frances Ziska Freouf Family. Back row: Vincent, Marie, Joe, Frank, Charlie. Middle Row: Millie, Frances, Frederick, Joseph, Anton. Front: Blanche and Emanuel. Taken about 1906.

into the cornfield, Joe's youngest daughter, Blanche, and the dog put them back into the pasture.

When the men came home from the field, Frances and the children began the milking while Joe took a hammer and staples and proceeded to repair the pasture fence where the cows had broken out. A shower came up. Lightning struck the fence some distance away, but it followed the wires and gave Joe a sudden jolt. This time, it only knocked him to his knees.

That evening he said to his wife, "That's the second time lightning has pursued me. You know what the old saying is— the third time it probably will get me."

"Don't be saying that!" exclaimed Frances.

And there *was* a third time. . . .

Emanuel called to his father Joe who was raking hay. "Stop the rakes. We're topping out this stack now because it looks like rain coming from the southwest."

Joe drove east, intending to unhitch the horses from the rake and move them to the wagon. Before he got there, a bolt of lightning—one that preceded the storm—struck.

The boys, knowing from the loud crack followed by

thunder that the bolt had hit someplace nearby, looked that direction. They saw their father's horses that had broken free from the rakes and were pounding madly across the meadow.

Joe was lying on the ground. The lightning had hit him on the back of his shoulder, burning a hole in his sweater. It then traveled through his body to his hip pocket where he carried an iron wrench; from there it went through the rake seat and down to a wheel of the rake. It blew a large hole where it entered the ground.

At home Blanche was pulling a child's wagon, loaded with freshly canned tomatoes, toward the cellar. The boys drove into the yard. As they lifted Joe out of the field wagon, Emanuel called to Blanche.

"Call the doctor!" Tears were trickling down his cheeks.

Blanche couldn't immediately get the doctor on the phone but did call neighbors. The Bouskas and the Tamses soon arrived. They helped Joe's sons who were attempting to revive their father by artificial respiration.

But this time he was dead.

About fifteen miles to the south, the Charlie Freoufs had been bombarded by hail. They collected hailstones to make a freezer of ice cream. The family was enjoying this rare treat when the Cliffords came, bearing the news of Charlie's father's death. (Charlie Freouf had no telephone.)

Medicine Creek Flood
June 1928, southwestern Nebraska

It was a wet spring, and Medicine Creek, which flows into the Republican River near Cambridge, was badly flooded. Herbert Mayo (John Teter's uncle) and a couple of neighbors, hurried to rescue the cattle. The men were able to reach the cows and were driving them through the swirling water toward higher ground.

To help guide the cows and urge them on, Herbert was swishing them with a sunflower stalk that he had yanked from the edge of a field. It was difficult for the men to keep their footing because the current was fast, and the water was deepening. Finally, they each grabbed a cow's tail in order to steady themselves. Herbert still had the stalk in one hand and was using it to keep the floundering cows moving.

Suddenly, he stepped into a ditch, lost his grasp on the

cows tail, and disappeared in the rushing water. For days, people dragged the flooded creek in a vain search for Herbert's remains. A month later there was a second flood which washed the body up onto the bank where it was found by neighbors.

Some days after the accident, Irene Teter, a sister of the drowned man, gave birth to a baby boy who was named Donald.

Until after 1948, when a dam forming Strunk Lake was built, Medicine Creek continued to flood during wet years. (The heavy machinery used to construct the dam was parked in the area when the Blizzard of '48-'49 struck, and it was pressed into service in order to remove the deep snow from the roads.)

Seven Turkeys
about 1928

Nettie Tasler reserved the seven turkeys she had raised in order to provide a better Christmas for their little girls, Alice and Mavis. When December arrived, Clarence placed a chicken crate in the wagon and loaded the turkeys.

Since he needed space for other articles he was hauling, he shoved the crate as far under the wagon seat as he could.

Clarence didn't hear any sounds of distress that the turkeys might have made, for hooves were clopping, harnesses rattling, and wheels rumbling as the wagon proceeded down the rough, trail road.

When Clarence arrived in Atkinson, he was shocked to discover seven lifeless turkey heads dangling on the outside of the wagon box. The creatures had poked their heads through the crate and out between the slat springs on the ends of the wagon seat. The bounce of the seat had broken their necks.

And what did the Taslers do for Christmas presents?

"I don't recall," said Clarence. "Nettie probably made something out of flour sacks—maybe rag dolls or new aprons."

Looking Ahead

Most of the people who had packed up their families and had moved from the Old World to the Nebraska prairies were, by the time of the late 1920's, reaching an advanced age, but they had lived to see their children slowly progressing toward a less harsh way of life. Young groves of trees dotted the once woodless plains and provided shade, shelter, and fuel. Windmills and flowing wells furnished water for stock and for gardens. The tanks in the milk houses were filled with farm produce: containers of cream, milk, cottage cheese, and butter hung from wires that dangled from above. Also, fresh vegetables might float in the cold water: perhaps a crisp head of cabbage or a watermelon, flanked by a bevy of cucumbers.

Many farmers had been freed from the exhausting task of walking back and forth across their fields behind their tilling equipment all day, for by now some had purchased riding plows and cultivators. These new machines, along with an increase in the number of horses on the farms, allowed a man to manage more acres.

Farm and ranch operators gazed longingly at the shiny, noisy, powerful tractors that were recent arrivals in the implement shops. A few men had already chosen one to drive home while others were saving their money in anticipation. Also, the Model T Ford had been joined by the faster Model A, and the Chevrolet Company (as well as other automobile companies) had equally speedy, enclosed vehicles!

Most women had sewing machines which were operated by foot pedals, and a few had wash tubs with agitators which, even though they were hand-powered, were an improvement over the wash board.

Children possibly found small toys in their Christmas stockings along with a package of candy, nuts, and popcorn.*

Days continued to be filled with long hours of muscle-tiring labor—but hope was in the air!

---

* In 1927 the children in one family each received a toy. The youngest got a rattle, but since he was only a few weeks old, he doesn't remember it. Then the family bought land, and after that the depression struck. The years ahead were so desperate that never again did those children get Christmas toys.

comes from the flowing well in the milk
d other perishable foods hang in the tank
es, or a watermelon might be floating in

t is full, the pipe will be lifted up and
ws back into the tank again.

Hand-Powered Washing Machine

Ella Dobrovolny had a machine similar to this one during the late 1920's and the early 'thirties. It was operated by grasping the stick, which can be seen extending up from its side, and swinging the entire tub back and forth in a cradle-like motion. The fifteen minutes required to wash a load of clothes seemed like hours to a six or eight-year-old. Then, like as not, Ella would say, "You'd better give it another five minutes. The men's clothes are greasy this time of the year." Once clean, the clothes were put through the wringer—two rubber rollers operated with a hand crank. Next, the washer was refilled with another load of clothes, and a child was called from play to swing the tub for another fifteen or twenty minutes!

The stone jar at the right of the washer is a churn.

Mary Regal Ziska
and her granddaughters, Monica and Pat.
The girls are the two elder daughters of her
son Freddie. Nancy was born later.
1928 photo.

Some of Joe Dobrovolny's Cattle

To a rancher, the cows come first, and wife and children soon learn to accept that fact. The income from the cows furnishes everything—clothes, food, rent, taxes, vehicles, fuel, haying equipment, land payments—everything! Cattle were—and are—to the rancher what the buffalo were to the Native American.

A Hay Stacker

A Wealth of Horses.

Top: Edd Ziska with his seven-horse team; middle: Jesse Dobrovolny with the horse Molly; bottom: Anton Dobrovolny's plow crew. The man with his legs crossed is Joe.

Jay, Lawrence, and Henry Dobrovolny and their uncle, Joe Dobrovolny.

Chapter 11

The Great Depression

Difficult Times
1929-1934

The Depression was caused by a succession of events. The aftermath of World War I along with governmental policies which encouraged inflation initiated the 1929 Stock Market Crash. When large companies shut down and people were thrown out of work, the demand for products dwindled.

As difficult as it was to deal with a slump in prices, most farmers and ranchers could have maintained their herds and could have survived until better times arrived had it not been for the drought and the searing temperatures of the early thirties. That period of hot, dry weather whisked away two essentials for crop and animal production: water and grass.

The dry years actually had begun in 1928, a year when one person reported that he got but half a yield. Then for a time, even though rainfall was not up to normal, enough moisture fell to allow people to produce some crops. However, the lack of rain in 1934 gave rise to a grim situation.

Because of a shortage of feed, farmers and ranchers were forced to sell their cattle and pigs, and the market was soon flooded. Since meat-packing plants could not accept any more animals, the federal government introduced a program through which they eliminated the excess livestock by buying cows for twelve dollars a head—in some cases, as much as fourteen dollars. Many of these animals were driven away, killed, and buried; others were shipped to cities and the meat given to people who were "on relief."

Picking Corn
1934

During the Dry Thirties, Ken Ziska went with his father Charlie (son of Joe) to pick corn—by hand, of course. Much of the field was covered with bare sand in which a few scrawny plants—perhaps eight or ten inches tall—whispered in the breeze. Only in the low spots were there any corn ears to pick.

Since the bang board must always be on the opposite side from the pickers, the wagon traveled in a circular pattern around a field rather than up one row and down the next.

"Our problem was," said Ken, "that the yield was so poor that we couldn't tell which rows we had picked and which ones we hadn't, and the drifting sand wiped out our tracks from one round of the field to the next. We solved our dilemma by marking the last-picked row with a piece of an old fence post.

"Speaking of sifting sand, there were high drifts of it along the fence rows. Tumble weeds will grow when nothing else does, and those years we had plenty of them. The wind rolled them into the fences, where they, in turn, caught the sand that blew off the barren fields. In some places these drifts of sand completely covered the fences.

"Our neighbor tried to sell his pigs because he had nothing to feed them. He took them to town, but no one would buy them because the market was flooded. He hauled them home and tried to give them to the neighbors, but *they* were trying to get rid of *their* starving hogs. Finally, he shot them."

There were no deep freezes then, and people could keep only that meat which they had time to can or otherwise preserve.

Ken's sister, Viola Ziska Kaup, remembers once when they were going to town in a Model A Ford and noticed that the road ahead was a different color.

"It looks like new gravel," said Charlie. "I didn't know that any of these roads were to be graveled."

When they reached the place that they had been scrutinizing, they discovered that the area was covered with a thick layer of huge, yellowish grasshoppers. The car skidded this way and that on "bug juice" until Charlie managed to slow it. The children worked frantically to close the windows, for the hoppers were bouncing everywhere, inside and out.

After a mile or two, they drove out of the horde of insects.

Buzz Herrick and the Cows
1934

During the Depression, V.J. Krysl sold most of his cows to the government (as did many other ranchers and farmers across the country) for twelve dollars each. Unlike most cattlemen who preferred not to know about the fate of their animals, V.J. inquired.

"Since there is no market for cattle," he said, "what becomes of all this stock that you fellows are collecting?"

"A few are sent to eastern markets," said a government agent, "but the most of them we simply take to a blowout."

The term, "take to a blowout," was one that everyone understood to mean, "we kill them," for the ranchers often buried dead animals in an eroded hole in the sand.

Knowing the fate of his livestock was not enough for the rugged V.J. He decided he wanted to *see* just what was happening. He and his sons accompanied the cattle drive to the blowouts. When they reached the designated area, the animals were shot, and as they lay dead in a tumbled heap, the agents covered them with a green liquid.

"I don't know what it was," said V.J.'s son Don who was a boy of eleven at the time. "Possibly it was something to control the flies."

V.J. had enough hay to keep some of his milk cows. Also, a neighbor, Gerald "Buzz" Herrick, agreed to keep ten of V.J.'s heifers in return for the calves they bore.

Herricks lived on the low, productive Brown quarter which is located a half mile north of the District 205 schoolhouse. They harvested the hay for Brown who baled and sold all of it that was marketable. However, Brown allowed Buzz to keep for himself all of the rushes that grew in the sloughs and also the weeds around the fields. It was this rough feed on which Buzz wintered the ten head of cattle.

The heifers gave birth to fall and winter calves, and Buzz and his wife broke the young cows to milk. Then the family received a small but welcome cream check (probably for the amount of a couple of dollars) each week which was, they often said, the only cash they had that winter.

In 1935, when rains and grass returned to the prairie, V.J. took the heifers home. It was difficult for Buzz to give up the milk cows, and the Krysl's, knowing how desperately the Herrick's needed the money from the cream, were sympathetic.

"But," said Anna Krysl years later, "a deal is a deal. At least they got to keep the calves."

Ed Krysl reported that some cows that were bought by the government were driven to town and shipped east on the railroad. Each evening one enterprising citizen went to the pens near the depot and milked the cows that were waiting to be loaded on the train. This action netted him milk for his family as well as some badly bruised shins, for most of the cows had never been milked before and would "kick like lightning."

Joe and the Depression

Since Joe began ranching at a later date than did his brothers, he was not as well established as they were, but by 1934 he had built his herd to about 310 head. However, with hay production down to less than twenty-five percent, he was preparing to ship 225 of them to Sioux City. To say that he was selling them would be misleading because the amount that he received for them would scarcely pay for the freight charges.

The day before the designated cattle drive to Atkinson, one of Joe's nephews (probably Lawrence or Jay Dobrovolny) came to help Joe and his teenage son LeRoy round up and sort the herd.

"First we'll bring the cows from the South Place," said Joe. "We'll cut the ones to be sold into the milk cow pasture, and the ones to be kept, we'll put in the east pasture. Then we'll bring the heifers from the Long Land."

Ella looked up in shock. She wasn't accustomed to questioning her husband's business decisions, but to sell the young cows was like selling their future! Her awed voice was little more than a whisper, and her eyes were dark with concern.

"Surely," she breathed, "you don't intend to let the heifers go!"

Joe's returned gaze was steady. His time of agonizing over the decision was in the past.

"I'm keeping eighty of the best cows," he said, "and I hope the hay will last until spring. If we also keep the heifers, the hay will be gone by January, and then we'd be forced to sell every critter on the place."

Ella turned back to the stove where, having removed a stove lid, she was toasting bread (skewered on a long-handled fork) over the hot coals in the firebox. She made no sound, but tears slid down her cheeks.

In addition to the eighty cows, Joe kept three bulls. That year was the first winter that he fed cottonseed cake as a supplement.

In 1925 Joe had moved his family from his little cabin south of Holt Creek to the Wright Place, the buildings of which sat on former Rosenberry land. It was about a quarter of a mile northwest of the lake which was once called Rosenberry Lake but had been renamed Wright's Lake. (Before the settlers came, it must have been a buffalo wallow, for Lawrence Dobrovolny said that when the construction crew was building the road around it, they dredged up scores of buffalo horns.)

Because in the thirties the lake was going dry, sportsmen in the area were instrumental in getting a second flowing well installed in it. (A flowing well is one which flows automatically without the aid of a pump. As in the case of a spring, the water is brought to the surface by underground pressure.)

Joe had two flowing wells near his home buildings. One was by the milk house where it filled a tank used for cooling perishable foods and also supplied water (carried in buckets) for household use. The other was in the corral where it watered the livestock.

The lowering of the underground water table had been weakening the wells, but when the new well in Wright's Lake was completed and the crystal clear water began to bubble over the end of the pipe, Joe's corral well completely stopped. The water stood near the top of the pipe, but did not slide over the edge into the tank. At Joe's request, the drillers came with pipe cutters and sliced off enough of the top portion of the pipe to again allow the well to flow.

Through the summer and into the fall the well produced adequately to water the livestock; then it again stopped. The only pump that Joe had available was a hand operated one. He set LeRoy, who was then in his mid-teens, to work at the grueling task of watering the livestock—eighty three head of cattle and fifteen horses. It takes only a few minutes of pumping to tire ones arms; LeRoy pumped for many hours each day.*
Finally, Joe constructed a mechanism which allowed the boy to

---

* "That was only half of it!" LeRoy said later. "During the times of the day when I had the tank full, I sawed wood by hand!"

stand on a crossbar and pump the well by teetering the bar with his feet. While he worked his legs, he stabilized himself by holding onto a support with his hands.

When the younger children came home from school, there he was—swaying back and forth above the well. While they carried in the cobs, wood, and water, and cared for the chickens, they could hear the chug-a-chug of the pump. After their chores were finished and they were inside, soaking in the warmth of the kitchen stove, they could look out of the window and see the rocking figure silhouetted against the darkening sky.

Joe later boasted about how LeRoy watered nearly a hundred head of cattle and horses that winter:

"He pumped that well each morning and each night and at intervals during the day. He never quit until every critter was satisfied and the tank was full."

In those days farm boys had no need for an athletic program to develop their muscles.

The Depression was a time when thousands of people lost their farms and ranches; thus there was a considerable amount of land on the market. However, scarcely anyone had the money or the credit to buy it. About fifteen miles south of Joe's place, a quarter of hay land was to be sold at auction.

The day before the sale, Joe went to the First National Bank in Atkinson and asked if he could borrow money to buy the land.

"Now, Joe," said Fred Swengley, the bank official, "I don't want to be a part of an act that would give you any more trouble than you already have. I just can't let you have additional money."

"Look at it this way," said Joe. "I already owe far more dollars against every acre in my place than this new land will cost me per acre. Let me have the money to buy the land, and when I spread my combined debt over all the acres that I own, I'll owe less per acre if I buy the land than if I don't buy it."

Swengley met Joe's steady gaze and considered for a moment. Then he slapped his knee.

"By golly, Joe! I'll do it!"

When Joe returned home from the sale, he stated simply: "I bought some more land."

Ella, who was the one faced with the daily struggle of clothing six children (Fred was born later) and of putting food on the table, burst into tears. "How can we buy land?" she asked,

"The kids need shoes—and I can't figure out how to get enough money to replace the worn out sheets on the hired men's beds.*

One of Leo Kramer's Early Inventions
as told by his brother Lawrence

The heat during the Dry Thirties was scorching, and any garden plants which were to grow needed a plentiful amount of moisture. Our brother Leo was interested in inventing things, and he devised an apparatus to water our mother's garden.**

We had a windmill near the edge of the corral which pumped water into the milk house tank where it cooled milk, butter, and the like. From there the water ran into two stock tanks outside.

Leo fashioned a mechanism which had two long wires attached to the mill. As the turning mill moved the pump stick up and down, it also pulled first one wire and then the other. The garden was by the house, and a well with a hand pump was near it. Leo ran the two wires from the mill to the garden and tied them to the opposite ends of a four-by-four inch piece of lumber that was, perhaps, three or four feet long. It, in turn, was fastened to the pump. As the mill turned, the wires teetered the four-by-four back and forth, thereby pumping the well.

Mother carefully ditched the water to the rows of plants.

We had twenty-five or thirty head of cows during the depression, but the pasture had no feed in it—it was as smooth as a wooden floor. So each forenoon we herded the cows on some strips of weeds and grass between patches of corn. I tell you, holding those cows out of the corn made a person scamper! The best grass was along the edge of the field, and when the cows were that close to the corn, they watched for a chance to slip in and get a few bites.

It was a long, hot, exhausting forenoon. In the afternoon, we put the cattle in the pasture even if it were empty of grass.

---

* Joe bought unbleached muslin, and Ella sewed sheets. She tried to sun-bleach them by repeatedly wetting them and spreading them on the grass in the sun, but with scant success.

** Later, Leo operated the Kramer Manufacturing Shop in Atkinson where he built customized ranching and farming equipment, inventing many of the machines himself.

Flat Broke
as told by Mae Hanel

What was the most difficult time in my life? There is no contest. It was the Depression when we were living in Denver in a one-room apartment with a pull-down cot. We shoved chairs together to make a bed for our four-year-old daughter, Bettye.

Frank had been laid off from his job, and every day he walked the streets looking for work while I did the best I could to take care of Bettye and keep her mind off the subject of food. What we mainly ate was green beans. For a long time after that, I hated the sight of a bean—we all got so sick of them! Since they were a cheap vegetable, I'd buy a can of them and some milk. I'd pour milk over the beans and thicken them with flour.

Little by little, we pawned our few possessions. First, Frank sold his shotgun, and later, his watch. I sold a nine-dollar pen for a mere seventy-five cents. Finally, we even pawned some silverware that we had received as a wedding gift.

One Sunday Frank was going through his tools, examining each one—hammer, pliers, screw drivers, and the like. I knew why. He was looking them over and trying to decide how much money they would bring.

"I think," I said, "that if we sold your tools and our household items, we'd have enough money to get home."

Frank didn't say a word—he just looked at me.

"Dad hires extra help this time of the year," I said, "and there is enough work on the ranch for us to earn our keep."

We went home and lived with my dad [Ed Schindler] for a while, after which we rented a place owned by my mother, Bertha Berger. For some years we had slim picking, but we finally got on our feet.

We've had our share of ups and downs—the same as other folks—but nothing else came near to being as bad as the Depression.

Newly-Oiled Floor
as told by Lawrence Dobrovolny

It was quite a surprise when the first dust storms came because we'd never seen anything like them before; however, people got used to them and took them in their stride. One particular storm, though, I'll never forget!

I was batching down on the O'Donnel Place which is

about five miles northeast of the home place. One evening I scrubbed my floors, and the next morning I oiled them. I heated up some linseed oil, thinned it a little to make it soak in, and brushed it onto the floor boards, after which I opened all the windows and doors in order to help with the drying process.

I hitched a four-horse team to the underslung [a large, low platform on wheels used to haul hay] and went a couple of miles away to get a load of hay. About the time I got the hay cabled on, I saw a black cloud rising from the north. I knew what it was—an approaching dust storm—and I'd left my house wide open!

What with being loaded like I was, there wasn't any way to hurry the horses, and the storm hit when I was about a half mile from home.

The way I remember it, I found about a half inch of dust on the floor, all stuck fast in that thick oil. Now that was a mess!

Lawrence's wife Phyllis said:

I was teaching school south of Bassett, and one Friday evening I rode the bus to Atkinson where my folks planned to pick me up. A dust storm hit and was so bad that they didn't come for me because they couldn't see to drive. The next day the wind let up, and I caught the west-bound bus back to Bassett.

LeRoy Dobrovolny said:

I recall one dust storm when it was almost black out. Car lights or a lantern didn't help much because the air was too thick with flying soil. The dust settled everywhere—on fields and ponds and inside of buildings and out. A thick coating gathered on the upper side of stringers and braces in barns and on the frames above windows and doors of outside buildings. In places like that where it wasn't disturbed, it lay for years; then when you happened to run into it unawares, it sure took you back to some awful memories.

I think that one reason we had such a bumper crop the year that the rains finally *did* come [1935], was because we had gotten all that rich topsoil from other regions. Sometimes we got red dust which people said was from western Oklahoma, and other times we got a yellowish dust, supposedly from South Dakota.

Mildred Findley was teaching in School District 210 when one of the storms rolled in. In those days there were no artificial lights in rural schools, and it was so dark that it was impossible for the children to read or write. After the teacher directed the pupils to put their books aside, she began teaching them by rote—all the grades in one class. They worked on the states and their capitals.

Walt Jones, a member of the school board, came to the door and told her to close school. The children walked home in the dim, eerie light and the choking dust. Upon reaching home, they proceeded to do their chores. When gathering the eggs, they found that the chickens were sitting on the roosts with their heads tucked under their wings, all of them sound asleep even though it was mid-afternoon.

It was a good time for children to write and draw in the dust—on vehicles, cellar doors, window sills, and furniture. Also, after the dust storms that year, there were some breathtakingly spectacular sunsets—a hodgepodge of all the brilliant colors that can be found on an artist's palette.

While most dust storms swept through in 1934, some came early the following year. The snow that winter was black because the flakes picked up dust as they passed through the atmosphere. Such snowstorms were called "black blizzards."

On April 30, 1935, the day that Warren Gilman was buried in Chambers, a dust storm engulfed the mourners as they drove from the cemetery toward the Gilman Ranch. (In those days there were no funeral homes in the area, and the body of the deceased lay in state in his own house where relatives and friends gathered before and after the funeral.)

"The car lights scarcely helped," said June Gilman, a daughter-in-law. "And to make matters worse, a few, large raindrops fell. Actually, they were mud drops, for they turned to mud as they passed through the dust-laden atmosphere. They splattered on everything including the windshields. Windshield wipers weren't so good in those days, and visibility was down to nearly zero. Luckily, everyone in the neighborhood had attended the funeral which meant that all the traffic was going the same direction.

"When we arrived at the ranch, we found everything coated with thick dust. The milk cows must have thought it was chore time, for they had come to the corral. They were a sorry sight—with dirty rings around their eyes, mouth, and nostrils. I recall that during those times, the livestock was prone to have respiratory problems—dust pneumonia and the like.

"My sister visited relatives in Kansas that year, and she said that the dust was even worse there because they had much more plowed ground than we did here. They fastened wet sheets over the windows in an effort to keep some of the dust out of the house, but nothing helped much."

A Hungry Horde
as told by Orval Monson*

One year in the Thirties when we completely dried out and the grasshoppers took over, we mixed sawdust, molasses, and arsenic and spread it on the fields with an end-gate seeder.** Since there wasn't much else for the hoppers to eat, they went right to work on the poisoned sawdust.

We hardly raised anything that season; I recall a forty-acre field from which we got a total of forty bushels of corn—and that was in rich Iowa soil! Any other year it wouldn't have been worth picking, but at that time, every kernel was precious. That was one winter when we almost starved!

A few years later we were infested with cinch bugs which seemed to have hatched out in a corner of our corn field. They devoured about two acres of corn before we figured out what to do.

We put tarpaper barriers between the infested area and the remainder of the field. Digging a trench by hand, we buried the bottom of the paper and let the rest stand up like a fence. Spraying the tarpaper with dip kept the insects from crossing it. When the bugs started traveling in a path along the barrier, we dug deep holes with a post hole digger. Whenever the holes filled with bugs, we poured kerosene on them.

The railroad tracks cut through our field diagonally, and the bugs began moving across them to a field on the other side. We tried to stop them by spraying insecticide along the tracks. It was a hot day, and I was so exhausted from the heat, the effort, and the fumes off the spray that I was afraid that I was going to pass out. Then an amazing event occurred: the bugs, having developed wings, rose into the air in an enormous, dark cloud

---

*Orval was the grandfather of Eve, Vince Jr., Adrienne & Renee.
** An end-gate seeder was a mechanism designed for scattering seed. It was fastened to the back end of a wagon box and was powered by a large sprocket which was attached to the rear wheel of the vehicle.

and flew away.

How we rejoiced over the miracle! However, our elation did have an edge of concern, for we knew that they would probably scatter to hundreds of other places to lay their eggs and to promote someone else's disaster.

The Stain on the Suit
1934

A certain Federal Land Bank representative (we will call him Simon Flint and say that he lived in Spade County) decided to foreclose the farm mortgage of a certain couple who had several small children. We will call the couple Peter and Beverly Helm.

"We tried to talk to him—tried to persuade him to rewrite the loan—but he refused," said Beverly, remembering. "He insisted we were so far in the hole financially that we'd never get out. When we said that the drought wouldn't last forever, and that we'd like to keep trying, he chuckled."

"'I'm doing you a favor to take this property off your hands,' he said. 'I've got the legal right to do it, and I assure you, I can make better use of it than you can. Why, you have so much debt against it that there isn't any way that you will be able to come up with the money to operate it.'"

Beverly continued to remember back to that event: "You know what a strong, robust man Peter is. Well, that day he was pale and whipped and was slumped in his chair. I'd never seen him look so bad—kind of a sickly yellow. We didn't know where we'd go or what we'd do.

"I glanced down at the baby on my lap and noticed a dark stain on the shoulder of the little sailor suit that he was wearing. It was the only Sunday clothes he had, and for a moment I couldn't collect my thoughts well enough to figure out how that spot got there.

"Then it hit me: A tear had slid out of my eye and had fallen on the baby. As soon as I realized what the stain was, the whole situation looked different to me. It was just as if I were a bystander looking in on this dreadful scene.

"There sat the Land Bank official in his neat, starched shirt, his head held high and his back straight. Outside was his shiny car, and up the street was his beautiful home. Slumped in front of him was the despairing, work-worn family with the mother whose tears were falling on the baby. How could that man look so boldly across his desk and tell them, destitute because of the terrible drought, that he meant to take their home? Probably, he gave the same awful news to some sad family every day, and was used to it.

"But suddenly, my fear and despair gave way to anger. I told him that I thought he was a poor choice for the representative of the Land Bank, and that he was working to fill his own pockets rather than to help the people that he was supposed to be serving. I said that I was going to write to the regional office and report what he was doing out here.

"Flint just laughed at me. 'Write if you want to,' he said, 'but it won't do you any good. This is my territory, and I make the decisions.'"

Beverly did write and ten days passed—ten days of worry and hopelessness. Preparing to leave the farm, the family packed their few possessions, including the empty fruit jars.

"I thought that surely this drought couldn't go on much longer," said Beverly. "In another year perhaps I again would have garden produce to fill the jars."

Early Monday morning there was a knock on the door, and there stood Mr. Flint and another man, both looking strangely out of place, standing there in their well-pressed suits in front of the tiny, weather-beaten farm house.

After greetings, the man spoke: "I'm Will Fawcett from the regional offices of the Federal Land Bank. I want to thank you, Mrs. Helm, for your recent letter to me, and to ask you if you will stand by what you said in it about Mr. Flint."

"Yes, I will!" exclaimed Beverly. "Every word!" She glanced at Simon Flint whose face was carrying a little more color than it usually did, and who now stood silent and ill-at-ease at Fawcett's elbow.

"In that case, I'd like you to come to Cowly to the county office and make a statement," he said.

Quickly, Peter and Beverly prepared the children for the trip. Beverly was so weak from her rising hope that she could hardly stuff the baby into that little sailor suit.

At Cowly they were again asked to repeat their story and to sign a statement, after which Fawcett said:

"We are closing the branch office in your town, Peter. The county office will assume responsibility for the area southeast of Cowly and if you still want that loan, we are prepared to make out the papers."

"I almost fainted with relief!" remembered Beverly. "I

thought the top of my skull would blow off my head! I have no idea what Peter said, for the room was turning around me. It is a good thing that I was sitting down, or I'd have surely dropped the baby!"

Since it was nearly noon, the office was locked while everyone went to lunch—everyone but the Helm family, that is, for they had no money. They waited in their little car where Beverly fed the baby.

"The other children were hungry, of course, but they accepted our explanation and didn't fuss," she remembered.

After the business was completed, they went home. Peter made a fire in the kitchen stove, Beverly fried some eggs, and they feasted, thankful that, for the moment, their land was safe—and that they had had enough gas in the car to get back to it.

"But, of course, that isn't really the end of the story," said Beverly. *"There is no way to explain the years and years of hard work and painful poverty in the time afterward. We didn't get that debt paid off until the children were nearly grown.*

"But don't give our names in this account! I don't want people to know how bad off we were in those times. It wounds me yet to think about it."

Other People Remember the Depression

"I got a job with the WPA," said Pete Weber. "It was a governmental program meant to give people work, and at the same time, construct roads, bridges, public buildings, and the like. Most of the brick streets found in towns today were built in the Thirties by WPA workers who labored with shovels and wheelbarrows. The first groves of trees referred to as "shelter belts" were also WPA projects. My job was to haul clay, using a team and wagon, from Bonenberger's Pit to Highway 11.

"At that time, I lost a quarter of land that we had already paid $3000 on, but we were able to save a section."

Helen Kubart Coufal said, "We bought the store in Stuart in 1935. The year before, Ed was on the committee for killing the excess hogs in the country. Now, that was a terrible thing. Terrible!

In the store, we sold eggs for ten cents a dozen and coffee for twenty-three cents a pound. You could go across the street and buy a hamburger in a bun for a nickel."

"In thirty-four I ran out of pasture early," said Fred Dobrovolny. "I was down from 500 head of cattle to about 150 head, and our pasture was as bare as a desert.

"The Dakotas had run out of grass a year or two before we did, and people from there had come south and had rented every acre they could find. Then when we ran short of pasture, there was no place for us to go but farther south.

"I went to Eight-Mule Kelly's. He was called Eight-Mule because he once hauled freight with a string of mules. After he baled the little hay he had, he took in my cattle on what was supposed to be after-grass—but the after-grass didn't grow that year. My cows ate his stubbles down to the roots."

Max and Marie Karo* drove their cattle over the hills to the Calamus River to find summer feed," reported Ralph Ries. "Max rode a horse and Marie took their small children in a spring wagon. I think it took them two days to get there, and a day to return.

"Mrs. Karo was a hard-working woman, both inside the house and out."

"Frank Noziska's house needed reshingling," said Walter Ries. "He cut tin cans apart and used the straightened tin to shingle his house."

"My dad and I were in Washington working in construction when the Depression hit," Lester Zarnfeller reported. "There were no contracts coming in and the whole industry—even the lumber mills—had to shut down. We came back to Nebraska and managed to exist on occasional odd jobs. Boy, those were some hard times!"

"During the Thirties," said George Hitchcock, "one of Frank Schaaf's quarters had so much cactus growing on it that the jack rabbits wouldn't venture off the cow paths. You would think that would be a situation that would make them easy prey for the dogs, but such wasn't the case. When a dog took up the chase, the rabbit ran down the cow path until he came to where it branched, and he'd turn onto the branch. Naturally, the dog thought he'd gain the advantage by cutting across, but instead, he'd get hung up in the cactus, and the rabbit would escape."

---

* Parents of Max II, Dorothy (Farr), and Delores (Seger)

Other Stories of the Early Thirties

When Jerome Kruger was a teenager, he worked for Ramm's Meat Market, and he often helped make bologna. One night after the meat was stuffed into the casings, Jerome discovered that his class ring was missing. It must have slipped off his finger when he was working with the meat which was mixed by hand in large tubs.

When Ramms sold the bologna, they told each customer about the lost piece of jewelry, and said that anyone who returned it would be given a couple of free rings of bologna.

One day V.J. Krysl came into the store, laughing and shouting even more loudly than was usual for him.

"Somebody owes me some bologna," he boomed as he tossed Jerome's ring on the counter. His wife, Anna, had bitten into it when they were eating.

(The Krysls were great bologna eaters. After the 200 rings which they made themselves each year were gone, they bought more—ten or fifteen rings at a time.)

Jerome later commented about V.J.: I'll never forget that laugh! He was the happiest guy I ever knew.

On some mornings the clatter of stove lids would be accompanied by Anna Krysl's scolding voice. She was angry because tobacco chewing guests of the previous night had sent their dark, juicy cuds flying into the cob basket.

The cobs were there to make a quick fire in the morning, but cobs that have been used as a spittoon do not burn well. An even worse problem was handling the cobs.

Ear corn was often tossed into the pigpen where the pigs ate the corn off the cobs. Children hated picking those dirty cobs from the pen, and mothers hated using them for fuel. However, Anna often commented that she would rather burn cobs from the pigpen than the ones that had been splattered with tobacco juice.

"During Prohibition, there was a bootlegger east of Elyria," said Philip Wentek. "He made whisky—if you could call it that. It was terrible! Pure poison! If you'da run it through a dirty stovepipe, it couldn't a been any worse.

"He gave me a drink of it one Sunday, and my mouth was still foaming on Monday. It seemed to do something to a person's salivary glands. Why, it was worse than poison! It could kill! I soon learned not to test folk's home-made brews!"*

When Ed Krysl married Mary Greger, Mary's father gave the young couple some young heifers to seed their herd. Ed was driving them to their own place when one of the more independent animals suddenly decided to turn back. While he was galloping to overtake her, his horse stepped into a badger hole and the two, man and horse, tumbled end over end. The horse struck Ed with his hind foot and broke Ed's collarbone.

When he told this story years later, a listener asked: "Did you go to a doctor?"

Ed laughed. "Oh, no."

"Well, what did you do then? Go to bed?"

"No. In those days I was peppy. I didn't need to go to bed with an injury like that."

Ed pulled his shirt collar aside to reveal his collarbone. There was a knot on it the size of a robin's egg. The bone obviously hadn't been in line when it healed.

Ruth Barnes reported that during the early thirties, she worked in the Night-and-Day Cafe in Atkinson. Her wages were nine cents per hour, an amount which she was glad to receive since it was during desperate times.

V.J. was an unparalleled optimist. Whenever he estimated how much oats he would get at harvest time, how much money he might realize from stripping blue grass seed, or how many pigs would be born to his eight or ten sows, his guess was always inflated.

His wife paid scant attention to yields and prices, but her much lower prediction would probably be a little closer than would his. One day she told how she figured her estimations:

"I take V.J.'s guess and cut it exactly in half. The actual number will be somewhere between the two guesses, and almost always it will be closer to mine than to his because usually his prediction will be more than twenty-five percent too high."

The Strawberry Roan

> *"He was the worst bronc I've seen on the range;*
> *He could turn on a nickel and leave you some change."*

Aloys Kaup worked for Max Karo before he started his

own ranch operation, and on winter evenings he and his wife Gertie sometimes visited V.J.'s family to play cards and to listen to the Krysls make music. One of the songs that they sang was "The Strawberry Roan," a long, delightful ballad about an ill-tempered bronc that couldn't be ridden.

"Say, Aloys," said Leo Krysl one night, "when are you going to toss your saddle on that strawberry roan colt* over at Karos?"

"Oh, she's too big for a saddle horse," answered Aloys. "Max says we're going to break her to the harness and use her in the hayfield."

"You shouldn't do that!" thundered V.J. "Since you have a strawberry roan, you should *ride* her. You've got to show that you're a better bronc buster than the feller in the song."

During subsequent visits, the banter continued until one spring day Aloys said that he planned to ride the roan, and he invited everyone to come and see him do it. On the appointed day, the Krysl men set forth, laughing and quipping.

Toward evening, they returned, proclaiming that Aloys was indeed a great bronc buster, for he had ridden the strawberry roan. It was difficult to tell from their comments whether they were relating actual events or simply paraphrasing the song when they told about the squealing, wild-eyed bronc. It was true, however, that the story got better with each retelling. Later, V.J. decided that he must have the roan for his own, and he managed to buy her from Karo.

Roanie was well-fitted for a draft horse, and she worked faithfully in the hayfield and on the plow for many years in spite of the fact that she was prone to develop collar sores. Bill (V.J.'s youngest son) used her on the hay rakes. However, it was obvious that Aloys had been successful in breaking her to ride, for at the end of the day, Bill often unhitched his team, hopped on Roanie's back, and (leading the other horses) rode her to where the wagon was parked.**

Creamed Ice

Marie Premer Moore belonged to the Busy Bees, a club

---

* A strawberry roan is a horse with a mixture of red and white hairs, giving the animal a speckled, rosy hue.
** The mirror wall hanging, constructed by Lou Laible from a horse collar and owned by Judy Krysl, is Roanie's collar.

in southwestern Nebraska whose members worked on whatever sewing project the host of the meeting chose, possibly embroidering, mending, or quilting. Each summer the group planned a picnic for the families of the club members.

During the winter, Marie's husband Lark harvested ice, sawing it on the river and packing it in sawdust in the ice house. Since the Moores had stored ice, they were the ones who furnished the ice cream for the picnic.

On this particular day, Lark put an ample amount of ice in a gunny sack and loaded it into the car. Marie packed the ingredients for the dessert in a box, but decided to keep the jar of cream cool by placing it inside the gunny sack with the ice.

When they reached the picnic spot on the Republican River, Marie carried the box of ingredients to the place where she planned to mix the ice cream. Lark removed the bag of ice from the car and unaware that there was a jar of cream inside, began to crush the ice by beating the sack with the broad side of an ax. After a few good whacks, the brown bag began to turn creamy white!

Marie may have been the first person to make iced milk, for she made the dessert without the benefit of cream. Lark is probably the only person who has ever frozen iced milk with creamy ice mixed with crushed glass! (For the benefit of young readers who aren't familiar with the making of home-made ice cream, do be aware that none of the ice gets into the ice cream.)

A Favorite Team

The best team of horses that Earl Moore ever had was a pair of heavy animals named Spike and Dot. Spike was gray, and Dot was black with a tiny white spot on her forehead. Because Earl bought a tractor before Lark did, Earl sometimes loaned horses to Lark.

Once when Lark was planting corn with a lister and was using a six-horse team, he hitched a newly trained colt on the outside next to the sturdy, dependable Spike. Suddenly, a frightened bird whirred up from its nest in the field and startled the colt. He reared up, came down on top of Spike, and scrambled around until he fell on the opposite side of his companion. There he floundered, ensnared in harnesses.

"And you know," said Lark with wonder in his voice as he told the story, "even though that colt was tangled in Spike's harness which was twisting and binding and pulling him out of shape, Spike stood firm and held him. Man, oh, man! There was the chance for the six of them to have gone six different directions and to have busted everything up. But trusty old Spike! He stood there as solid as a mountain."

Restoring order was a tedious task with harness straps stretched so tightly that it was difficult to unhook them, particularly when one had to wedge between horses who were frightened and might kick. Finally, though, the six-horse team was again arranged in proper order.

"But oh-h-h boy," said Lark. "A person really appreciated a dependable horse when he was in an emergency like that!"

Pheasant for Supper

Boyd and his father, Frank Teter,* were cutting wood near the river and were loading it on a wagon. Neva, Boyd's wife, had driven a 1928 Whippet car to the scene to help. When evening came, Boyd and Neva went home in the car in order to start chores on time. Frank, the mules, and the loaded wagon followed at a slower pace. There was a hammer hanging by the claws on the front of the wagon.

Suddenly, a rooster pheasant raised his head out of the grass and crowed. Grabbing the hammer, Frank hurled it. It happened to hit the pheasant in the head and knocked him dead.

"You've never seen a happier man," said Boyd in telling the story. "He was about sixty years old, but he was as tickled as a little kid who had just caught his first fish. We had pheasant for supper."

Teter's Threshing Accident

The earth-shaking tractor thundered into the Teter field, pulling the monstrous thresher, and as it did so, brought all the excitement, the commotion, and the urgency that is common to threshing time. Every person had an assigned task. The able-bodied men, as well as the neighborhood youths, were in the field pitching bundles, hauling grain, overseeing the machine, and perhaps stacking straw. The old men might be tending the bins or helping to set up outside, make-shift tables. The

---

* Frank Teter, who lived near Bartley in southwestern Nebraska, was the great-great-grandfather to Stephanie and Robert Krysl.

grandmothers could be peeling vegetables while the younger women cooked the mountain of food. Periodically, the children would be pulled from their play to carry wood, cobs, or water into the house—or to carry dish water or vegetable peelings out.

Earl Teter was one of the men who was pitching bundles. After loading his hayrack, he drove it to the machine and positioned it on the belt-drive side of the feeding platform. (Another man was feeding bundles from the other side.)

As Earl reached his pitchfork back and forth over the endlessly moving band that carried power and motion from the tractor to the thresher, he made a single but unfortunate mistake: he swung the fork too low, and one of the tines caught in the whirring belt.

With a motion as fast as the crack of a whip, the handle of the pitchfork snapped toward Earl's face. It made a wide, gapping hole all the way through his cheek and knocked him flat. Luckily, he didn't fall on the spinning belt.

The machine operator was the first to reach him. Earl was unconscious and remained so for about twenty minutes. His face with the torn cheek was a shocking sight.

He was driven to Cambridge where a doctor stitched the wound.

Chauffeuring a Pig

There was no hint in the morning that this day would be a most unordinary one—one that Gene Kramer would remember all his life. It began as usual: after the milking chores were completed, Gene leaped onto the pony and rode to a neighbor's farm where he supposed that he would spend the day splitting wood, forking manure, or pitching hay. When dusk came, he, young shoulders hunched from handling loaded shovel or fork, would ride home to supper and warmth.

However, when he arrived at the neighbor's place on this particular day, his boss (here called Jeb) said: "As soon as you put your horse away, Boy, help me lift the back seat out of this Model A. We're going to Battle Creek to buy a boar pig."

Gene led the pony toward the barn, his mind a whirl of disbelief and hope. Who did Jeb mean by *we*? It wasn't likely that he meant himself and his family, for his wife and his growing number of small children would not accompany him on such a trip. But why would he take Gene, the hired boy, along when there were sheds to clean?

Farm people didn't move around much in those days, particularly a boy like Gene who was from a family of twelve children. His knowledge of the surrounding area was limited to a couple of towns on either side of their farm.

Soon Jeb and Gene were seated in the Model A with a box of sandwiches between them, and were chugging eastward down the highway. Battle Creek, Jeb informed Gene, was about a hundred miles away.

A hundred miles! Gene had never before been that far east!

When they arrived in Atkinson, the first town along the way, Jeb stopped in front of a tavern. "You wait here," he directed. "I have to go inside and see a feller."

A half hour went by quickly while Gene examined the road map and watched the people on the street. What would it be like, he wondered, to live in town and not have cows to milk and pigs to slop? Maybe when he got a little older, he would get a job in town.

After Jeb's return, the journey resumed; but when they reached O'Neill which was twenty miles farther, Jeb had to see another man in another bar. This time the wait was longer, and when Jeb finally reappeared, he brought the smell of whisky with him. He came to the passenger side of the car.

"Slide over," he said. "You might as well drive."

Automatically, Gene obeyed; but once under the steering wheel, he hesitated. "I'm not old enough," he said, "and I don't have a license."

Jeb exploded. "Dad gum it!" he shouted. "You've driv' all over two farms for years and have dodged chickens and pigs by the hunnerds! There's scarcely a car on the road now in the middle of the week, but if we do meet some, you can dodge them a durn sight easier than you can a dumb animal. Drive, I say!"

Gene drove. Actually, he knew it was the safer option.

When twice more Jeb had to stop "to see a man in a bar," Eugene welcomed the chance to rest his arms which were tense from gripping the steering wheel too tightly. It was dusk by the time they located the hog farm near Battle Creek.

Jeb wandered through the pen full of milling hogs, wanting to make a wise selection. Since he and his neighbors usually traded boar pigs with each other, he was seeking to add to the local hog gene pool, and he felt the weight of great responsibility. His problem now was that he couldn't see clearly, and this difficulty was not the result of the sinking sun. Gene watched from the sideline, and was relieved when Jeb pointed to a large animal that possessed well-rounded hams. The farmer and Gene wrestled the pig and tied his feet, after which they rolled him over the folded front seat into the back seat of the car. The boy's ears rang and his spine tingled from the shrill squealing of the frightened hog.

"You fellows are welcome to come in and have a bite of supper with us," offered the farmer as Jeb counted some dollar bills into his hand.

Supper! The prospect sounded good to Gene. It had been a long time since sandwiches, and his stomach was empty.

"Much obliged for the invite," said Jeb, "but we need to be on our way."

At first they made better time on the return trip. Gene felt more confident, and the car purred along nicely at thirty miles an hour. Both passengers had settled down: Jeb was nodding and snoring, and the pig was grunting softly. The situation, now quite peaceful, was ridiculously unreal to Gene. Usually at this time of the evening he was riding his pony home, but here he was—a hundred miles away—chauffeuring his sleeping boss and a Hampshire hog!

Suddenly the lights blinked and then went out. Gene stopped the vehicle and roused Jeb.

"Try to get to the next town," said Jeb. "If we can't find a mechanic, we will at least have light from the street lamps to work on the problem ourselves." He reached through the crack between the two front seats and patted the pig. "Nice ol' feller!" he crooned. "Good ol' boy. We'll get you home by and by!" Then he promptly went back to sleep.

Gene rolled down the window. Only a few stars penetrated the overcast sky and he wondered how he could possibly drive in the darkness. Then he noticed that he could see the faint outline of the old snow along the roadside. Perhaps — using it as a guide—he could manage to move ahead slowly. Jeb had been right about one thing; there was scarcely any other traffic on the road. Gene inched the car forward.

After a few minutes, a light appeared on the road ahead. Gene did the best he could to stay to the far right, and the two cars passed safely. Later another light appeared. When the two cars met, the other stopped, and Gene did likewise.

"Are you having trouble?" called a man's voice. Gene explained.

"I'll turn around and you can follow my tail light,"

offered the man. "Neligh is only a couple miles down the road. Perhaps you can get help there.."

Gene was immensely relieved when they drove into the lighted streets of Neligh.

After inquiry they located a mechanic, Dewayne Frady, who was working late. Gene watched as the man skillfully checked the lights, and was surprised when the mechanic began explaining the problem to him. In those days, kids usually were not told *anything* and, what is more, they didn't *expect* to be told anything. Could it be that he was crossing the boundry between boyhood and adulthood?

Once the lights were repaired, Dewayne slid into the driver's seat to try them. The pig, startled, let out a loud grunt. The mechanic, equally surprised, turned around.

"Is that a *pig?*" he asked.

"It shore is," said Jeb, who had been leaning against a fender, waiting. "I don't have a pickup, and this beats payin' shippin'"

Once again on the road, the little car rumbled along. Although the stop had done nothing to ease the hunger pangs gnawing under Gene's rib cage, it had erased his weariness. Jeb had revived as well. He chatted first with the boy and then, in crooning tones, to the pig. Every little while he reached back to pat the animal reassuringly.

However, yet another problem would test Gene's skills, for great, fluffy snowflakes began to fall. When snow settled on the windshield, he turned on the wipers, only to discover that they were so old and bent that they simply stirred the snow a little, but didn't clean it off. Again Gene pulled to the roadside.

"Just wait a little," directed Jeb. "These big flakes won't last long."

After a few minutes, the falling snow thinned, and Gene got out and cleaned the windshield. They pulled back onto the road, but soon flakes as big as feathers began floating down, and they were again forced to stop. Jeb, unconcerned about the wait, went back to sleep.

Gene proceeded, alternating the starts and stops in accordance with the snowfall. Hemmed in by the surrounding darkness, he felt strangely alone. Who was he, anyway? Even to himself, he seemed a strange being in an odd little vehicle creeping along on the dark surface of the earth. He didn't seem to be the same boy who was pitching manure the day before.

Finally, the snow stopped falling, but by the time they

arrived at Jeb's place, it was about two-thirty. They wrestled the pig out of the back seat and into the pen, after which Jeb trudged slowly toward the house. Gene moved through the corral to the barn where his pony was stabled. The thick blackness inside was made more sinister by the shifting and grunting of the disturbed animals that were housed there, but Gene found his horse and the bridle. He was soon outside the building, mounted, and heading through the cold night toward home. The last part of the journey was cheered a little by the fact that his mother had left a kerosene lamp burning in the kitchen.

Upon arrival, Gene again braved the blackness of the barn while he tended his pony. Once inside the kitchen—now cold because the fires in the stoves had burned themselves out— he raided the bread box and blew out the light. In the bedroom, he undressed and crawled into a bed which already held two of his brothers. While he shivered himself warm, he reviewed the happenings of the incredible day. Would Jeb think of it as an unpaid holiday, or would he pay him the ordinary wage in spite of the fact that Gene had done none of the usual work expected of him? Gene decided that it didn't matter, for he would treasure in memory every detail of the unexpected journey. Before this day, it had seemed to him that he would never outgrow a boy's body; but now he knew that manhood lay only a short distance ahead.

Hauptmann's Murder Trial

Joe Dobrovolny closely followed the newspaper accounts of the Bruno Hauptmann murder trial and often remarked that, incriminating as the evidence was, it was circumstantial, and he repeatedly proclaimed that the accused man should not be given a death sentence. This statement was in conflict with general opinion, both local and national.

Hauptmann was accused of the 1932 kidnapping and slaying of the baby son of the hero, Charles A. Lindbergh, who five years before, had made the first solo flight across the Atlantic Ocean. Hauptmann had been apprehended after passing some of the bills from the ransom money, more of which were found in his garage. Also, his ladder fit the imprints of the ladder used in the kidnapping. Most people insisted that his guilt was unquestionable.

One evening during supper, one of Joe's children asked him why he objected so strongly to Hauptmann's execution.

"Because," said Joe, "the death sentence is irrevocable. It is true that the man is most probably guilty, yet can we be positive?

"Back around the turn of the century when I worked in South Dakota for Jim Mitchell, Jim said that when he was a young feller—I suppose about 1868 or 1870—he came west through Omaha, and he witnessed a lynching there. One of the local settlers had been murdered, and the people in charge arrested a man who was in the vicinity. He was a stranger who was passing through.

"According to the evidence, it seemed that the prisoner was the one who had committed the crime. Even though he swore that he was innocent, a quick trial sentenced him to be hanged. It seems that his wife was traveling with a second group of people who were a few days behind, and he asked that the execution be delayed until she arrived so that he could say good-by to her. People in the area were not in a mood to grant favors, however, and his request was denied.

"Well, they hanged him. Years later, Jim Mitchell was reading an account about various innocent people who'd been executed, and that man in Omaha was among them. The actual murderer made a death-bed confession and said he'd been in the crowd on the day of the hanging. Jim always said that a court shouldn't sentence a person to death on circumstantial evidence, and I figure that he was right."

Hauptmann was executed in 1936.

Joe Sells His Steers

"Now that we're finally getting some moisture," said Charlie Bumgart of Humphry, Nebraska, "I have a bumper grain crop, and I'd like to corn-feed some steers. Can you guide me to a ranch that has some good ones for sale?" He was visiting his cousin, Fred Braun, who lives in Atkinson, Nebraska.

"You've come to the right area," answered Fred. "We should be able to find whatever you want."

They drove a Model T Ford to the Joe Dobrovolny Ranch. Charlie had taken a bottle along, and he offered Joe a drink which Joe politely declined. First of all, Joe wasn't a drinking man, and secondly, he was not going to let liquor paralyze his brain at a time when the year's income was at stake. Charlie also ignored the contents of the bottle.

Charlie was pleased with the beautiful herd of Herefords,

but he didn't like Joe's price. After three hours of dealing, Joe continued to hold firm, and Charlie, since he truly wanted the steers, bought them. The bottle of liquor remained full.

The next year, Charlie reported to his cousin that Joe's Herefords had gained more weight per pound of feed than had the animals that he had purchased elsewhere. He reappeared at Joe's ranch to deal for a new crop of steers, but this time he did not bother to bring a bottle.

After the Depression

The return of adequate rainfall did not immediately bring an end to depressed times; however, it rekindled hope among the sprinkling of people who had managed to remain on the farms and ranches. As might be supposed, it took years of hard work to climb out of the depths of debt and to peek over the rim to brighter days.

After the drought ended, people were preoccupied with the immediate struggle of rebuilding their herds and their businesses, and paying the interest on their debts. Even though they were concerned about the noises that Hitler was making in Europe, it was easy to put aside the disturbing news which arrived from afar, for they had enough problems of their own.

It was a time when America was fiercely isolationistic. The adults (who were, in most cases, the sons of the pioneers) were apt to comment: "When we fought the World War,* we thought it was to be the last war because President Wilson said that we would thereafter have a world court to settle the arguments between countries. But those European nations never could get along, and aren't of a mind to listen to any world court. One of the reasons that our parents came to this country was to get away from the constant wars. If people over there want to fight, let them go to it! We're going to stay out of it!"

Four years after the Drought of Thirty-four, Hitler put into motion his desire to conquer the world by inventing an excuse to over-run Czechoslovakia after which, in quick succession, he gobbled up a half dozen other countries.

In the meantime, the aggressive Japanese (who had trained their youth for war from the time they were children) were looking for lands rich in minerals and had their eyes on the

---

* There was no need to say "World War I" before the Second World War.

Dutch East Indies and on French Indochina. Since Hitler had advanced across the mother countries (Netherlands and France), the Japanese thought that they could conquer such lands easily— if it were not for the U.S. Naval vessels docked in the Hawaiian Islands at Pearl Harbor. The Japanese surprise attack on Pearl Harbor snapped the unprepared United States out of her snug nest of isolationism and plunged her into the dark days of World War II—and into the middle of world affairs.

More than a mere chapter would be needed to describe those war years from 1941 to 1945 when the quickly trained American boys fought both in the Pacific against Japan and in Europe against Hitler. There is no space here for those accounts of sacrifice and victory—nor for stories from the lives of the generation (in many cases, the grandchildren of the pioneers) who fought the war.

It has often been said that this country's greatest asset is the enterprising spirit of her people. How can that statement be true, since most Americans are descended from the same ancestors as are the people in the countries from which the pioneers came?

But it is true, for Americans are descended from courageous, energetic, adventuresome people. Had the pioneers lacked any of these qualities, they would not have packed their possessions, said good-by to friends and relatives, and moved across the ocean to a strange, untamed land. In spite of the tales about "golden America" and in spite of the "homestead fever" that swept the European nations, they would have remained in their "Old Country" homes.

Theirs is an unparalleled legacy—a legacy which yet lives on in their descendants.

Appendix

Photo Album

Family of V.J. and Anna Hytrek Krysl

The four older children of V.J. and Anna
Hytrek Krysl. Behind: Leo;
front: Josephine, Christine, Amelia.
About 1922.

Right, V.J. and Anna's two younger children with a cousin from Kansas: Bill Krysl, Bill Stroda (son of Anna's sister Mary), and Don Krysl. 1932.

Below: Leo & Margaret Krysl's eldest son, Dan, and family: Dan, Gina, Lean, Nancy, Brad, Steve, & Brian. About 1990.

(Leo Krysl family con't)
Top: Ed and Cheryl Krysl Stubbs, Jason, Sandy, and David.
Center: Bill and Dianne Prenosil, Jessica and David.
Bottom: Mike and Lori Krysl, Jeremiah, Lucas, Joshua, and Caleb. 1990.

Top: Family of Paul and Amelia Krysl Kaup. (Amelia is V.J. and Anna's second child.) Back row: Milton, Dan, Randy, Francis, Phillip. Front: Amelia, Paula, Vencille, and Paul. About 1980. Lower left: Milton and Naoka Kaup with children, Vincent and Jim, and grand-children, Kelli and Kevin. Lower right: Dan and Lucina Kaup with children Joseph, Regina, and Daniel. 1990.

Randy and Sherry Kaup and their son, Ryan. 1990.

Center: Children of Francis and Deb Kaup: Matthew, Christi, and Justin. 1990.

Left: Phillip & DeeAnn Kaup and their children, Jason, Nicole and Doug.
1993 photo.

Top: Fernando and Paula Kaup Leos and children Monica and Fernando II. 1991 photo.

Center: Lloyd and Vencille Kaup Hipke and Paul, Cody, and Logan. Bottom: V.J. & Anna's third child, Josephine, married Bernard Kaup. (Brothers married sisters.) Their family, from left: Jerry, Josephine, Rodger, Bernard, and Bernie. 1954 photo.

Top, left: Jerry and Barb Kaup and children, Tammy, Kristin, Jered, & Brian. 1980. Top, right: Rodger and Sandie and children, Sharon, Julie, and Brad. 1986. Bottom: Bill and Bernie Kaup Coventry with children Kathleen and Brett. 1987.

V.J. and Anna Hytrek Krysl's three youngest: Christine, Don (right) and Bill. Christine did not marry.

Center: Don and his two son's, Don Jr. (the younger) who was the Kearney High School band director but now is studying optometry; and Vincent who is a commercial artist. 1982 photo. Right: Don's daughter, Judy, an artist/illustrator. 1988 photo.

Donald Krysl, 1923-1983.

Drawn by his son, Vincent.

Top: V.J.'s youngest child, Bill, with his wife Theresa. Middle: Bill and their dog. (A Krysl portrayal would not be complete without an antic with a dog!) Bottom: Bill's son Kevin with wife Trish and, to their right, their children, Jennifer and Adam.

Top: Bill and Theresa's second child, Mary Jo, her husband, Dr. Mark Serbousek, and their children, Matthew and Kimberly. Center: The third, Tom, with wife Bonnie and children Sarah and Nick. Lower: Bill's youngest, Chuck, with niece Kimberly. About 1990 photos.

The Family of Joe and Ella Ziska Dobrovolny

Top, from left: Marie, Tony, LeRoy, a guest on the pony, Ella, Tom, and Albena. 1932. Lower left: Joe and Ella's two youngest children, John (on the heifer, Nancy) and Fred. About 1946. Right: LeRoy and his wife Dorothy, 1947.

Bride and groom: Ron Bennetts and Rita Dobrovolny*. Left: Francis* and Lorrie with their children Cory and Lisa. To the right of the bride: Rita's father LeRoy; Linda* and Daryl Baker; Mary* and her friend Roy; Ellen and Gerald* with (inset) their son Nathan. *LeRoy's children.

Top: Joe's second child, Albena Dobrovolny Kramer, her husband Lawrence, and their family. Center: Dan and Jan Kramer, and their children Erin, Kory, and Matt. Bottom: Greg & Val. 1987.

Rollin and Judy Kramer with children (by age) Nathan, Jeremiah, twins Noah and Joshua, and Cassidy.

Right: Joe and Ella's third child, Marie. Below: Marie's first husband, Don Krysl (1923-1983), using an out-dated walking plow to prepare the ground north of their house for planting trees. 1946. By now there is a thick grove there.

Don and Marie's children as youngsters. Top: Judy and Lambo, 1952. Center: Don Jr. (on the left) and Vincent with a puppy. 1964.

Right: Two beauties, Stephanie (daughter of Don Jr. and Shirley Krysl) and their dog Bitsy. Steph plays the piano, draws, and likes science. 1991.

Top, left: Don and Shirley's son Robert likes sports and driving his go-cart. 1991. Top, right: Vince Jr. on his paper route. He is interested in space. Lower, left: Vince and Patti's daughter, Eve Willadsen, studies speech and Spanish; lower, right: Vince and Patti's two youngest, Renee (the happy singer) and Adrienne (who reads and writes.) 1992.

Marie's second husband, Ray Kramer, with five of his seven children. From left: Ray, Ed, Donna, Rose Ann, Mary Ann, and Joe. Not shown, Patrick and Jerry. 1991.

Tony is the fourth of Joe and Ella's seven children. At right: Tony with his wife Greta and their sons, Mike and Lee. Below: Joe's fifth, Tom, with his wife Joan.

Left: David (Tom and Joan's elder son.) 1991. Inset; Dave's wife, Brenda.

Right: Dick (Tom and Joan's younger son), his wife, Cindy, and their boys, Travis and Zach. 1991.

Below: Joe & Ella's sixth child, John, with his wife Mary Ann; their daughter, Mary Kay; and (behind) sons Joe with wife Pam; and Steve with wife Betty.

Dustin, 3, and Kurtis, 8 months, are Steve and Betty's sons. 1992 photo. Jaymi is Joe and Pam's little girl. 1993.

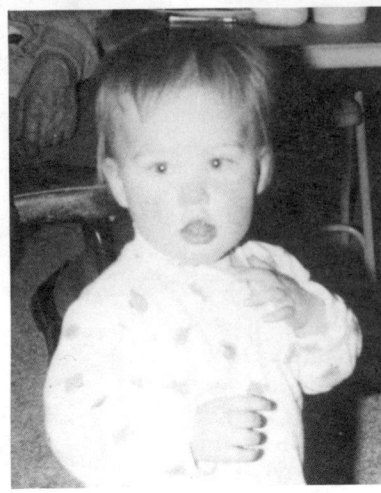

Lower: Fred Dobrovolny is the youngest of Joe and Ella's seven children. With him here are his wife, Dixie, and their children, Tammy and Fred Jr. 1980 photo.

Ella's Kolac Recipe

Ella Dobrovolny often delighted her grandchildren with pans of delicious *kolace* made from a recipe handed down from her Czech ancestors in Europe. Whenever she was asked for the recipe, she was glad to oblige: "Use a couple handsful of this and quite a bit of that—depending on the size of the batch you want to make." She never measured anything; rather, she tossed the ingredients together, with only hand and eye as guides.

One day her daughter-in-law, Mary Ann, measured an ample amount of the various ingredients, placed them in bowls on the kitchen table, and asked Ella to mix a batch of *kolace*. After the *kolace* were finished, Mary Ann measured the amounts of the remaining ingredients and subtracted. Now, Mary Ann is the champion kolac baker in the family. Here is the recipe:

1/2 cup warm water in a small bowl (perhaps a 3-cup bowl.) Add 1 tsp sugar and 2 pkg. yeast. Set aside for it to "rise".

2 cups powdered milk (dry)
1 1/2 cups hot water
1 1/2 tsp. salt
3 eggs
1/2 cup sugar
6 tbs. oleo, melted
5 or 6 cups flour

Mix powdered milk and water together. Beat eggs, add the milk mixture, the salt and sugar, the oleo, and beat.
Pour the yeast mixture into the second mixture. Add 5 cups of flour to begin with. Mix. You may add up to another cup of flour as you mix in order to make a soft dough. Knead by hand for ten minutes. Then rub margarine around the upper edges of the bowl, and cover with wax paper. Place a towel over all in order to retain warmth. Let rise an hour. Punch down. Let rise 45 minutes.

Flour a cutting board and line pans with shortening. Ella used margarine. *Take dough in small parts (3 or 4 at a time, and in pieces about the size of a large egg) and place on cutting board. (Cover the remaining dough in the bowl.) Flatten each piece into a square and place a spoonful of filling in the middle of it. Twist each corner of the square, bring the four corners to the center over the filling, twist and pinch them together, and fasten the resulting bit of twisted dough to the side of the *kolac*. Place in pan. Go back to the star above, and repeat the process. As you work, butter the sides of the *kolace* where they touch each other. Cover the kolace in the pans with waxed paper and let rise 1 1/2 hours. Bake at 360 degrees for 15 or 16 minutes. Remove from pan, place upright on a cooling rack, and brush lightly with margarine.

Kolace Filling: Cook 2 pounds of dried fruit (in enough water to cover) until tender. Cool, drain, and pit if necessary. Mash well. Add 1 cup sugar, 1 tsp vanilla, and 1/4 tsp. cinnamon.

(Ella usually made two batches of fruit mix, one from 2 lbs. of prunes, and another from 2 lbs. of apricots. Also, she had adapted her mother's recipe to modern times by substituting powdered milk for fresh milk—and margarine for butter.)

John Ziska's Egg Soup

John Ziska lived alone on his farm in Green Valley for the five years (1883-1888) prior to his marriage. Since he worked long hours in the field, he didn't care to spend much time at cooking. His usual supper was egg soup. Following is his method for making egg soup:

As soon as the fire is kindled, place the water kettle (called the teakettle) on the front of the stove to heat. Break bread (it may be fresh bread or dry bread*) into a bowl, and also break two or three eggs over the bread. When the teakettle of water is boiling, pour hot water over the bread and eggs.** Eat.

The Jim Ziska family lived with John until John's death in 1941. One of his grandsons, also named John, said that whenever their mother was gone, Grandfather John usually made egg soup for supper. "He always asked us kids if he should make some for us," he said, "but we never cared for any. We looked around and found something else to eat."

* Since there was no such thing as plastic wrap and also no handy roll of waxed paper, bread was wrapped in brown wrapping paper or in a towel. It soon "dried out." The older bread that had dried was used for bread soup, bread pudding, etc.
** Anyone wishing to make bread soup should heat the water in a pan, break the eggs into the boiling water, and let them cook a minute or so before pouring them over the bread. It is now known that people sometimes get food poisoning from eating raw eggs. Why didn't the pioneers get food poisoning? Occasionally, they did. "Summer complaint" was common at that time, and many children died from it. Some cases of that malady—which was actually food poisoning—may have been caused by raw eggs!

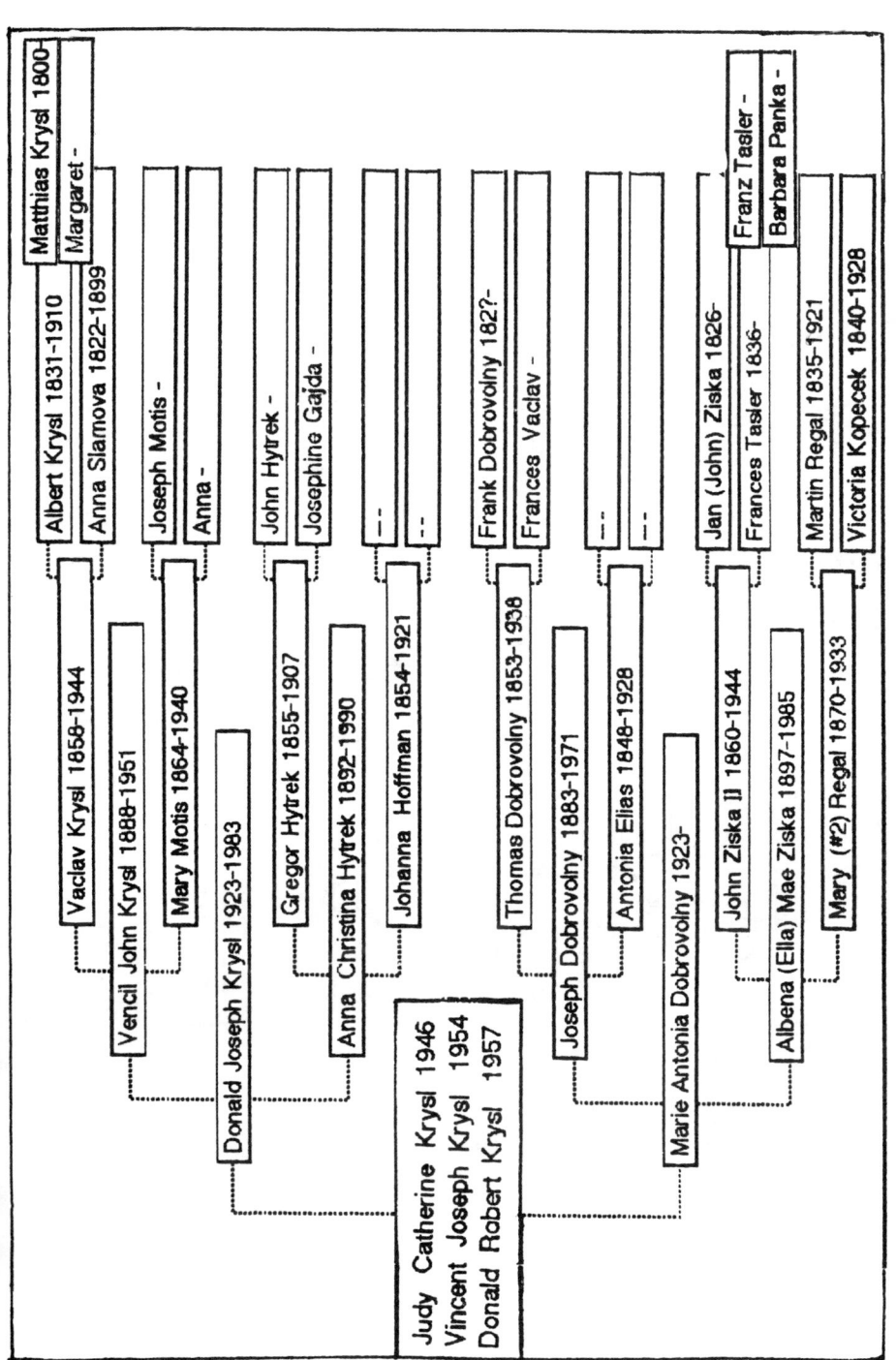

KRYSL, DOBROVOLNY, HYTREK, and ZISKA ANCESTORS

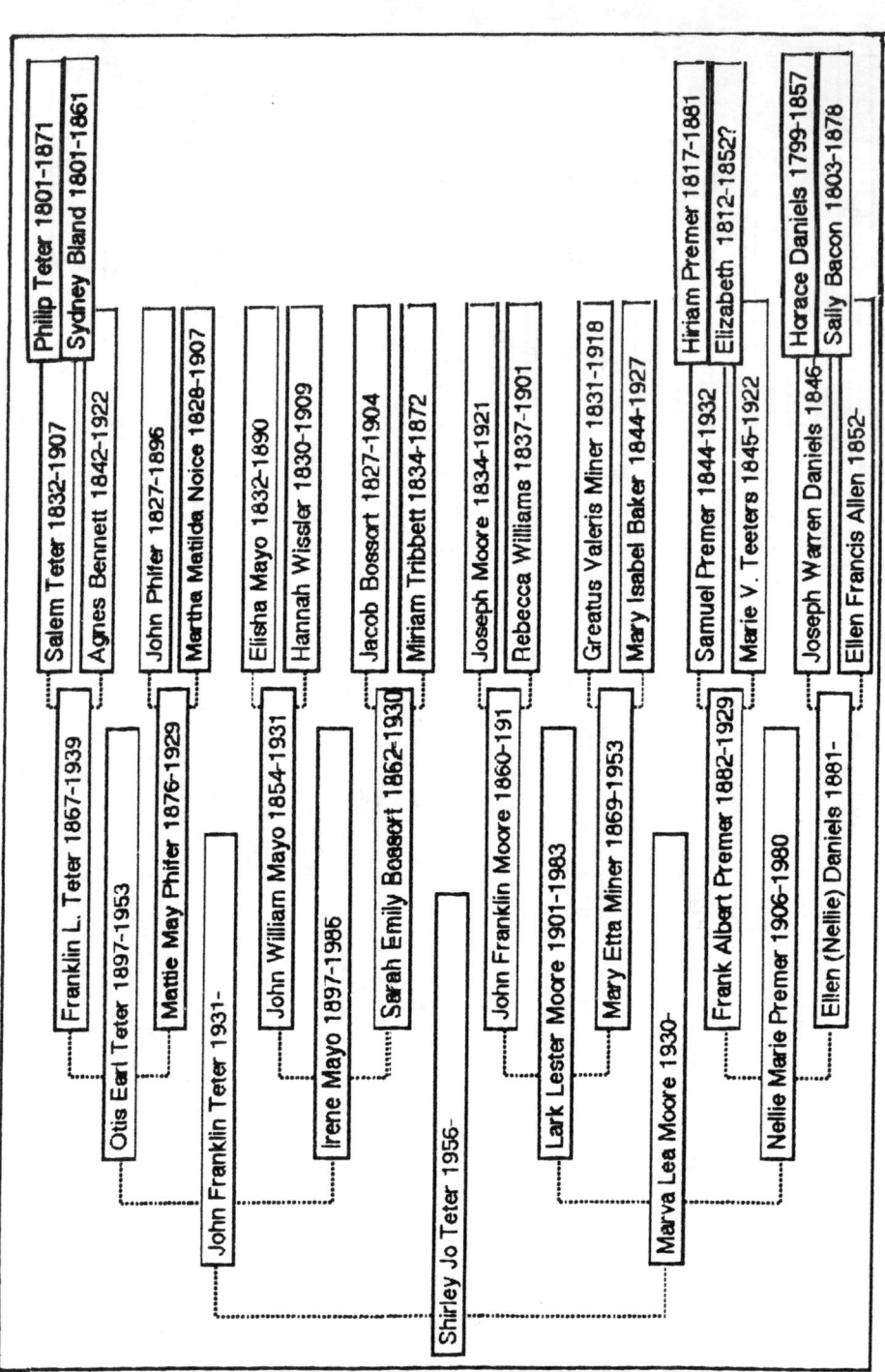

TETER and MOORE ANCESTORS

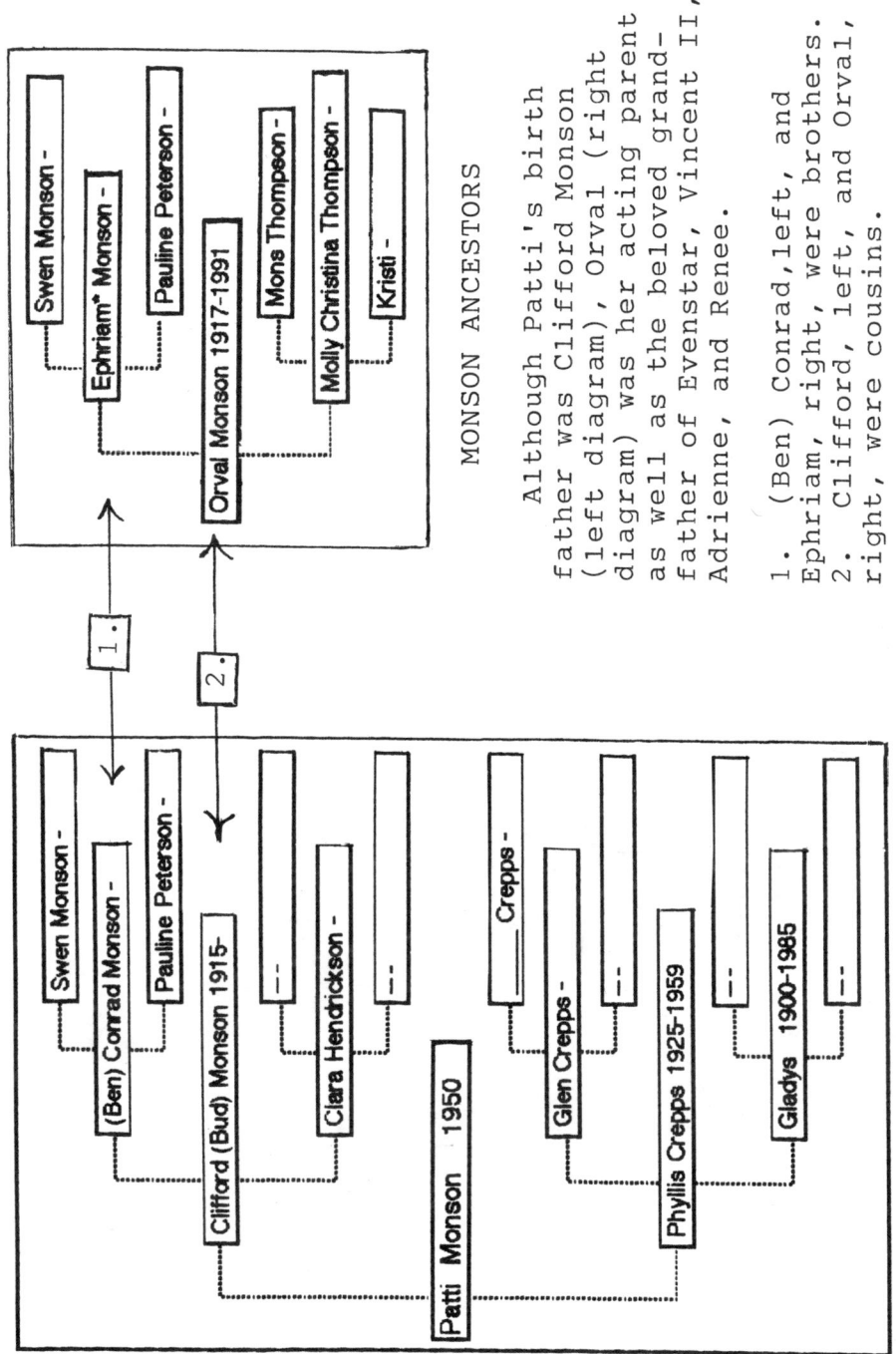

MONSON ANCESTORS

Although Patti's birth father was Clifford Monson (left diagram), Orval (right diagram) was her acting parent as well as the beloved grand-father of Evenstar, Vincent II, Adrienne, and Renee.

1. (Ben) Conrad, left, and Ephriam, right, were brothers.
2. Clifford, left, and Orval, right, were cousins.

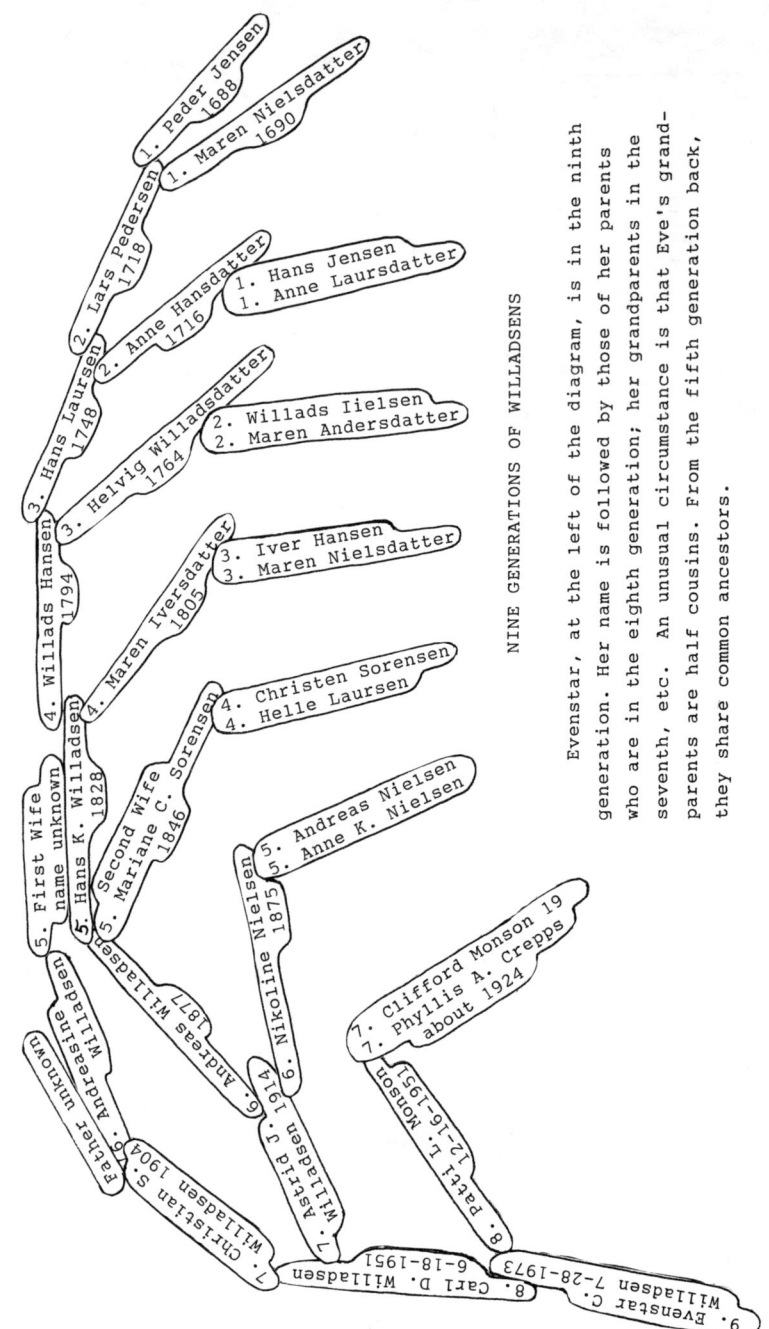

NINE GENERATIONS OF WILLADSENS

Evenstar, at the left of the diagram, is in the ninth generation. Her name is followed by those of her parents who are in the eighth generation; her grandparents in the seventh, etc. An unusual circumstance is that Eve's grandparents are half cousins. From the fifth generation back, they share common ancestors.